THE CHRONOLOGY
of the
LIFE OF PAUL

THE CHRONOLOGY
of the
LIFE OF PAUL

GEORGE OGG

WIPF & STOCK · Eugene, Oregon

Wipf and Stock Publishers
199 W 8th Ave, Suite 3
Eugene, OR 97401

The Chronology of the Life of Paul
By Ogg, George
Copyright©1968 Methodist Publishing - Epworth Press
ISBN 13: 978-1-4982-8050-1
Publication date 2/7/2016
Previously published by Epworth Press, 1968

Every effort has been made to trace the current copyright owner
of this publication but without success. If you have any information
or interest in the copyright, please contact the publishers.

Preface

IN RECENT times many points in the Pauline chronology have been discussed in contributions to theological journals and in works on Paul, and some of these discussions have issued in a brief chronological outline of the apostle's career. Considerable attention has also been paid to this subject in recent Commentaries on the Acts of the Apostles, alike in the introduction and in appropriate places in the body of the commentary proper. But so large a subject requires a separate volume—a book devoted entirely to it and dealing with it in all its compass. There has been no study of the kind since the appearance in 1918 of Plooij's book *De chronologie van het leven van Paulus*. In several respects it is an excellent work; and although I find many of its conclusions unacceptable, I gratefully acknowledge an indebtedness to it much greater than my references to it may indicate.

GEORGE OGG

THE MANSE OF ANSTRUTHER EASTER
Scotland

If we claim only reasonable probability, it will be as much as men who love the truth can ever at any given moment hope to have within their grasp.

>William James
>*The Varieties of Religious Experience*

Contents

Preface	v
Bibliography	xi
1 When was Paul Born? His Early Years	1
2 The Martyrdom of Stephen	11
3 Damascus and Arabia	13
4 Paul's Flight from Damascus	16
5 The Date of Paul's Conversion	24
6 Paul's First Visit to Jerusalem after his Conversion	31
7 The Silent Years	36
8 Agrippa's Persecution of the Church and his Death	39
9 The Famine-Relief Visit to Jerusalem	43
10 The First Missionary Journey	58
11 The Jerusalem Conference	72
12 Paul's Collision with Peter and his Separation from Barnabas	89
13 Claudius's Expulsion of the Jews from Rome	99
14 Gallio's Proconsulship of Achaia	104
15 The Second Missionary Journey	112
16 Paul's Return to Syria, Acts 18:18-23	127
17 The Third Missionary Journey	133
18 The Date of Festus's Entrance on Office as Procurator of Judaea—(1) The Antedated Chronology	146
19 The Date of Festus's Entrance on Office as Procurator of Judaea—(2) The Traditional Chronology	160
20 To Rome	171
21 The Sequel to Acts 28:30-1	178
22 The Date of Paul's Martyrdom	194
Chronological Outline	200
Index of Authors	201
Index of New Testament Passages	205

Bibliography

PRE-REFORMATION

Eusebius, *Chronicle*.
This survives in two versions, one in Latin by Jerome and one in Armenian. For the former, see *Die Chronik der Hieronymus*, ed. R. Helm, vol. VII.i of the works of Eusebius in *Die griechischen christlichen Schriftsteller der ersten drei Jahrhunderte*, hrg.v.d,kgl. preussischen Akademie der Wissenschaften; for the latter (the Armenian in a German translation), see *Die Chronik*, ed. J. Karst, vol. V of the works of Eusebius in the same corpus. For both versions (the Armenian translated into Latin by H. Petermann), see *Evsebi Chronicorum Libri Dvo*, ed. A. Schoene (Berlin, 1866).

Chronicon paschale.
The author is unknown. The work appears to have been published before the end of the reign of Heraclius (610–41). Ed. Dindorf in *Corpus Scriptorum Historiae Byzantinae* (Bonn, 1831).

Georgius Syncellus, *Chronographia*.
Author lived in Constantinople in the eighth century. Ed. Dindorf in *Corpus Scriptorum Historiae Byzantinae* (Bonn, 1829).

FROM THE REFORMATION TO THE END OF THE EIGHTEENTH CENTURY

Caesar Baronius, *Annales ecclesiastici a Christo nato ad annum 1198*, 12 vols (1588–1607). Ed. Theiner, 37 vols, of which vol. 1 brings the history down to A D 67.

Dionysius Petavius, *De doctrina temporum* (1627, nova ed. Antwerp, 1703). See Ch. 18 below.

James Usher (or Ussher), *Annales Veteris et Novi Testamenti*, 2 vols. (1650–4). Ed. of his works by Elrington and Todd, the *Annales Novi Testamenti* in vol. X, pp. 473–598 and vol. XI, pp. 1–113.

John Pearson, *Annales Paulini*, (1688).
An English translation of this work with geographical and critical notes taken from many sources was published at Cambridge in 1825.

Johann Albricht Bengel, *Ordo temporum a principio per periodos oeconomiae divinae historicus atque propheticus*, 1741.

FROM THE BEGINNING OF THE NINETEENTH CENTURY

E. Burton, *Attempt to Ascertain the Chronology of the Acts* (1830).

R. Anger, *De temporum in Actis Apostolorum ratione* (1833).

K. Wieseler, *Chronologie des apostolischen Zeitalters* (1848).

T. Lewin, *Fasti Sacri : or a Key to the Chronology of the New Testament* (1865).

BIBLIOGRAPHY

J. B. Lightfoot, *Biblical Essays* (1893), pp. 215–33.
W. M. Ramsay, *The Church in the Roman Empire* (1893) ; *St. Paul the Traveller and the Roman Citizen* (1st ed., 1894, 14th ed., 1920) ; *Pauline and other Studies in the History of Religion* (1906).
A. Harnack, *Geschichte der altchristlichen Litteratur bis Eusebius* II.i : *Die Chronologie der altchristlichen Litteratur bis Eusebius* (1897).
C. Turner, ' Chronology of the New Testament : ii. The Apostolic Age '. Hastings, *A Dictionary of the Bible* I (1898), pp. 415–25.
G. H. Gilbert, ' The New Chronology of Paul's Life ', *Bibliotheca Sacra*, LV (1898), pp. 244–58.
C. W. Votaw, ' Recent Discussions of the Chronology of the Apostolic Age ', *The Biblical World* N.S. xi (1898), pp. 112–9, 177–87.
B. W. Bacon, ' A Criticism of the New Chronology of Paul ', *Expositor* 5th Ser., VII (1898), pp. 123–36, X (1899), pp. 351–67, 412–30.
Th. Zahn, *Einleitung in das Neue Testament* (2nd ed., 1900) II, 629–43.
G. Hoennicke, *Die Chronologie des Lebens des Apostels Paulus* (1903).
C. Clemen, *Paulus, sein Leben und Wirken* (1904) I, 349–410.
O. Holtzmann, *Neutestamentliche Zeitgeschichte* (2nd ed., 1906).
J. Wellhausen, ' Noten zur Apostelgeschichte ', *Nach.v.d.kgl. Gesellschaft der Wissenschaften zu Göttingen*, 1907, pp. 1–21.
E. Schwartz, ' Zur Chronologie des Paulus ', *Nach.v.d.kgl. Gesellschaft der Wissenschaften zu Göttingen*, 1907, pp. 263–99.
M. Goguel, ' Essai sur la chronologie Paulinienne ', *Revue de l'Histoire des Religions* LXV (1912), pp. 285–339.
F. Prat, ' La Chronologie de l'âge apostolique ', *Recherches des Sciences religieuses* III (1912), pp. 374–92.
H. H. Wendt, *Die Apostelgeschichte* (5th ed., 1913), pp. 57–64.
A. Brassac, ' Une inscription de Delphes et la chronologie de Saint Paul ', *Revue Biblique* N.S.10(22), 1913, pp. 36–53, 207–17.
D. Plooij, *De chronologie van het leven van Paulus* (1918).
K. Lake, 'The Chronology of Acts ' in Jackson and Lake, *The Beginnings of Christianity* I.v. (1933), pp. 445–74.
C. J. Cadoux, ' A Tentative Synthetic Chronology of the Apostolic Age ', *Journal of Biblical Literature* LVI (1937), pp. 177–91.
J. Knox, *Chapters in a Life of Paul* (1950).
E. Haenchen, *Die Apostelgeschichte* (12th ed., 1959), pp. 53–64.
G. B. Caird, ' Chronology of the New Testament : (b) The Apostolic Age ', *The Interpreter's Dictionary of the Bible* i (1963), pp. 603–7.

CHAPTER ONE

When was Paul Born ? His Early Years

PAUL BEGAN his eventful life in Tarsus, a city of Cilicia (Acts 22:3), but the year of his birth is not given in any ancient writing and cannot be determined with any absolute certainty.

According to Pseudo-Chrysostom, *Oratio Encomiastica in Principes Apostolorum Petrum et Paulum*,[1] he served the Lord for thirty-five years, and having finished his course he entered into rest when sixty-eight years of age. These figures are not without interest. But, taken by themselves, they throw no light on the precise year of Paul's birth.

At one point [2] in his *Commentary on Philemon* Jerome introduces a story which he had heard possibly during his stay in Bethlehem. 'It is said', he writes, 'that the parents of Paul the apostle were natives of Gischala, a district of Judaea, and that when the whole province was laid waste by the Roman arms and the Jews were scattered throughout the world, they were carried away to Tarsus, a city of Cilicia.' This tradition is somewhat confused in its chronology. It may nevertheless rest on a substratum of truth. When Varus the governor of Syria came into Palestine to quell the uprisings that followed the death of Herod the Great, he burned Sepphoris and sold its inhabitants as slaves.[3] Gischala was not far distant; and if it was dealt with in the same way, Paul's parents may have been

---

[1] Migne, *P.G.*, LIX.494. The unknown author of this sermon probably lived in the fourth century. The text was first edited by G. Vossius in 1580.

[2] In discussing the words 'Epaphras, my fellow prisoner' in verse 23. Jerome also gives the story, in an abbreviated and less satisfactory form, in *De vir.illustr.* 5. The texts are assembled in Zahn, *Einleitung in das Neue Testament* I, 49, note 16.

[3] Josephus, *Ant.*, xvii.289. Whiston's trans., new edn. by Margoliouth, is used throughout.

carried away to Tarsus at that time. On this view his birth could not be put earlier than 4 B C. But if this tradition has roots in history, it may originally have referred not to Paul's father and mother, but to certain of his somewhat less immediate ancestors ; and perhaps all that ought to be gathered from it is that these ancestors were Galileans.

The views entertained regarding the time of Paul's birth may be gathered into three classes according as they put it : (1) some years before the commencement of the Christian era, (2) very near to its commencement, and (3) some years after it.

I

In a contribution [4] which he made to the *Zeitschrift für die neutestamentliche Wissenschaft* in 1926 J. Jeremias adduces what he considers evidence that before his conversion Paul was an ordained rabbi ;[5] and since according to the Babylonian Talmud [6] the minimum age for ordination was forty years, he concludes that by the time of his conversion Paul was already a middle-aged man.[7] Since he puts his conversion in A D 31 or 32, hardly in 33,[8] it follows that he puts his birth some years before the commencement of our era. We consider first the passages which he adduces.

(*a*) Acts 9:1–2 ; 22:5 ; 26:12. According to Jeremias these passages indicate that Paul set out for Damascus charged with a commission that comprised responsible judicial functions such as could be exercised only by an ordained rabbi. But, as will be shown below,[9] there is reason to think that the work in Damascus for which Paul was recommended by the high priest

---

[4] ' War Paulus Witwer ? ', *ZNTW* XXV.(1926).310–12.

[5] On Ordination (סְמִיכָה) see Strack and Billerbeck, *Commentar zum NT*, II.647–61.

[6] b. *Sotah*, 22b. See Strack and Billerbeck, *ibid.* II.652.

[7] Cf. A. Schlatter, *Geschichte der erster Christenheit*, p. 114 (E.T., p. 95) : ' Presumably he was more than forty years old.'

[8] Jeremias, *The Eucharistic Words of Jesus* (E.T. of *Die Abendmahlsworte Jesu*, 2nd edn., 1949 ; cf. 3rd edn., 1963, p. 33, note 5) p. 12, note 3.

[9] Page 8.

was of a humbler order and did not involve for him such a high degree of responsibility.

(b) Acts 13:15. In the fact that Paul was formally invited to preach in the synagogue in Pisidian Antioch, Jeremias finds a suggestion that he was recognized there as an ordained rabbi. But any fit person could be invited, and perhaps Paul was chosen on this occasion simply because it had got abroad in the city that he and Barnabas had come there claiming that they had a message to deliver. The invitation on this particular Sabbath was extended to a visitor, and for that reason, and no other, it may have been somewhat more formal than usual.

(c) Acts 26:10. Gathering from this verse that Paul was a member of the college of judges and acted as a judge in cases involving sentence of death, Jeremias finds in it evidence that he was an ordained rabbi.

But did Paul exercise judicial functions? The question is investigated by A. Oepke,[10] who answers it in the negative. When a Jew was brought before a local court on the ground that he had become a Christian, Paul can have had no official part in the proceedings that followed, for, not being resident in the district, he can have had neither a seat nor a vote in the court. Christians were sometimes done to death by fanatical Jewish mobs, and some doubtless died under the floggings which the Jewish authorities had power to inflict; but, as Oepke points out, a Roman governor out of whose hand the power of life and death had been completely taken away is an impossible figure. The words of the Jews in John 18:31, ' We are not allowed to put any man to death ',[11] were therefore fundamentally true. In consequence if a Jew was arrested because he had become a Christian and was brought before the Sanhedrin and that court decided that he ought to be put to death, it had then to refer the case to the procurator. If Paul was a member of the Sanhedrin, he doubtless denounced the prisoner when his case

[10] 'Probleme der vorchristlichen Zeit des Paulus ', *SK* CV.(1933).387–424.
[11] Here and frequently the New Testament is quoted in the rendering of the *New English Bible*.

was under discussion and then cast his vote against him. But there is no compelling reason to believe that he ever was a member of that court. It seems very likely that the words, 'and when they were condemned to death, my vote was cast against them', which many have regarded as evidence that he was a member of it (and so was over thirty years of age) at the time of the martyrdom of Stephen or shortly thereafter, have been attributed to him by the writer and merely show us one aspect of the conception that he had of Paul as a persecutor of the early church. Even if the words are Paul's own, they may mean merely that he approved of the decisions of the Sanhedrin, and so cannot be said to *prove* that he was a member of that court.[12]

The ceremony of ordination can be traced back to the first century of our era, since according to b. *Sanh.* 1:19a, R. Johanan b. Zakkai, who died *c.* A D 80, ordained two of his pupils.[13] But it is far from certain that the regulation as to age given in the Babylonian Talmud was of considerably earlier date, and E. Fascher[14] attaches little worth to this part of Jeremias's argument. Moreover Paul is described as a νεανίας at the time of the stoning of Stephen (Acts 7:58) and so shortly before his conversion; and this term, while certainly applied to men of a considerable age, was not rightly applied to such as were over forty.

There is one passage, Josephus, *Ant.*, xviii.197, which may seem to disprove this. In it a certain German, in addressing Agrippa I through an interpreter, is reported to have used the words ὦ νεανία. Agrippa's age at the time is not known exactly, but he must have been at least forty and may have been as many as forty-six years old.[15] The speaker may, however, have had regard to courtesy; he may have allowed himself to be guided

---

[12] So F. F. Bruce, *The Acts of the Apostles*, p. 443.
[13] See Strack and Billerbeck, *Comm. zum NT*, II.650.
[14] 'Zur Witwerschaft des Paulus und der Auslegung von 1 Kor. 7', *ZNTW* XXVIII.(1929).62–9.
[15] See Schürer, *The Jewish People in the Time of Jesus Christ*, I.II.152, note 7.

merely by Agrippa's appearance; or it may be that the use of this term discloses a false element in the story that Josephus tells here.[16]

II

As has just been stated, Paul is described as a νεανίας at the time of the martyrdom of Stephen. Ordinarily this term was used ' of men between twenty-four and forty years of age ',[17] and so had a considerably wider range of meaning than the rendering ' a young man ' suggests. In Philemon verse 9 Paul refers to himself as a πρεσβύτης. This term is usually rendered ' an old man '. But it is sometimes difficult to determine what that means. There have always been men who have grown old more rapidly than their contemporaries, men who have been regarded as old and men who have even referred to themselves as old men when they were still in their fifties. The possibility that Paul may have aged prematurely in the service of Christ complicates the question as to what precisely may have been in his mind when he applied this term (it being assumed that he applied it in the sense ' an old man ') to himself. There need, however, be little doubt that normally a πρεσβύτης was a man who had passed the sixtieth milestone. Taking the term in Philemon verse 9 in this sense and assuming that the epistle was written c. A D 62, many have concluded that Paul was born very near to the commencement of our era.

It has, however, been conjectured that here πρεσβύτης is only an alternative spelling of πρεσβευτής and means ' ambassador '. This rendering of the word has been widely accepted.[18] It is suggested by Ephesians 6:20 and it is well suited to the context. J. B. Lightfoot,[19] one of the earlier authorities to advocate this rendering, apparently thought that its adoption involves no serious loss so far as the chronology of Paul's life is concerned.

---

[16] So Holzmeister, *Historia Aetatis Novi Testamenti*, p. 131.
[17] Grimm-Thayer, *Lexicon, s.v.*; Arndt and Gingrich, *A Greek Lexicon of the New Testament, s.v.*
[18] Margin of R.V.; text of *R.S.V.*; and of *N.E.B.*
[19] *St. Paul's Epistles to the Colossians and to Philemon*, p. 339.

'On any showing', he writes, 'he must have been verging on sixty at this time and may have been some years older.' Actually, however, its adoption means that we are without any direct indication of Paul's age in the closing years of his life, and indeed that the only direct indication of his age contained in the New Testament is the one in Acts 7:58—at the time of Stephen's martyrdom he was a νεανίας.

III

In Commentaries on Acts and in Lives of Paul it is generally assumed that he spent his youth in his native Tarsus. In those days Tarsus was a centre of commercial enterprise, and there was resident in it a considerable community of Jews. If not taught privately, Paul will have begun to attend the school attached to their synagogue when about six years of age. Later, probably when in his teens, he will have been apprenticed to a trade. In recent years, however, the common assumption as to the place of Paul's youth has been challenged, and reasons have been given for believing that, soon after his birth, his parents left Tarsus and settled in Jerusalem.[20] If they did so, then it was there, in a predominantly Jewish *milieu*, that he spent his impressionable early years, received his elementary education and learned a trade.

A new and important chapter of his life opened when he entered the theological college, the House of Interpretation, in Jerusalem to be educated in the learning of the scribes.[21] There he sat at the feet of Gamaliel (Acts 22:3). This is the Gamaliel who on a memorable occasion (Acts 5:34 ff) counselled the Sanhedrin to maintain a waiting attitude toward the Christian movement. Peculiarly little is known about him, many of the sayings and doings once considered his being now attributed to

[20] See W. C. van Unnik, *Tarsus of Jeruzalem*.
[21] Some have maintained on the ground of Galatians 1:22 that Paul was never in Jerusalem before his conversion. For a telling refutation of that theory see J. Weiss, *History of Primitive Christianity* (E.T. of *Das Urchristentum*) I.186, note 9.

his grandson. In particular there is uncertainty as to the period when he ministered in Jerusalem as a member of the Sanhedrin and as a teacher. In the *Jewish Encyclopaedia* [22] this period is given as the second third of the first century of our era; according to Haenchen [23] it was A D 25–50; and according to Oepke [24] A D 20–50. If, following the last named of these authorities, we assume that it began not earlier than A D 20 and if we further assume, as usually is done, that Paul was fifteen years old when he entered the House of Interpretation, then he cannot have been born earlier than A D 5. Since moreover he was at least twenty-four years of age at the time of Stephen's martyrdom (A D 37 at the latest),[25] he cannot have been born later than A D 13.[26]

If now he was born in the interval A D 5–13, he may have been in his twenties at the time of the martyrdom of Stephen and also at the time of his conversion, which apparently took place soon afterwards.[27] But is that likely?

Decisive help in settling this matter can hardly be expected

---

[22] V.559.

[23] *Die Apostelgeschichte* (12th edn., 1959), p. 554; cf. Hopfl and Gut, *Introductio in Novum Testamentum*, p. 294.

[24] Op. cit. (note 10, *supra*), p. 418.

[25] Since Aretas died in A D 40 (see p. 16, *infra*) and Paul was three years in Damascus after his conversion.

[26] The birth of Paul is put in A D 10 at the earliest by Oepke (op. cit., p. 423), about A D 10 by B. Rigaux (*Saint Paul et ses Lettres*, p. 134), in A D 10 or 12 by Renan (*Les Apôtres*, p. 163; E.T. p. 77), in A D 10–15 by Knopf (*Probleme der Paulusforschung*, p. 10). Adopting a division of the ages of man found in Philo and derived from Hippocrates, T. Lewin in his *Fasti Sacri*, p. 150, no. 1,025 puts Paul's birth *c*. A D 9. In his *Life and Epistles of St. Paul*, I.4, note 20, he abandons this division as 'highly artificial' and puts Paul's birth in A D 2.

[27]

		A D	A D	A D	A D
	Conversion	34	35	36	37
24 years old at Conversion:	Birth	10	11	12	13
25 ,, ,, ,, ,,	,,	9	10	11	12
29 ,, ,, ,, ,,	,,	5	6	7	8
30 ,, ,, ,, ,,	,,		5	6	7
31 ,, ,, ,, ,,	,,			5	6
32 ,, ,, ,, ,,	,,				5

from the psychology of religion. Oepke [28] quotes the conclusion of Starbuck that conversions belong to the years between ten and twenty-five and that few occur outside these limits. But, as Oepke recognizes, the conversion of Paul goes back to an objective factor that is fixed to no special time. Let that factor be operative, and a revolution will take place in a man's inner life whether he be younger or older. Thouless [29] has rightly noted that the formula, by which psychologists have been so much captivated, *Conversion is an adolescent phenomenon*, is an over-simplification. 'Their omission', he writes, 'to consider conversions which do not fall under this formula is rendered serious by the fact that these exceptions have often been the most important conversions in history.'

Many consider it quite unlikely that the responsible duty to discharge which Paul proceeded on his memorable journey to Damascus can have been entrusted to a man who was still in his twenties. Here it needs to be noted that onwards from the time of Herod the Great the jurisdiction of the Sanhedrin was restricted to Judaea in the narrow sense and did not extend to Galilee or to foreign parts. The Sanhedrin had no authority over the synagogues in Damascus.[30] That being so, one must read with considerable reserve the verses in Acts in which it is stated or implied that Paul proceeded to that city invested by the high priest with full authority and power to arrest the Christians he found there and bring them bound to Jerusalem; the Roman government would have defended Christians in Damascus who appealed to it against such treatment. These verses must then be put down to a striving either in the tradition used by the writer or on his own part to present an impressive picture of Paul as the arch-persecutor of the early church.

---

[28] Op. cit. (note 10, *supra*), pp. 410 f.
[29] *An Introduction to the Psychology of Religion*, p. 187.
[30] Those who deny this adduce 1 Maccabees 15:15–21, Josephus, *Ant.*, xiv, 190–5, and *Bell. Jud.*, I.474. But on these passages see Haenchen, op. cit. (note 23, *supra*), p. 268, note 4. Christians arrested in Damascus would have been dealt with by the synagogue authorities there.

It needs, however, also to be noted that the moral influence of the Sanhedrin and in particular of its president, the high priest, was not confined. In the period with which we are here concerned a person coming to Damascus with letters of introduction from the high priest would undoubtedly have been received by the Jews there with very considerable respect.

Paul, it is clear, was not invited or ordered to go to Damascus by the high priest and Sanhedrin; the initiative was taken not by them but by him. 'He went', it is recorded, 'to the high priest and applied for letters to the synagogues at Damascus.' (Acts 9:1-2). This consists with the accounts which he gives in his epistles of his activities as a persecutor of the church. In them he nowhere refers to or suggests or pleads any obligation laid upon him by those then in authority to act as he did, but lays the burden of responsibility for his conduct entirely on his own shoulders. It is therefore unlikely that in the letters which he carried he can have been designated a plenipotentiary or special commissioner of the Sanhedrin or that in them there can have been an instruction to the Damascene Jews to receive him in some such capacity. In them the high priest can only have commended him to them as one whose success in spying upon Christians in and around Jerusalem, in hunting them out and in bringing them to the law-courts was ample proof that he was well fitted to undertake such work in Damascus also. The high priest and Sanhedrin were fully aware of the importance of this work. Part of their aim in recommending Paul to the synagogue authorities in Damascus may well have been to communicate to them their sense of its urgency. But if it involved no more than what has just been stated, then, important as they reckoned it, they cannot have regarded it as beyond the competence of a man still in his twenties. Moreover Paul was in all likelihood no longer a raw youth. It may be assumed not only that he had already finished his theological course but also that he had already served for a period as a rabbi and in doing so had gained some experience. With his learning and his knowledge of men together with the zeal of a volunteer and the drive of one still in his twenties, he may well have seemed to the high priest and his colleagues *the* man for this work.

There are several indications that physically Paul was not cast in a Herculean mould, that he was not a particularly strong man, and that at times he was not at all in good health. Set over against that, his services, sufferings and achievements as a servant of Christ impart a certain dramatic character to his life. The fact that with his modest resources he proved equal to a long catalogue [31] of severe demands upon physical strength is not easily explained; but we may perhaps find it somewhat more understandable if he entered on his missionary career when a younger rather than an older man.[32]

[31] 2 Corinthians 11:23 ff.
[32] On the subject-matter of this paragraph see Goguel, *Introduction au Nouveau Testament* IV.i.128–45, and Clavier, ' La Sante de l'Apôtre Paul ', *Studia Paulina in honorem Johannis de Zwaan* (1953), pp. 66–81.

CHAPTER TWO

The Martyrdom of Stephen

IN ACTS the earliest mention of Paul occurs in the account of the arrest, trial and stoning of the protomartyr Stephen (6:8–8:3). This account has figured prominently in discussions regarding the powers of the Sanhedrin in capital cases throughout the period when Palestine was subject to Rome. It has been gathered from it that that court, after it had tried Stephen, passed sentence of death upon him and then of itself proceeded to execute the sentence. The case was not referred to the Roman procurator, and he apparently did not take the Sanhedrin to task for its action; and this is taken as indicating that in all that it did the Sanhedrin proceeded in strict accordance with its judicial powers.

Many,[1] however, point out that it is not recorded that the Sanhedrin condemned Stephen to death. According to the narrative, as they understand it, Stephen, when speaking in his own defence, was interrupted by an incensed multitude, and thereupon the proceedings gave place to a riot which culminated in his being stoned to death. It is not possible, they maintain, to determine whether or not, had the trial run a full, normal course, the Sanhedrin would have referred the case to the procurator. Yet other scholars think it very likely that there were no proceedings before the Sanhedrin. According to Haenchen [2] the proceedings against Stephen were an act of lynch justice and were first associated with the supreme court by Luke; and Goguel [3] concludes from the presence in the narrative of a number of doublets that in it two traditions have

[1] See J. Blinzler, *Der Prozess Jesu* (2nd edn., 1955), p. 119.
[2] *Die Apostelgeschichte* (12th edn., 1959), pp. 244, 246.
[3] *Introduction au Nouveau Testament*, III.194; cf. Spitta, *Die Apostelgeschichte, ihre Quellen und deren geschichtlicher Wert*, pp. 96 ff.; also Moffatt, ' Stephen ', *Encyclopaedia Biblica* IV, col. 4,788 f.

been combined, according to the earlier of which Stephen was not tried by the Sanhedrin, but simply laid hold upon by a fanatical mob and taken outside the city and there stoned to death.

On each of the last two of these views the Jews involved were guilty of disorderly behaviour and of murder, and certain writers consider that they would not have ventured on such conduct at any time in the procuratorship of Pilate. Accordingly some of them conclude that this riot must have taken place after Pilate's departure from Palestine in A D 36 and before the arrival of his successor Marcellus. The murder of Stephen would then have a historical parallel in the murder of James the Lord's brother, for it also took place at a time when Roman rule in Palestine was somewhat relaxed, namely, in the interval between the death of Festus and the coming of Albinus in his room.[4] Others of them think it likely that the riot took place when Marcellus was in office. They consider that Pilate's actual successor was Marullus and that Marcellus merely acted as procurator pending the arrival of the emperor's nominee. Marcellus was a friend of Vitellius the governor of Syria and apparently owed this temporary appointment to him; and since, as Josephus[5] clearly indicates, Vitellius was favourably disposed to the Jews, the likelihood is that Marcellus was so also.[6]

But, as Goguel[7] points out, the stoning of Stephen, as the issue of an outburst of fanaticism, is ' no more unlikely under the harsh government of Pilate than under the milder administration of Marcellus '. That being so, attempts such as those mentioned above to determine its date can lead us nowhere.

---

[4] Josephus *Ant.*, xx.200. This passage may, however, be an interpolation.
[5] *Ant.*, xviii.90.
[6] Westberg, *Die biblische Chronologie nach Flavius Josephus*, p. 64, suggests that Marcellus and Marullus may have been one and the same person.
[7] Op. cit. (note 3, *supra*), IV.1.87, note 1.

CHAPTER THREE

Damascus and Arabia

IN THE autobiographical portion of the Epistle to the Galatians Paul records that after his conversion, without consulting any human being and without going up to Jerusalem to see those who were apostles before him, he went off at once to Arabia, and afterwards returned to Damascus; also that after three years he did go up to Jerusalem (1:16 ff).

It has been suggested [1] that here 'Ἀραβία is a mistake for "Ἄραβα and that from Damascus Paul went to ערב, the modern 'Arrabat-el-battof, a place in Galilee in the vicinity of Sepphoris and Cana and not far from Gischala, the town from which, according to a precarious tradition already referred to,[2] Paul's parents had been carried away in a time of civil commotion. But this suggestion has no solid foundation; and if Paul went to Galilee, he is not likely to have returned to Damascus. It is much more probable that by Arabia is meant the kingdom of the Nabataean Arabs, which in the period of their greatest prosperity extended east and south of Palestine from the Euphrates to the Red Sea. The part to which Paul betook himself may not have been far from Damascus. The picture that some have drawn of Paul travelling all the way to the Sinaitic peninsula, tarrying there like Moses and Elijah in the mount of the Lord and learning there that the law had been a temporary institution and that prophecy had been fulfilled in Christ, has been rightly dismissed by G. S. Duncan [3] as 'an imaginative reconstruction for which there is no justification'. In modern times many have supposed that he went to

---
[1] By S. A. Fries, 'Was meint Paulus mit 'Ἀραβία, Galatians 1:17?', ZNTW II.(1901).150 f.
[2] Page 1, supra.
[3] The Epistle of Paul to the Galatians (The Moffatt New Testament Commentary), p. 29.

Arabia so that for a season he might devote himself to prayer and meditation, but it may be that the early fathers were right who held that his purpose in going there was to preach the Gospel. That agrees with what we know about Paul, and perhaps it also explains how he incurred the displeasure of the Nabataean authorities.

The visit to Arabia is not mentioned in Acts, and commentators are not agreed as to whether it should be regarded as having been paid before or after the preaching activity in Damascus referred to in Acts 9:19b–22. Neither view is satisfactory. To insert it between 9:19a and 9:19b is to make a gap in a verse the two parts of which are obviously very closely connected— Paul stayed some time with the disciples in Damascus, not after returning from Arabia, but after his strength had returned ; and to insert it between verses 22 and 23 is to ignore the word ' immediately ' ($εὐθέως$) in Galatians 1:16. The view preferred by Alford [4] and Knowling [5] that the Arabian visit ought to be put between verses 21 and 22 is also at variance with Paul's statement, ' I went off at once to Arabia '.

How long Paul remained in Arabia is not known. Some who think that his purpose in going there was that through communion with God he might be prepared for the work to which he had been called, also think it not unlikely that his stay there may have occupied most of the three years mentioned in Galatians 1:18 ; and they suggest that the writer of Acts may have passed over it in silence because it belonged to Paul's private life. But it might at least equally well be suggested that he has made no mention of it because it was of brief duration or, on the assumption that Paul went to Arabia as a missionary of Christ, because his mission proved unsuccessful. If the part of Arabia to which he went was near to Damascus, his missionary activity there may be included in his public preaching in the synagogues mentioned in Acts 9:20.[6] That, however, is doubtful. Moreover

---

[4] *The Greek Testament* II.103.
[5] *The Expositor's Greek Testament*—II.239.
[6] So Lagrange, *L'Epître aux Galates*, p. 16.

he was away from Jerusalem for three years (Galatians 1:18) and it must be acknowledged that the vague expression ' many days ' ($\dot{\eta}\mu\acute{\epsilon}\rho\alpha\iota$ $\acute{\iota}\kappa\alpha\nu\alpha\acute{\iota}$) in Acts 9:23 hardly suggests so long an interval.[7] On the whole it seems best to conclude that the writer of Acts had not heard of the Arabian visit. That explains not only why he is silent regarding it, but also why, as pointed out above, it is so difficult to find room for it in his account of Paul's sojourn in Damascus, why he seems to represent that sojourn as shorter than it was, and also why the ethnarch of Aretas does not figure in his account of Paul's flight from Damascus.

[7] Paley, *Horae Paulinae* (new ed. by Binnie, 1880), p. 88, quotes 1 Kings 2:38 and 39 ; but the Septuagint translators, as though conscious of a difficulty, substituted *three years* for *many days* in verse 38.

CHAPTER FOUR

Paul's Flight from Damascus

IN 2 Corinthians 11:32 f Paul relates that when he was in Damascus, the ethnarch of Aretas the king kept the city with a garrison so as to have him arrested, but that he was let down in a basket, through a window in the wall, and so escaped his clutches. In Acts 9:23-5 it is recorded that during Paul's stay in Damascus after his conversion, the Jews hatched a plot against his life, but that their plans became known to him. They kept watch on the city gates day and night so that they might murder him; but his converts took him one night and let him down by the wall, lowering him in a basket. The following verse (26) indicates that, having thus escaped from Damascus, he proceeded to Jerusalem.

These two passages sufficiently resemble one another to leave us in no doubt that they relate the same episode, and consequently that what is recorded in 2 Corinthians 11:32 f took place on the occasion not of Paul's first departure from Damascus but of his second, which was also his final, departure from that city three years after his conversion. At the time of the episode there was in Damascus an official who is referred to as 'the ethnarch of Aretas the king' (ὁ ἐθνάρχης Ἀρέτα τοῦ βασιλέως). This Aretas was Aretas [1] IV, king of the Nabataeans. The most probable date of his accession appears to be 9 B C.[2] From two well-preserved inscriptions [3] and also from coins [4] it is known that he reigned for forty-and-eight years. Consequently Paul's flight from Damascus cannot be put later than A D 40.

The function of the official who is styled 'the ethnarch of

---

[1] חרתה in the inscriptions.
[2] This is the conclusion of von Gutschmid in Euting, *Nabatäische Inschriften*, p. 89.
[3] Ibid. p. 56, nos. 16 and 17.
[4] Ibid. p. 85.

Aretas the king' has been much discussed. Three views may be distinguished.

(1) One is that he was the sheikh of a band of Arabs, subjects of Aretas, who were encamped outside the walls of Damascus.[5] At his instruction they kept an eye on the entrances to the city (ἐφρούρει τὴν πόλιν), whilst the Jews resident within it kept an eye on the exits from it (παρετηροῦντο δὲ καὶ τὰς πύλας). This sheikh may have been called the ethnarch. In certain places the word denotes a prince of lower rank than a king.[6] Literally it means the founder or the ruler of a people; and since the organization of the Nabataean kingdom was essentially tribal, it may have been applied to the chieftains of its tribes. Indeed that it was applied to them is clear from Greek inscriptions found in the Hauran. These inscriptions relate to the conditions that obtained in the first half of the second century when the Arabia that belonged to Petra [7] had become a Roman province; and though the fact that the heads of tribes were then called ethnarchs does not prove that they were so earlier, it nevertheless points to that as a possibility. But it cannot be allowed that 'he kept an eye on the entrances to the city' is an adequate or correct rendering of ἐφρούρει τὴν πόλιν. It is inadequate because it does not indicate clearly, as ἐφρούρει does, that the ethnarch was armed with military power.[8] And it is incorrect for two reasons. In the first place Paul's statement that it was by being let down in a basket through a window in the wall that he escaped the ethnarch's clutches shows clearly that the ethnarch was not encamped in the neighbourhood of the city, but was resident in it and so watched it not from the outside but from the inside. In the second place, while φρουρεῖν means sometimes 'to watch from the outside' and sometimes 'to watch from the inside', the latter meaning is to be preferred

---

[5] So Loisy, Lake, Plooij, Haenchen.
[6] See 1 Maccabees 14:47; 15:1–2; Josephus, *Ant.*, xiv.191, xvii. 317; *Bell. Jud.*, ii.93; Lucian, *Macrob.*, 17.
[7] Dion Cassius, lxviii.14.
[8] Moffatt's rendering of ἐφρούρει τὴν πόλιν is 'he had patrols out in the city'.

here. There are passages in which the former meaning is undoubtedly in order. One such passage is adduced by Field,[9] others are adduced by Zahn.[10] But the sense in which Paul uses the verb here is in all likelihood the one in which it is used in the Septuagint, and with regard to that it is sufficient to quote these words of E. L. Hicks : ' The word for garrison is uniformly φρουρά, φρουρεῖν, the soldiers are φρουροί. The verb occurs in its literal sense in 2 Corinthians 11:32 : ἐν Δαμασκῷ ὁ ἐθνάρχης Ἀρέτα τοῦ βασιλέως ἐφρούρει τὴν Δαμασκηνῶν πόλιν πιάσαι με (where the R.V. seems less accurate than the A.V. Marquardt, Röm. Alterth., IV.247, takes the word in its strict sense). I do not wish to dogmatize nor to impose this one meaning upon φρουρεῖν semper et ubique ; but a glance at the literature and documents of the Hellenistic period will show that the word in this sense was in perpetual use, and can hardly have been employed in the New Testament without a reminiscence of it. φρουρά = garrison, 2 Samuel 8:6, 14 ; 1 Paral. 18:13 ; 1 Maccabees 9:51, 11:66, 12:34, 14:33 ; φρουρεῖν = to garrison, Judith 3:6 ; 1 Esdras 4:56 ; similarly φρούριον and φρουρός in LXX. Indeed I think the meaning of garrison is universal in the Old Testament. '[11] Hicks quotes Galatians 3:23, 1 Peter 1:5 and Philippians 4:7, the three verses in which the verb occurs in the epistles of the New Testament. In the first of them he prefers the notion of a garrison town, and he is fairly certain that in the other two also that is the better meaning.

(2) Another view is that the ethnarch mentioned in 2 Corinthians 11:32 was the head of the Nabataean community resident in Damascus.

Josephus in *Ant.*, xiv.117, quotes a passage from Strabo in which, referring to the Jews in Alexandria, he says : ' There is also an ethnarch allowed them, who governs their nation, and distributes justice to them, and takes care of their contracts,

---

[9] F. Field, *Notes on the Translation of the New Testament*, p. 187.
[10] Th. Zahn, *Die Apostelgeschichte des Lucas*, p. 329.
[11] ' On some Political Terms employed in the New Testament ', *Classical Review* I.(1887).7 f.

and of the laws to them belonging, as if he were the ruler of a free republic.' In an edict to the Alexandrians preserved in Josephus, *Ant.*, xix.281-5, the emperor Claudius observes that ' when the Jewish ethnarch was dead, Augustus did not prohibit the making such ethnarchs '. Origen also in his *Epistula ad Africanum*, § 14, writes that in his own day the Jewish ethnarch in Palestine had so great powers that he differed in little from a true king. Some have thought that likewise the ethnarch referred to by Paul was the head of the Jewish community in Damascus. Thomas Lewin, for instance, in his work *The Life and Letters of St. Paul* [12] considers that there can be little doubt ' that ὁ ἐθνάρχης in 2 Corinthians 11:32 was the *Jewish* chief magistrate '. But then he would have been called not the ethnarch of Aretas but the ethnarch of the Jews (in Josephus, *Ant.*, xiv.117, ' their ethnarch ' ; in xix.283, ' the Jewish ethnarch ' ; and considerable as his authority may have been he could not have kept the city with a garrison.

Several more recent scholars [13] prefer to think that at the time of Paul's flight from Damascus the city was in the hands of the Romans and that the ethnarch was the head of the resident Nabataean community, exercising in it functions similar to those which the Jewish ethnarchs in Alexandria and Palestine exercised in theirs. If Aretas was allowed by the Romans to nominate this official, that might explain why he is designated the ethnarch of Aretas. But it is not certain that he was nominated by Aretas ; he may have been so by the Damascene Nabataean community itself ; and however he may have been nominated, he certainly did not have power to keep the city with a garrison.

(3) Yet another view is that at the time when Paul escaped from Damascus Aretas was in possession of the city and that the ethnarch was his viceroy there.

[12] I.(4th edn.).72, note 60 ; see also Lewin *Fasti Sacri*, nos. 1533 and 1580.
[13] E.g. E. Schwartz, ' Die Aeren von Gerasa und Eleutheropolis ', *Nachr. v.d. königl. Gesell. d. Wissen. zu Göttingen*, (1906), pp. 367 ff ; E. Meyer, *Ursprung u. Anfänge des Christentums* III.346.

This view obviously consists both with the description of the ethnarch as the ethnarch of Aretas the king and with the statement that he kept the city with a garrison. Two objections have been made to it: (*a*) If the ethnarch exercised sovereign rights in Damascus, he could without more ado have had Paul arrested in the city; (*b*) Since the government of the Nabataean kingdom was by tribes, it is likely that the person chosen to be the king's representative in Damascus was the head of the tribe occupying the territory within which that city was situated, accordingly that his powers were not confined to the city and that Paul, once he was beyond its walls, was not beyond his reach. The contention that the ethnarch was the head of this tribe merits consideration and may be sound.[14] It explains the title ἐθνάρχης where we would expect ἔπαρχος or στρατηγός, and it brings its use here into conformity with its use in the inscriptions from the Hauran referred to above. But of the first objection it may be said that it ignores the difference that there may be between what an official has power to do and what he finds himself capable of doing in a given situation, and of the second that it ignores the extent to which, by strategy and in the dead of night ' when the eye of caution is sealed in sleep ', the friends of a man whose enemies seek his life may prove his helpers.

This view involves the assumption that during part at least of his reign Aretas IV was in possession of Damascus. The history of the city from the beginning of the Roman period to A D 106 has been much debated. According to Marquardt and Mommsen it remained subject to the Nabataean kings throughout the whole of that time. Marquardt[15] maintains that in 62 B C, when M. Aemilius Scaurus, the first governor of Syria, made a treaty with the Nabataean king, Damascus became in fact subject to the Romans. But he holds that the Nabataean kings were given possession of it, doubtless on payment of

---

[14] See Schürer, ' Der Ethnarch des Königs Aretas ', *SK*, LXXII.(1899). 95–9.

[15] *Organisation de l'Empire Romain*, II.349.

a tribute, and that it was only in A D 106, when Arabia Petraea became a Roman province, that the city passed into the power of the Romans, being attached, however, not to Arabia but to Syria. Mommsen [16] notes that in the time of the last of the Seleucids the city voluntarily submitted to the Nabataean king, and he thinks it probable that its dependence on the Nabataean kings subsisted so long as there were such kings. If it did so, then, as Mommsen writes, ' the attempt to find a chronological basis for the history of Paul's life in the sway of the Nabataean king of Damascus, and generally to define the time of Paul's abode in this city, must probably be abandoned '.

On the whole, however, the view that Damascus remained subject to the Nabataean kings continuously from 62 B C to A D 106 seems unlikely. The evidence against it is assembled by Schürer [17] under five heads. Peculiarly compelling is the evidence provided by coins of Damascus which bear the heads of Augustus, Tiberius, and Nero. Mommsen argues that while from the fact that the city had such coins there follows its dependence on Rome, there does not follow its non-dependence on the Roman vassal-prince. But it is significant and needs to be underlined that these coins do not bear upon them any allusions to a native prince such as are invariably found on the coins of vassal-States. In the words of Schürer, ' these coins are very unfavourable to the idea of a contemporary subjection to the king of Arabia '.

The coins which bear the head of Tiberius run on to the year 345 of the Seleucid era, i.e. A D 33–4, and those which bear the head of Nero begin with the year 374 of the Seleucid era, i.e. A D 62–3. That there are no coins of the kind for the intervening years may be purely accidental; it does not prove that throughout the whole or some part of that interval Damascus was subject to Aretas, but it permits the possibility of that.

---

[16] *The Provinces of the Roman Empire*, II.148–50, note 4.
[17] *The Jewish People in the Time of Jesus Christ*, I.ɪɪ.354 f, note 14 ; cf. von Soden, ' Aretas ' *Encyclopaedia Biblica*, I, cols. 296 f.

Josephus [18] records that a war broke out between Aretas IV and Herod Antipas. Its occasion was in part the action of the latter in divorcing his wife, the daughter of the former, and in part certain differences about boundaries. Antipas was defeated and appealed to Tiberius, who wrote to Vitellius, the governor of Syria, instructing him to make war upon Aretas and either to take him alive and send Aretas to him in bonds or to kill him and send him his head. Vitellius accordingly prepared an expedition against Aretas. His army marched by way of the great plain, while he himself with Aretas and his friends went up to Jerusalem. On the fourth day of his stay there, word came of the death of Tiberius. The mandate for the expedition thereupon lapsed *eo ipso*, and nothing more came of it. Tiberius died on 16th March, A D 37. Vitellius was in Jerusalem at the time of ' an ancient feast of the Jews ', apparently Passover, which in that year fell *c*. 19th April.[19] The expedition thus belongs to the spring of A D 37. It seems quite unlikely that in the interval A D 34–7 and prior to this expedition Aretas had seized Damascus. Such an act on his part would have been a major reason for the campaign that was launched against him, and it would hardly have been left unmentioned by the Jewish historian. Moreover, if Damascus had been in the hands of Aretas, Vitellius, on setting out to go to Petra, would have proceeded against it and not have left it in his rear. It may accordingly be concluded that in the spring of A D 37 Damascus was still in Roman hands. If then the term ἐθνάρχης in 2 Corinthians 11:32 is understood in the last of the three ways mentioned above, Damascus must have passed into the hands of Aretas—it was probably handed over to him by Caligula [20]—between A D 37 and A D 40 ; Paul's flight

---

[18] *Ant.*, xviii.109–26.
[19] Lewin, *Fasti Sacri*, p. 255. The dates of the Jewish feasts given by Lewin are based on the times of the astronomical full moon, and not upon those of the appearing (phase) of the new moon of Nisan. They are, therefore, not always correct, but are often a sufficient guide.
[20] So Schürer, op. cit. (note 17, *supra*), I.II.357 ; also A. H. M. Jones, *Cities of the Eastern Roman Provinces*, p. 292. According to S. Perowne, *The Later Herods* (1958), p. 83, ' during the years 37 to 40 it [Damascus]

from the city must have taken place in the same interval, and therefore his conversion, three years earlier, between A D 34 and A D 37. In the following chapter, reason will be given for dating his conversion in the first rather than the second half of this interval.

was leased by Caligula to Harith IV, King of the Nabataeans'. The view of Renan and some others that Aretas seized Damascus on hearing of the death of Tiberius, is less likely. Such an action on the part of Aretas would have been such a defiance of the power of Rome that Vitellius, a governor of whom Tacitus (*Ann.*,VI.32) wrote that 'in the government of provinces he acted with the virtue of ancient times', would almost certainly have marched upon Damascus before returning to Syria.

CHAPTER FIVE

The Date of Paul's Conversion

IT IS NOT until the reader of Acts reaches its ninth chapter that he comes upon the account of Paul's conversion. That may give him the impression that there was a considerable time between the Lord's resurrection and that decisive turning-point in Paul's life. It needs, however, to be noted that dialogue, prayer and address occupy much of the first eight chapters, that the events recorded in them are not numerous, and that each of a fair proportion of these events took place within one day or two days at the most. Moreover the intervals between certain of the events were not, or can scarcely have been, long. Whilst allowance needs perhaps to be made for exaggeration, the numbers mentioned in 2:41 and 4:4 clearly indicate that in those early pentecostal days there was a rapid increase in the membership of the Church. That carries with it the likelihood that soon there was in it a considerable body of Hellenists, that the needs of the latter mentioned in 6:1 were soon felt, and consequently that the appointment of the Seven (6:5) was soon made. This gave Stephen an opportunity of using his gifts in the service of Christ which, it may be assumed, he at once redeemed; and that a man whose doctrine was so disquieting and who was so outspoken and irresistible in his presentation of it was soon stoned to death, is very likely.[1] The persecution spoken of in 8:1 was an issue of the same spirit of opposition that occasioned the murder of Stephen and doubtless followed immediately upon it. Paul had part in this persecution from its beginning, and no long time need have passed before he set out for Damascus.

---

[1] Moffatt, in the article 'Stephen' in *Encyclopaedia Biblica*, IV, col. 4796, note 1, mentions a tradition that put the ascension and Stephen's martyrdom in the same year. See p. 30, note 12, *infra*.

According to the dates given by certain authorities for the crucifixion and for Paul's conversion there was a considerable interval (one of four or five or six or even of ten years)[2] between these two events. For the present what calls for consideration is not their determination of these dates, but the points which some of them have made in seeking to confirm their conclusion that this interval was a fairly long one.

(1) Attention is called to the fact that there were already Christians in Damascus when Paul arrived there; and it is maintained that since that implies an expansion of the Church beyond the borders of Palestine, sufficient time must be allowed for that.

There is no good reason to question the existence by this time of a company of Christians in Damascus. According to Matthew 4:24 f our Lord's fame reached the whole of Syria and great crowds followed Him not only from Galilee and Jerusalem and Judaea but also from the Decapolis and Transjordan. It is then likely that there were Damascene Jews in these crowds, and that some of them returned home impressed by what they had seen and heard.[3] Again, since the large Jewish community in Damascus was doubtless represented at all the major religious feasts in Jerusalem, it is likely that it was so in the multitude that heard Peter's sermon on the day of Pentecost and also in the many who then became believers. Yet again, it may be that of those who left Jerusalem on the outbreak of the persecution that followed the murder of Stephen some fled to Damascus. In ways such as these the fact that there was already a group of Christians in Damascus can quite well be accounted for. Nothing necessitates the conclusion that it was the issue of a missionary campaign of some years duration. Moreover these Christians

---

[2] E.g. Lightfoot, A D 30–4; Zahn, A D 30–5; Turner, A D 29–35; Wieseler, A D 30–40.

[3] This of course does not mean acceptance of the theory of Lohmeyer in his book, *Galiläa und Jerusalem*, that the Christianity of Damascus stemmed from a Galilean Christianity that was distinct from the Christianity of Jerusalem.

were apparently still living in happy relations with the Jews and had not yet separated from the synagogue (Acts 9:2, 22:12). Nothing suggests that they had already gathered themselves into an organization such as could have been built up only in the course of several years. Indeed there is no indication that at this time there were any organized Christian communities outside Jerusalem.[4]

(2) It is maintained that in the period covered by Acts 1-8 there was a change in the attitude of the Pharisees towards the Church in Jerusalem, and that this can have come about only after some considerable time.

From Acts 4 it is clear that in the first attempts made by the Jewish authorities to suppress the new faith the Sadducees played a leading part. In 4:1 they are mentioned along with the controller of the temple and the priests who arrested Peter and John. In 4:5 f attention is called to the fact that in the Sanhedrin that met on the following day the Sadducean members were present in full force. The account given in Acts 5:17-42 may or may not be a doublet of that given in Acts 4:1-22,[5] but it also testifies to the prominent part played by the Sadducees in measures taken against the Church (see verses 17 f and 21).

At the outset it was mostly in the temple area that the apostles taught; and since the Sadducees were responsible for good order there, their actions against the apostles may be put down to fears of disorder. But they had also other and more compelling reasons for dealing with them as they did. They were profoundly disquieted by the proclamation of the apostles that Jesus of Nazareth, in securing whose crucifixion they had taken a large part, was the holy and righteous One, the Source of life and

---

[4] Cf. W. L. Knox, *St. Paul and the Church of Jerusalem*, p. 12, note 3; Goguel, *The Birth of Christianity* (E.T. of *La Naissance du Christianisme*), p. 463.

[5] See Harnack, *The Acts of the Apostles* (E.T. of *Apostelgeschichte, Beitr. zur Einleitung in das N.T.* III), pp. 162-202; Jeremias, ' Untersuchungen zum Quellenproblem der Apostelgeschichte ', *ZNTW*, XXXVI.(1937).205 ff; Haenchen, *Die Apostelgeschichte* (12th edn., 1959), pp. 209 f; Dupont, *Les Sources du Livre des Actes*, pp. 33-50.

salvation, and jealousy provoked by the popularity of the apostles also goaded them into action.

But from the fact that the Sadducees took a leading part in the first attempts to repress the new movement it by no means follows that others did not co-operate with them. The Pharisees secured permission to have representatives in the Sanhedrin probably in the reign of Alexandra (79–69 B C), and by the time of Herod the Great they had become a very influential party within it. Pharisees then were undoubtedly present in the Sanhedrin that met to examine Peter and John (Acts 4:5 ff), and it is to be assumed that they joined with the Sadducees in ordering these two apostles to refrain from all public speaking and teaching in the name of Jesus (Acts 4:18). So too there were Pharisees in the Sanhedrin that met on the day after the arrest of all the apostles, and the statement, ' They wanted to put them to death ' (Acts 5:33) applies to them as well as to the Sadducees. It is true that one of them, Rabbi Gamaliel, counselled them to adopt a waiting policy, and true that the members of the Sanhedrin took his advice (Acts 5:40a). But they did so only after a fashion and not for long. If they discharged the apostles, they did so only after flogging them and ordering them to give up speaking in the name of Jesus (Acts 5:40b) ; and when discussions began in the synagogues of the Hellenists—and that, as has already been indicated, may have been soon afterwards—the Pharisaic party showed almost at once and quite unmistakably how little prepared it was to maintain the ' wait and see ' attitude recommended by Gamaliel.

Allowance must of course be made for individuals. Reference is made later to some of the Pharisaic party who had become believers (Acts 15:5). But the wording of this reference itself testifies to general Pharisaic unbelief. The Pharisees had also been party to the crucifixion of Jesus. They too must have viewed with apprehension the emergence of the Christian community. From the outset there must have been in them a spirit of opposition, and, alarmed by the rapid growth of the Church, they must soon have given expression to it. If in Acts prominence is given first to Sadducean rather than to Pharisaic opposition to Christianity, that is because the scene of proclamation and debate was first the temple and then the synagogue, and not because opposition on the part of the Pharisees came later or because their attitude changed gradually from friendliness to neutrality and then gradually from neutrality to active hostility.

(3) On the ground that in Romans 16:7 Paul says of Andronicus and Junias that they were Christians before he was, it is maintained that he numbered himself not among the believers of the earliest years but among those of a somewhat later time.

Here, however, Paul singles out significant facts with regard to these two: members of a Gentile Church, they were his fellow-countrymen; they had suffered imprisonment for Christ's sake as he also had done; and they were men of note among the apostles (perhaps the itinerant evangelists). What he adds is doubtless significant also, and that they had become Christians before he did is significant only if the number of those who by then had done so was not very large. Paul himself was converted in the early days of the Christian community, but, even so, these two had already by that time become members of it.

The question as to what time there was from our Lord's resurrection to the conversion of Paul is discussed by Harnack in an article entitled ' Chronologische Berechnung des " Tags von Damaskus " '.[6] There he points out that, besides the teaching of Acts 1:3 that there were forty days between the resurrection and the ascension, two other views of the length of this interval were current in early times, the one that it was an interval of one and a half years and the other that it was one of twelve years.

The latter view,[7] which is found in gnostic writings preserved in Coptic and is not earlier than the third century, emerged out of the tradition that after the resurrection the apostles remained

---

[6] In *Sitzungsberichte der kon. preussichen Akademie der Wissenschaften zu Berlin* (1912), pp. 673–82.
[7] On this view see especially von Dobschütz, ' Das Kerygma Petri ', *TU*, XI.I.(1893).52 ff and 136 ff.

together in Jerusalem for twelve years before they went out on their several ways to preach the Gospel in other lands. It was assumed that the Lord had tarried with them and taught them throughout these years. The other view, that the interval was one of one and a half years, is attested no fewer than three times.

(1) Irenaeus in *adv. Haer.*, I.xxx.14, gives the following as part of the teaching of the Ophites :

But after His resurrection He tarried (on earth) eighteen months ; and knowledge descending into Him from above, He taught what was clear. He instructed a few of His disciples, whom He knew to be capable of understanding so great mysteries, in these things, and then was received up into heaven.[8]

(2) Irenaeus in *adv. Haer.*, I.iii.2, gives the following as part of the doctrine of the disciples of Ptolemaeus, whose school he describes as a bud from that of Valentinus :

The other eighteen Aeons are made manifest in this way: that the Lord (according to them) conversed with His disciples for eighteen months after His resurrection from the dead.[9]

(3) In the *Ascension of Isaiah* (9:16), which belongs to the second century, we read :

And when He (the Son of man) shall have despoiled the angel of death, He will rise again on the third day and will remain on the earth for five hundred and forty-five days.[10]

The *Ascension of Isaiah* is an apocryphal writing, but its author was neither a heretic nor a gnostic. Here then we have a datum that had a place alike in ecclesiastical tradition and in gnostic tradition, and which in consequence must be very early. It does not owe its existence to metaphysical speculation, and must be rooted in history ; and what Harnack suggests is that originally it referred to the period between the Lord's resurrection and His appearance to Paul on the Damascus road. According to 1 Corinthians 15:8 that appearance was the last one of its kind and marked the end of a distinct period. It is possible,

---

[8] Ante-Nicene Library trans.
[9] Ibid.
[10] 545 days = one year (365 days) plus six months (6 × 30 = 180 days).

Harnack thinks, that when in his teaching Paul referred to his conversion he sometimes gave the length of this period ; and this information may have been transmitted to the Valentinians by a disciple of Paul, Theodas by name, who is mentioned by Clement of Alexandria,[11] but is otherwise unknown.

In spite of all that Harnack urges in support of his interpretation of the eighteen months, there may well be a measure of doubt as to its soundness.[12] But that interpretation certainly harmonizes with the conclusion which other considerations necessitate, namely that there was no long interval between the resurrection and Paul's conversion. We assume that the resurrection took place in A D 33.[13] Fourteen years after his conversion Paul attended the Jerusalem Conference (Galatians 2:1). He then set out on what is commonly called his Second Missionary Journey and in the course of it arrived in Corinth, as we shall see,[14] early in A D 50. Thus only three or four years remain for the period from the resurrection to Paul's conversion plus the period from the Jerusalem Conference to Paul's arrival in Corinth. This means that Paul's conversion can hardly have taken place later than A D 35 and must be dated either in that year or, less probably, in A D 34.

---

[11] *Strom.* VII. xvii.106. That Theodas was acquainted with Paul (γνώριμος δ' οὗτος γεγόνει Παύλῳ) seems improbable. See article ' Valentinus ' in *Dictionary of Christian Biography*, IV.1076.

[12] The eighteen months have been put down by some to a misunderstanding of IH M′ HMC (= 'Ιησοῦς μ′ ἡμέρας) as IH′ MHCI (= ιη′ μησί), and eighteen months may later have been given as 545 days. In the *Excerpta latina Barbari* (*Evsebi Chronicorvm Libri Dvo*, ed. A. Schoene, I.230), Paul's conversion is put eight months after the ascension :

> *Paulus au
> tem apostolus post ascensionem dni et post
> passionem Stephani dierum in apostulatum or
> dinatur VI Idos Januarias sub consolato Rubellio
> nis· post ascensionem saluatoris nostri men
> ses VIII post dies XI passionis Stephani pridie
> Epiphaniae.*

[13] Ogg, *The Chronology of the Public Ministry of Jesus*, pp. 244-77.

[14] Page 115, *infra*.

CHAPTER SIX

Paul's First Visit to Jerusalem after his Conversion

AN ACCOUNT of Paul's first visit to Jerusalem after his conversion is given in Galatians 1:18–24 and also in Acts 9:26–30. In the first of these passages Paul states that he paid this visit three years after his conversion, that his purpose in making it was 'to get to know' (ἱστορῆσαι)[1] Cephas, that he stayed with him for a fortnight, without seeing any other of the apostles, except James the Lord's brother, and that he then went to the regions of Syria and Cilicia. 'I remained', he adds, 'unknown by sight to Christ's congregations in Judaea. They only heard it said, " Our former persecutor is preaching the good news of the faith which once he tried to destroy "; and they praised God for me.' According to the passage in Acts, Paul, on reaching Jerusalem, found it difficult to make contact with the body of disciples there since they doubted the reality of his conversion. But through the good offices of Barnabas he secured an introduction to them. He then stayed with them and moved about freely in Jerusalem, speaking boldly and openly in the name of the Lord and debating with the Hellenists. But they planned to murder him, and the brethren, on learning of this, escorted him to Caesarea and saw him off to Tarsus.

These accounts present a considerable number of difficulties. In Acts the purpose of the visit is not stated, and Barnabas is assumed to have an acquaintance with Paul which has not previously been accounted for. In Galatians no reference is made to the service which, according to Acts, Barnabas rendered Paul. Whereas according to Acts, Paul appears to have been introduced to the apostles generally, he himself solemnly affirms

---

[1] On this verb see a contribution by G. D. Kilpatrick to *New Testament Essays : Studies in Memory of T. W. Manson*, ed. by A. J. B. Higgins, 1959, pp. 144–9.

that of the apostles he saw only Cephas and James the Lord's brother. Whereas in Acts he is represented as having engaged in public preaching in Jerusalem, his own description of his visit to the city suggests that it was entirely private in character. The account in Acts gives the impression that the stay in Jerusalem was longer than the fortnight mentioned in Galatians. Since of the churches in Judaea the foremost was the one in Jerusalem, the statement in Acts that Paul preached publicly in that city seems to be at variance with his own statement that he remained unknown by sight to these churches.

F. C. Baur and other members of the Tübingen School maintained that the account in Acts, both of the sojourn in Damascus and of this visit to Jerusalem, has been written up against the representation in Galatians. No mention has been made of Paul's stay in Arabia and he has been brought back to Jerusalem soon after his conversion so that his activity as a preacher of the Gospel may follow upon his recognition by the apostles. On the ground of the difficulties which it presents certain scholars of a later date have concluded that the story told in Acts 9:26-30 has been adapted to its present situation, but referred originally to a later visit of Paul to Jerusalem. This visit was paid after Barnabas had become acquainted with Paul through having him as his colleague in the work of the Church at Antioch, and may be the visit referred to in Acts 11:27-30, 12:25.[2] More recently the historicity of Acts 9:26-30 has been denied. It is maintained that on leaving Damascus Paul proceeded to Tarsus, and the Jerusalem visit recorded in Acts 11:27-30, 12:25 is identical with the one recorded in Galatians 1:18-24. This identification is discussed in Chapter 9 below.

Two arguments are adduced in favour of the view that Acts

---

[2] So J. Weiss, *History of Primitive Christianity* (E.T. of *Das Urchristentum*), I.200, note 17. Weiss ventures the suggestion that the visits of Acts 9:26-30 and 11:27-30, 12:25 may be identical. Cf. D. F. Robinson, ' A Note on Acts 11:27-30 ', *JBL*, LXIII.(1944).169-72. On Robinson's argument, see F. W. Beare, ' Note on Paul's First Two Visits to Jerusalem ', *JBL*, LXIII.(1944).407-9, to which Robinson replies (ibid., pp. 411 f).

9:26–30 may be an adapted version of an account of the famine-relief visit to Jerusalem recorded in Acts 11:27–30, 12:25. The one is that then the acquaintance of Barnabas with Paul can occasion no surprise : Barnabas had already got to know Paul personally through working with him in Antioch. But it may be pointed out here that this acquaintance assumed in Acts 9:26–30 is also assumed in Acts 11:25. The other argument is that by the time of the famine-relief visit the Hellenists in Jerusalem must have heard of Paul's missionary work in Syria and Cilicia, and so it is more likely that, as recorded in Acts 9:29, they planned to murder him. But Stephen, so far as is known, confined his proclamation and defence of the Gospel to Jerusalem, and it was Hellenists there who took the initial steps that led to his being stoned to death (Acts 6:9 ff).

Attempts are made to account for, and to reduce, the differences and seeming discrepancies that have been listed above. It is noted that the two accounts of this visit come from different authors, that they were written with different ends in view, and that whereas the one in Galatians gives the inner history, the other in Acts gives the outer history of Paul's doings in Jerusalem on this occasion. Attention is also called to two obvious facts : that the writer of Acts may have omitted certain happenings simply because he had never heard of them, and that he could not give precise information about matters of which he had no more than a general knowledge. Full consideration ought assuredly to be given to these points, but many remain far from convinced that they suffice to harmonize the two accounts.

It is easy to suggest when and where Barnabas may have come to know Paul before the latter's conversion. They may have met in Jerusalem at the time of one of the great feasts. Since Paul belonged to Cilicia and Barnabas to Cyprus, which lay near to Cilicia, the two may have met either in Cyprus or in Cilicia. In particular they may have done so in Tarsus when one or both of them were students in the university there.[3] J. N.

---

[3] Since Paul's parents were Jews of the stricter sort, it seems unlikely that he attended the university in Tarsus, a seat of pagan culture.

Sanders [4] makes a suggestion which, while it rests on suppositions that are certainly debatable, carries down the commencement of Barnabas' acquaintance with Paul to a time after the latter had become a Christian. He considers it very probable that Barnabas was not sent to Antioch by the church in Jerusalem as recorded in Acts 11:22, but that he was one of the men of Cyprus and Cyrene who, after the persecution that arose about Stephen, came to Antioch preaching the Lord Jesus (Acts 11:20); and he suggests that he met Paul during the 'many days' (Acts 9:23) between his conversion and his first visit to Jerusalem thereafter. All these suggestions are, however, no more than possibilities, and it remains true that the writer of Acts assumes in 9:27 an acquaintance of Barnabas with Paul the beginnings of which he has not recorded earlier in his narrative.

To avoid the discrepancy between the statement in Acts that in Jerusalem Paul spoke boldly and openly in the name of the Lord and his own statement that he remained unknown by sight to Christ's congregations in Judaea, it has been suggested that the phrase 'in Jerusalem' (εἰς 'Ιερουσαλήμ) in Acts 9:28 should be regarded as a gloss and both that verse and the one following be read as a continuation of what Barnabas reported about Paul's conduct in Damascus. But this involves a certain amount of needless repetition, and the phrase 'in Jerusalem' rests on good manuscript authority. The suggestion made more commonly that in Galatians 1:22 Paul may distinguish between the provincial Churches in Judaea and the church in Jerusalem is regarded by many as far-fetched.

No fully satisfactory reconciliation of the two accounts seems possible. It may be of course that in certain of its particulars Paul's own account is not correct and that he is responsible for some of the difficulties that present themselves. But his state-

---

[4] 'Peter and Paul in Acts', *New Testament Studies*, II.(1955).133-43. For a discussion of the considerable rearrangement of events suggested in this article and a refutation of the arguments advanced in support of it, see J. Dupont, 'Pierre et Paul dans les Actes', *Revue Biblique*, LXIV.(1957).35-47.

ment, 'What I write is plain truth', coupled with the asseveration, 'Before God I am not lying', forbids the thought. 'Such asseverations', writes Weizsächer,[5] 'serve to establish truth in sacred matters.' From Galatians 1:20 it has been inferred that in part at least Paul's purpose in Galatians 1:18–24 was to refute certain rumours that were in circulation to the effect that he had had many contacts with the apostles and the members of the church in Jerusalem on the occasion of his first stay there after his conversion. It is then added that while the writer of Acts thought that what he has recorded in 9:26–30 was sound tradition, it was in fact merely a precipitate of these rumours. However that may be, it is to be concluded that while the account in Acts 9:26–30 is that of Paul's first visit to Jerusalem after his conversion, it is not fully informed or entirely free from error, and that Galatians 1:18–24 should be accepted as the more reliable record of what happened. It was then three years after his conversion, therefore in A D 37 or 38, that Paul returned to Jerusalem. This, his first visit to the city since his conversion, was a private one. It lasted only a fortnight, and it ended with his departure to Syria and Cilicia.

According to some, Paul paid this visit to Jerusalem in A D 40. In that year the minds of the members of the Sanhedrin were fully occupied with the mad attempt being made by Caligula to have his statue set up in the temple at Jerusalem; and it is urged that only if Paul visited the city in that year, can the fact that during his stay he remained unmolested be accounted for. That, however, is to forget that his visit was private in character and of brief duration.

---

[5] *The Apostolic Age of the Christian Church* (E.T. of *Das apostolische Zeitalter der christlichen Kirche*), I.95.

CHAPTER SEVEN

The Silent Years

IN ACTS the story of Paul is broken off at 9:30 with the words, 'They [the brethren in Jerusalem] escorted him to Caesarea and saw him off to Tarsus', and it is not resumed until 11:25, where it is recorded that Barnabas went to Tarsus to look for him and, having found him, brought him to Antioch to be his colleague in the work of the church there. The intervening period must, we reckon, have been one of seven or eight years: for, so we have concluded, Paul was in Jerusalem for the first time after his conversion in A D 37 or 38; and since, as will be shown below,[1] the probable date of the famine-relief visit to Jerusalem is winter A D 45–6, the year in which Barnabas and Paul worked together in Antioch is probably A D 45. No account is given of Paul's activities during these seven or eight years,[2] and only two statements of a fairly general nature can be made about them. The one, based on Galatians 1:23, is that he spent at least part of that time in Syria and Cilicia preaching the good news of the faith which once he had tried to destroy. The other, based on Acts 15:41, is that his preaching resulted in the founding of churches in both these regions. It may be assumed that, whilst thus engaged, Paul also sought time for study; and W. C. van Unnik,[3] who maintains that Paul spent his youth in Jerusalem, suggests that it was during this period that he gained not only the acquaintance which he exhibits with Greek culture but also that mastery of the Septuagint which is manifest in his epistles.

---

[1] Page 53.
[2] J. Weiss, *History of Primitive Christianity* (E.T. of *Das Urchristentum*), I.205, notes that not even the author of the *Acta Pauli* has ventured by an exercise of his imagination to fill up this gap in our knowledge of Paul's career.
[3] *Tarsus or Jeruzalem*, p. 37 (E.T., pp. 56 f).

The fact that history is so largely silent regarding this period does not justify such a redistribution of Paul's later recorded activities as would bring some of them within it. Before entering upon the great work for which they are now remembered, many of God's servants have served a long and rewarding apprenticeship, engaging in a narrow sphere for many years in labours of which no detailed account has been preserved. The writer of Acts may be silent about what Paul did in this period because he had practically no information about it. Another possibility is that he did have information about it, but chose not to record it. It may be, as G. G. Findlay [4] maintains, that 'Paul's work in his homeland lay outside the main course of the Church's development which Luke made it his business to sketch'.

Paul had an ample opportunity of engaging in missionary work in Syria and Cilicia. In the former of these regions such work was possible not only in several inland towns but also in all the coast towns from Ptolemais in the south to Seleucia in the north, and in the latter not only in Tarsus but also in such centres as Anazarbus, Mopsuestia and Corycus. In some quarters it has been assumed that Paul's statement, 'I went to the regions of Syria and Cilicia', does not mean that he confined himself to these regions, but merely indicates that these were the regions from which his work at this time began and so leaves open the possibility of his having passed beyond them. J. Weiss [5] suggests that Paul may have spent part of this period on a missionary journey to Cyrene. But he does so with considerable hesitation. 'Of course', he writes, 'we cannot come to any conclusion about a possibility which is so vague and shadowy.' John Knox in his book, *Chapters in a Life of Paul*,[6] maintains that at this time the apostle engaged in missionary work not only

---

[4] 'Paul the Apostle', *HDB*, III.704a; cf. Dibelius, *Studies in the Acts of the Apostles* (E.T. of *Aufsätze zur Apostelgeschichte*, ed Greeven), p. 209: 'It seems that only those evangelizing activities were important to him which were directed toward the west and finally led to Rome.'
[5] Op. cit. (note 2, *supra*), p. 204.
[6] Pages 74–85. On Knox's conclusions see G. Ogg, 'A New Chronology of Saint Paul's Life', *Expository Times*, LXIV.(1953).120–3.

in Syria and Cilicia but also in Galatia, Macedonia, Greece, and Asia, and that he ' must have first reached Corinth hardly later than A D 45, perhaps several years earlier'. But according to Acts 18:12 ff Paul was in Corinth for the first time when Gallio was governor of Achaia, and from the Delphi inscription it is known that Gallio entered on that office not earlier than May A D 51.[7] In consequence Knox is obliged to suggest that the writer of Acts has made a considerable mistake : he has assigned the trial before Gallio to Paul's first visit to Corinth, whereas, if there was in fact such a trial, it must have taken place on the occasion of a later visit. That, it is extremely difficult to allow. Moreover Paul's statement, ' I went to the regions of Syria and Cilicia ', must be considered along with his reason for making it. That reason seems to be rightly given by Bonnard : ' Paul's supreme purpose in mentioning his activity in Syria and Cilicia is to lay stress upon his remoteness from Jerusalem '.[8] That being so, then, had it been possible, would he not have underlined his separation from Jerusalem still further and have written, ' I went to the regions of Syria and Cilicia and then beyond them to Galatia, yes and still farther afield into lands west of the Aegean Sea ' ? On the whole it seems unlikely that in the interval between his first visit to Jerusalem after his conversion and his arrival in Antioch (Acts 11:26) he travelled beyond the borders of Syria and Cilicia.

[7] Page 111, *infra*.
[8] *L'épître de saint Paul aux Galates*, p. 34. Cf. J. Dupont, ' Notes sur les Actes des Apôtres ', *Revue Biblique*, LXII.(1955).47 ff.

CHAPTER EIGHT

Agrippa's Persecution of the Church and His Death

IN ACTS 11:27-30 it is recorded that at some time in the course of the year during which Barnabas and Paul worked together in Antioch certain prophets came there from Jerusalem, that one of them, Agabus by name, predicted a severe and worldwide famine, that the disciples then agreed to make a contribution, each according to his means, for the relief of their fellow Christians in Judaea, and that, having done this, they sent it off in the charge of Barnabas and Paul to the elders. In Acts 12:25 it is added that these two, their task fulfilled, returned from Jerusalem. In the intervening paragraph, Acts 12:1-24, an account is given first of a persecution of the church at Jerusalem by Herod Agrippa I and then of that king's death. For the present we confine our attention to the question: What are the dates of these two happenings?

Herod Agrippa I was a grandson of Herod the Great and, through his grandmother Mariamme, a descendant of the Hasmonaean princes. An adventurer in youth and early manhood, he cultivated the friendship of Caligula, who, soon after his accession on 16th March A D 37, bestowed upon him the tetrarchies of Philip and Lysanias with the title of king (Josephus, *Ant.*, xviii.237). Later, when Caligula deprived Herod Antipas of his kingdom, he bestowed it upon Agrippa (*Ant.*, xviii.252). Later still, when Claudius became emperor, he added Judaea and Samaria to what Agrippa already possessed, thus making him king over all the territory that had belonged to his grandfather (*Ant.*, xix.274). After telling the story of Agrippa's death, which occurred when he 'had reigned three years all over Judaea' (*Ant.*, xix.343), Josephus adds: 'He departed this life, being in the fifty-fourth year of his age, and in the seventh year of his reign; for he reigned four years under

Caius Caesar, three of them were over Philip's tetrarchy only, and on the fourth he had that of Herod added to it, and he reigned besides these three years under the reign of Claudius Caesar ' (*Ant.*, xix.350 f).

In A D 37 the month Nisan has already commenced by 16th March.[1] Consequently the second year of Agrippa's reign, as Josephus has reckoned it,[2] was A D 38 (1st Nisan)—39, and the seventh A D 43 (1st Nisan)—44. Since Claudius became emperor on 25th January A D 41 and Agrippa reigned three full years under him, the death of Agrippa must have taken place between 25th January and 1 Nisan A D 44. According to Lewin (*Fasti Sacri*, p. 282), Passover in A D 44 was 1st April, and therefore 1st Nisan was 19th March. According to Parker and Dubberstein (*Babylonian Chronology*, p. 46), a second Adar (19th March–17th April) was intercalated in this year and 1st Nisan was 18th April.

A coin of Agrippa's eighth year is discussed by Reifenberg in the *Palestinian Exploration Fund Quarterly Statement* (LXVII. [1935].80). The conclusion just reached that Agrippa died near to the close of the seventh year of his reign, suggests the likelihood that this coin was minted in anticipation.

When Agrippa was stricken with the sickness of which he died a few days later, a festival was being held in Caesarea ' in honour of Caesar, on behalf of his well-being '.[3] It has been suggested [4] that this festival was in celebration of Claudius' birthday. It has also been suggested [5] that it was a celebration of the day of his accession. But there does not appear to have been a regular observance of his birthday even in Rome, and

---

[1] According to Lewin, *Fasti Sacri*, p. 255, Passover in A D 37 was 19th March.
[2] See Wieseler, *Chronological Synopsis of the Four Gospels* (E.T. of *Chronologische Synopse der vier Evangelien*), pp. 48 f.
[3] Josephus, *Ant*, xix.343—εἰς τὴν Καίσαρος τιμὴν ὑπὲρ τῆς ἐκείνου σωτηρίας.
[4] Wieseler, *Chronologie des apostolischen Zeitalters* (p. 132), carries this suggestion back to Nonne.
[5] According to Hoennicke, *Die Chronologie des Lebens Apostels Paulus* (p. 43), by Kellner in *Der Katholik*, (1887), p. 139.

that day was 1st August,⁶ which would place the celebration later in the year than 1st Nisan. It may also be objected to both suggestions that Claudius, if he did not actually forbid, appears to have very largely disapproved of festivals in his own honour.⁷ Josephus notes that the festival in Caesarea was attended by ' a great multitude of the principal persons and such as were of dignity throughout the province '. The fact that he does so and more especially the expressions ' in honour of Caesar ' and ' on behalf of his well-being ' which he uses, seem to indicate that he intends not a regularly recurring festival, but one that had a certain joyous occasion. It may be then that the reference is to a festival held in Caesarea to mark the victory of Claudius over the Britons and his safe return to Rome. The date of his return is not known precisely. But it was in the consulate of C. Passienus Crispus II and T. Statilius Taurus,⁸ therefore in A D 44 and before 4th May in that year, since on that day the consul suffectus P. Pomponius Secundus took the place of Crispus.⁹ The fact that in Dion Cassius the return of Claudius is the first event recorded under the consulate just mentioned indicates that it took place early in the year. It is true, as Haenchen ¹⁰ observes, that all the authorities speak only of a celebration in Rome. But it may be assumed that there were celebrations also in the provinces and that these took place soon after the one in Rome. Lewin ¹¹ adduces a passage from Philo which, he claims, implies that after the safe return of Caligula from Gaul ' rejoicings were expected not only from the Romans but also from the provincials '. The fact that Agrippa owed much to Claudius and would hardly have neglected such an opportunity of extolling him, makes it the more likely that there was a celebration in Caesarea. That this did not take place

⁶ Suetonius, *Claud.*, 2.
⁷ Dion Cassius, lx.5.
⁸ Dion Cassius, lx.23.
⁹ Liebenam, *Fasti consulares imperii romani von 30 v.Chr. bis 565 n.Chr.*, p. 12.
¹⁰ *Die Apostelgeschichte* (12th edn., 1959), p. 54, note 3.
¹¹ *Fasti Sacri*, p. 280.

until the summer—an inference made by some from the statement of Josephus (*Ant.*, xix.344) that on its second day Agrippa came into the theatre 'early in the morning' (ἀρχομένης ἡμέρας) [12]—seems unlikely.

The foregoing is the view that has perhaps been most generally entertained. But there is another [13] which also merits consideration. It is that the festival in question was a celebration of quinquennalia which had been instituted in 9 B C [14] by Herod the Great and commenced on the foundation day of Caesarea. That day was 5th March;[15] and since these quinquennalia were held every fourth year, a celebration of them fell in A D 44.[16]

Agrippa's persecution of the church at Jerusalem took place at the time of a Passover (Acts 12:3). If then the conclusion reached above that he died between 25th January and 1st Nisan A D 44 is sound, the persecution must be dated Passover A D 43 at the latest. If it is assigned to this Passover, there was an interval between it and the king's death of several months. There is no good reason why that may not have been the case. In Acts 12:19 it is plainly stated that he left Judaea and resided for a time (διέτριβεν) in Caesarea. According to verse 23 his death was a punishment for his impiety in usurping the honour due to God. But if he died shortly before the Passover next following the one referred to in Acts 12:3, the fact that he was cut off and not suffered to see it and on it to resume his attempt to lay violent hands on the apostles, may well have occasioned the thought, which perhaps lies concealed in the narrative of Acts 12:1–24, that his death was also a punishment for his persecution of the Christian community and a divine intervention on its behalf.

---

[12] See Holzmeister, *Historia Aetatis Novi Testamenti*, p. 133.
[13] On this see E. Schwartz, 'Zur Chronologie des Paulus', *Nach.v.d. könig. Gesell.d.Wissen. zu Göttingen* (1907), pp. 265 f.
[14] See Lake in Jackson and Lake, *The Beginnings of Christianity* I.v.451.
[15] Eusebius, *Mart. Pal.*, xi.30.
[16] The first celebration was in 9 B C = 745 a.u.c., therefore the first celebration in the reign of Claudius took place 52 (= 4 × 13) years later, i.e. in 797 a.u.c. = A D 44.

CHAPTER NINE

The Famine-Relief Visit to Jerusalem

THE FAMINE-relief visit to Jerusalem accounted for and briefly reported in Acts 11:27–30, 12:25 is in Acts Paul's second visit to that city after his conversion. But in his own enumeration in Galatians of his visits to Jerusalem after his conversion the second is a conference visit (Gal 2:1–10) which resembles, and is generally identified with, the conference visit reported in Acts 15:1–29. In Galatians then the famine relief visit is not referred to, and indeed it seems that no room for it can be found there. Hence the considerable chronological problem which the mention of this visit in Acts occasions.

(1) Of the solutions of it that have been proposed at least one may be discarded at once. It is the suggestion that although Paul was commissioned to accompany Barnabas, he did not go with him all the way, but parted from him at a point some distance short of the Judaean border and later rejoined him on his return journey to Antioch. It is admittedly possible that Paul may have acted in this way and have had good reason for doing so. But Acts 12:25 implies that he accompanied Barnabas throughout, both to and from Jerusalem.

(2) H. Schlier in *Der Brief an die Galater* [1] dismisses Acts 9:26–30 as unhistorical and identifies the visit to Jerusalem recorded in Acts 11:27–30, 12:25 with the one mentioned in Galatians 1:18–24. He suggests that, on escaping from Damascus, Paul went to Tarsus, that later he joined Barnabas in Antioch, and that the famine-relief visit which he paid with him to Jerusalem was his first visit to that city after his conversion. According to Galatians 1:18 Paul visited Jerusalem that he might get to know Cephas, but according to Acts 11:30 he did so that along with Barnabas he might deliver to the elders the

[1] Edn. of 1951, pp. 74–6.

collection that had been made in Antioch. Schlier notes this difference. He considers, however, that it involves no contradiction, since Paul merely states the purpose that was decisive for him on this occasion. The famine-relief visit appears to have been of brief duration [2] and to have involved no intercourse of Paul with the whole body of the apostles and no public appearance of Paul in the city. In both these respects it resembles the visit recorded in Galatians 1:18–24.

The other arguments which Schlier adduces in favour of the identification which he proposes are, however, less convincing. There were three years between Paul's conversion and his first visit after it to Jerusalem (Gal 1:18), and that is admittedly sufficient time for a sojourn in Damascus and Arabia, a visit to Tarsus and a stay in Antioch before the journey to Jerusalem. But writing in support of his contention that he was an apostle not by human appointment or human commission, Paul was under obligation to give an account of all his movements from the time of his conversion up to the time of his going to Syria and Cilicia (Gal 1:21). He has taken care to record that, having gone from Damascus to Arabia, he returned from there to Damascus (Gal 1:17), and had he later visited Tarsus and Antioch before proceeding to Jerusalem, he would not have omitted to say so. In Galatians 1:21 he states that after his visit to Jerusalem he went to the regions of Syria and Cilicia. According to Schlier Syria and Cilicia there designate the field of Paul's first missionary journey (Acts 13, 14), just as they do in Acts 15:23 and 41. But in each of these three verses Syria and Cilicia mean no more than these two regions. An enlargement of their meaning which would bring Cyprus and the inland parts of Asia Minor visited by Paul on his First Missionary Journey within their compass is without justification. Indeed it is

---

[2] There is no need to infer, as Ramsay (*St. Paul the Traveller and the Roman Citizen*, p. 51) does, from the use of the word διακονία in Acts 11:29 (A.V.: ' relief ') and 12:25 (A.V.: ' ministry ') that Paul and Barnabas remained in Jerusalem throughout the time of the famine, acting as ' providers and distributors '.

possible that in the New Testament, so far from comprehending Pamphylia, Pisidia and Lycaonia, the term ' Cilicia ' in the combination ' Syria and Cilicia ' may refer only to Cilicia Campestris. Schlier thinks that the chronological difficulties which the identification he proposes may occasion are overcome if, from the parenthetical statement that the predicted famine in fact occurred in the reign of Claudius (Acts 11:28b), it is inferred that the prediction of it, the collection made in Antioch and the sending of it to Judaea all took place in the reign of Caligula, therefore prior to 25th January A D 41. But that inference is very precarious ;[3] and it is to be noted that although Zahn makes it so far as the prediction is concerned, he puts the relief mission to Jerusalem in the reign of Claudius.[4]

(3) Influenced by the writings of W. M. Ramsay, many scholars in this country and some elsewhere have identified the famine-relief visit with the visit about which Paul writes in Gal. 2:1-10. They maintain that when in Jerusalem for the purpose stated in Acts 11:30, Paul and Barnabas took the opportunity to discuss with the apostles there the question of the admission of Gentiles to membership in the church. The silence of Acts does not of itself exclude the possibility of their having done so ; and although in the account of the visit given in Acts the only office-bearers mentioned are the elders, it does not follow that at this time all the apostles were absent from the

---

[3] ' I do not believe ', writes Alford (*The Greek Testament* II.129), ' that the words ἐπὶ Κλ. [i.e. ' in the reign of Claudius '] imply that *the events just related were not also in the reign of Claudius* ; but they are inserted to particularize the famine as being that well-known one and only imply that the author was not *writing* under Claudius.' Haenchen (*Die Apostelgeschichte* [12th edn., 1959] p. 56) observes that in adding these words the writer's aim was not to provide a date, but to give prominence to the fulfilment of the prophecy. Plooij (*De chronologie van het leven van Paulus*, p. 15) and Hoennicke (*Die Chronologie des Lebens des Apostels Paulus*, p. 45) point out that the inference from Acts 11:28b that it was in the reign of Caligula that Agabus prophesied the famine goes back beyond Zahn to Bengel and Süskind.

[4] See *Zeittafel* in his *Einleitung in das Neue Testament* (2nd edn., 1900), II.644.

city or that Paul and Barnabas had no contact with such of them as were there. On the other hand, if this identification is made, a matter was discussed on this occasion that had a large bearing on Paul's future labours and on the subsequent expansion of the church as a whole; and even if the discussion took place in private, it is difficult to believe that its findings were kept secret and that the writer of Acts can have restricted himself so completely to one portion of the work that Paul and Barnabas did when on this visit to Jerusalem. Ramsay rightly emphasizes the part that the handing over of the relief fund must have played in binding together the mother-church in Jerusalem and the church in Antioch and indeed in deepening the sense of unity among Christians everywhere. But it is assuredly wrong so to underscore this as to make it appear that the conference supposed to have been held at this time was merely an incidental and private discussion and so did not reach ' the proper level of importance ' [5] to be reported in Acts.

The scholars whose position is at present under consideration distinguish between Galatians 2:1–10 and Acts 15:1–29 and hold that, on returning from the First Missionary Journey, Paul and Barnabas attended the Jerusalem conference reported in the latter passage. To the question—Why, in his enumeration in Galatians of his visits to Jerusalem after his conversion, has Paul stopped at the second and not also mentioned this third visit and the contact that he had then with the apostles ?—they give two answers. Some of them say that it was sufficient for him to make clear to the Galatian Christians how independent, so far as his gospel was concerned, he had been of the apostles up to the time when he first preached it to them. But that answer can satisfy only those who accept the so-called South Galatian theory.[6] Others of them say that Paul wrote Galatians at a time when the conference of Acts 15 was still in the future. But it is widely held that First and Second Corinthians, Galatians and

---

[5] Ramsay, *St. Paul the Traveller and the Roman Citizen*, p. 58.
[6] See p. 117, note 10, *infra*.

Romans were all written about the same time, several years after the conference of Acts 15.[7]

Ramsay held that in Galatians 2:1–10 there is a reference to the task to fulfil which the Antiochean Christians had asked Paul and Barnabas to proceed to Jerusalem.[8] He found it in verse 10, which, with expansions to bring out the meaning, he rendered : ' One charge alone they gave us, to remember the poor brethren at Jerusalem, a duty which as a matter of fact I at that time made it my special object to perform.'[9] But that rendering of the verse cannot be allowed ; as Haenchen points out, there is no τότε [= at that time] in its second half. Paul refers there not to a purpose which he was at the time fulfilling, but to one to fulfil which was always with him a heartfelt desire.

(4) According to a considerable number of scholars [10] no

---

[7] ' The view of Lake, Emmet and others that the ep. [Galatians] was written at the close of the First Journey (preceding the Conference of Ac. 15) and was the earliest of Paul's letters, seems to be losing some of its favour.'—A. J. Grieve, *Supplement to Peake's Commentary* (1936), p. 34a. According to Dupont, *Les Problèmes du Livre des Actes* (1950), pp. 53–7, those who have written in the interval 1940–50 in support of an early dating of Galatians have added nothing decisive.

[8] According to Hopfl and Gut (*Introductio Specialis in Novum Testamentum*, p. 299, notes 4 and 5) this was the view also of V. Weber in his earlier writings. Later he maintained that the visit of Galatians 2:1–10a is not mentioned in Acts, that it was followed by the famine-relief visit, and that Galatians 2:10b is a brief reference to the latter. T. M. Manson (' St. Paul in Ephesus : 2. The Problem of the Epistle to the Galatians ', *Bulletin of the John Rylands Library*, XXIV.[1940]. 59–80) holds that the visit of Galatians 2:1–10 is not mentioned in Acts and that it corresponds neither to the visit of Acts 15 nor to the famine-relief visit, but was paid about the same time as the latter ; cf. V. Bartlet, ' Some Points in Pauline History and Chronology ', *Expositor*, 5th ser., X.(1898).263–80. Paley (*Horae Paulinae* [ed. Binnie (1880), p. 88]) suggests that Paul's visit to Jerusalem recorded in Galatians 2:1–10 may be one of which Acts has taken no notice.

[9] Ramsay, *St. Paul the Traveller and the Roman Citizen*, pp. 56 f.

[10] Besides Funk and Haenchen, who are mentioned in the text, others who may be named are Clemen (*Paulus* I.215 and 371–3) ; Goguel (*Introduction au Nouveau Testament*, III.220–2) ; Dibelius, (' Das Apostelkonzil ', *Theologische Literaturzeitung*, LXXII.(1947).193–8) ; and John Knox (*Chapters in a Life of Paul*, pp. 69–72).

collection was made in Antioch such as is mentioned in Acts 11:29 and consequently there was no famine-relief mission to Judaea. They share the view that for the story that he tells the writer of Acts used tradition which he did not fully or accurately understand, tradition which referred to a visit paid to the capital at a later time and which he has in some measure distorted in adapting it to the earlier place in which he has set it.

This is the conclusion of R. W. Funk [11] in a contribution to the *Journal of Biblical Literature*. From the statement, ' Only they would that *we* should remember the poor ' (Gal. 2:10a), he infers that at the Jerusalem Conference both Paul and Barnabas were asked to make a collection for the poor Christians in Jerusalem. He suggests that they both did so in the churches which they founded and that in due course they carried what they had collected to Jerusalem, returning there not necessarily together. This return, he then suggests, may be referred to in Acts 12:25, in which verse he accepts the well-attested reading εἰς. The writer of Acts, he observes, gives much more heed to geographical order than to temporal sequence ; and here he has apparently used a tradition which referred to a Jerusalem visit paid at a time near the close of the history which he records, but that visit he has carried back to the point where he is about to round off his account of the development of the church in Syrian Antioch.

It is also the conclusion of Haenchen.[12] He maintains that in some quarters the collection about which present-day readers of the epistles of Paul to the Corinthians and the Romans are well informed was little known or understood, and that instead of it getting abroad that this collection was made in the Gentile churches which Paul had founded and was conveyed by him to the mother-church in Jerusalem when he returned there at the close of his Third Missionary Journey, it got abroad that it was made in Syrian Antioch and was conveyed to Jerusalem by Paul and Barnabas on the occasion of a visit which these two

---

[11] ' The Enigma of the Famine Visit ', *JBL*, LXXV.(1956).130–6.
[12] *Die Apostelgeschichte* (12th edn., 1959), pp. 319–23.

were believed to have made, and in fact did make, together from Antioch to the capital. The writer of Acts 11:27–30, 12:25, Haenchen holds, used this tradition and along with it another tradition, the substance of which was that Agabus had foretold the grievous famine which afflicted Judaea in the reign of Claudius and which is mentioned by Josephus in his *Antiquities* (iii.320 f, xx.51–3, 101). Working these two traditions together, the writer brought Agabus down from Jerusalem to Antioch so that he might make his prophecy there and thereby move the Antiochean Christians to decide upon the collection which they were reputed to have made. Accounting for the story of the famine-relief visit in this way, Haenchen finds in it only one reliable fact, namely that on one occasion Paul and Barnabas went up together from Antioch to Jerusalem; and this occasion he takes to be that of the Jerusalem Conference of Acts 15.

But there may be more history in this story than these scholars allow.[13] Someone—not necessarily Agabus, but someone who came later to be identified with Agabus—may have foreseen and foretold the great famine with which Judaea is known to have been visited in the reign of Claudius. There were famines in several other parts of the civilized world in his reign. In one year of it there was according to Pliny [14] an unusually high Nile, and that must have been followed by scarcity throughout Egypt. Papyri from Tebtunis [15] mention conditions which point to a bad harvest in Egypt in the spring of A D 45 or the spring of A D 46. Suetonius [16] refers to 'incessant dearths' which marked the reign of Claudius and says that the emperor devised all the means he possibly could to bring provisions into Rome even in the winter season. There was famine in the city in the

---

[13] While maintaining this, we think it precarious to conclude, as is sometimes done, from the words συνεστραμμένων ἡμῶν, 'when we were gathered together', of the Western text of Acts 11:28 that in Acts 11:27–30 we have to do with the account of an eye-witness and so with a story that may be accepted as trustworthy.
[14] *H.N.*, v.58.
[15] See p. 52, *infra*.
[16] *Claud.*, 18.

beginning of his reign, probably from AD 41 to AD 43,[17] and again according to Tacitus [18] in its eleventh, according to Orosius [19] in its tenth and according to Eusebius [20] in its ninth or tenth year. According to Eusebius [21] famine occurred in Greece in the eighth or ninth year of the reign. Ramsay [22] mentions an inscription which perhaps refers to famine in Asia Minor at some time in the same reign, and according to Tacitus [23] there was a deficiency of military supplies in Armenia in AD 51. Admittedly a number of famines in different lands and in different years, even although they all occur within the period of one reign, do not constitute a single famine occurring simultaneously in all lands. But about the time of the great famine in Palestine in the reign of Claudius the people there must have heard reports of famines that had recently occurred elsewhere; and it seems not unlikely that they synchronized these other famines and their own and lumped them all together in one, and that thus in tradition the original prophecy of a famine to occur in Judaea may have become a prophecy of a great famine that would be 'throughout all the world' (ἐφ'ὅλην τὴν οἰκουμένην).[24] That, as some think, there was already a certain tension between the church at Antioch and the motherchurch in Jerusalem, may be questioned. But if there was, it needs to be remembered how seldom it is that tensions stay the impulse in Christian men to stretch out a helping hand to

[17] Dion Cassius, lx. 11; Aurelius Victor, *Caes.* 4; coins of Claudius in Eckhel, vi. 238–40.
[18] *Ann.*, xii.43.
[19] vii.6.17.
[20] *Chronicle*, ed. Schoene, II.152 f.
[21] Ibid.
[22] *St. Paul the Traveller and the Roman Citizen*, p. 49.
[23] *Ann.*, xii.50.
[24] Cf. Hoennicke, *Die Chronologie des Lebens des Apostels Paulus*, p. 44. The view of certain older scholars that ὅλη ἡ οἰκουμένη denotes simply the whole land of Palestine is now abandoned. De Zwaan in Jackson and Lake (*The Beginnings of Christianity*, I.II.59) rejects with good reason the suggestion of Torrey that it is due to a misunderstanding of the Aramaic כל ארצא, by which Palestine is meant.

brethren who are threatened with starvation. If this famine was predicted in Antioch, it may be assumed that the Christians there made a collection for the relief of their brethren in Judaea and in due course sent it to them by the hands of Barnabas and Paul.

In Josephus, *Ant.*, iii.320, the great famine that afflicted Judaea when Claudius was emperor is also dated in the high priesthood of Ismael. Unhappily this does not enable us to determine the time of it more closely. When Valerius Gratus became procurator of Judaea in A D 15, he appointed one Ismael, son of Phabi, to be high priest, but deprived him of the office in a little time (Jos., *Ant.*, xviii.34). Another Ismael, son of Phabi, was appointed high priest by Herod Agrippa II (Jos., *Ant.*, xx.179) and was in office from *c.* A D 59 to *c.* A D 61. Besides these two no other high priest of New Testament times is known to have borne the name Ismael. Attempts to make room for an Ismael among those who were high priests in the reign of Claudius and also attempts to identify with Ismael some one of those who held the office in that reign, have all proved unsuccessful. It would thus appear that the name in *Antiquities*, iii.320, is a mistake, perhaps, as Schürer [25] suggests, ' a fault of memory on the part of the historian '.

After telling what befell the Jews in the time of Cuspius Fadus' government, Josephus proceeds : ' Then came Tiberius Alexander as successor to Fadus. . . . Under this procurator (ἐπὶ τούτου) that great famine happened in Judaea, in which queen Helena bought corn in Egypt at a great expense, and distributed it to those that were in want, as I have related already ' (*Ant.*, xx.100 f). The reading ἐπὶ τούτου found in the *Epitome antiquitatum* is the one adopted by both Niese and Naber in their editions of the text of Josephus. But some scholars prefer the reading ἐπὶ τούτοις which has the support of the Greek manuscripts, the Latin translations and Eusebius (*H.E.* II.xii.1). This they take to mean in the time of the procurators Cuspius Fadus and Tiberius Alexander (A D 44–8). But, leaving

---

[25] *The Jewish People in the Time of Jesus Christ*, II.1.200, note 553.

aside the question whether that is not rather the meaning of ἐπὶ τούτων, we may claim for the reading ἐπὶ τούτου that it alone fits the context and alone makes sense. In *Ant.*, xx.17–96, Josephus tells the whole story of the conversion to Judaism of Helena queen of Adiabene and her son Izates, of her presence in Jerusalem at the time of the great famine, of her liberality on that occasion, and of the subsequent fortunes of her son. That story he sets in the procuratorship of Fadus because it began then. But it continued beyond that time; and when Josephus comes to record the happenings under Tiberius Alexander, he notes that it was in his time that the great famine occurred in Judaea in which Helena came to the help of the starving population in Jerusalem as he has already related.

It is not known when exactly Tiberius Alexander entered on his procuratorship. A rescript of Claudius addressed to the Jews and preserved in Josephus, *Ant.*, xx.II ff, runs as follows: ' Claudius Caesar Germanicus, tribune of the people the fifth time, and designed consul the fourth time, and imperator the tenth time.... I have written about these affairs to Cuspius Fadus, my procurator.... This was dated the fourth day before the kalends of July, when Rufus and Pompeius Sylvanus were consuls.' Now Claudius was tribune for the fifth time from 25th January A D 45 to 24th January A D 46, and the consuls named were the *suffecti* of A D 45.[26] It is clear, therefore, that Fadus was still in office on 28th June A D 45. As he is likely to have continued in it for some time after that, the coming of Tiberius Alexander as his successor may perhaps be put in A D 46. This narrows the period within which the great famine must have occurred to A D 46–8.

Papyri from Tebtunis in Egypt indicate that famine conditions obtained in that land in August, September and November of A D 45.[27] The high price of corn in those months points to a bad harvest in the spring of A D 45 or to an anticipated bad

[26] Liebenam, *Fasti consulares imperii romani*, p. 12.
[27] See K. S. Gapp. ' The Universal Famine under Claudius ', *Harvard Theological Review* XXVIII.4.(1935).258–65.

harvest in the spring of A D 46. In the one case there must have been famine conditions in Egypt from the fall of A D 44 to the spring of A D 46, in the other from the fall of A D 45 to the spring of A D 47, and in either case from the fall of A D 45 to the spring of A D 46. In consequence Helena's servants can have bought corn in Egypt at the earliest only after the harvest there in A D 46.

By the time Helena arrived in Jerusalem many people were dying for want. Conditions were then apparently at their worst, and that they would be in the spring of the year following the one in which the harvest in Judaea had failed and immediately before the new harvest was cut. If the queen's servants bought corn in Egypt in the spring of A D 47, there was a bad harvest in Judaea in the spring of A D 46; if they did so in the spring of A D 48, the bad harvest in Judaea was in A D 47. It is to be assumed that the Antiochean Christians retained the collection they had made or were still making until they learned that the brethren in Judaea were beginning to feel the need of it, but forwarded it immediately they had word to that effect. That word must have reached them in the fall of A D 45 or in the fall of A D 46. The famine-relief visit is then to be dated either winter A D 45-6 or winter A D 46-47. The earlier date is the more satisfactory; it shortens somewhat the interval between the events recorded in Acts 12:1-24 and this visit; also it leaves somewhat more time for what took place between this visit and the Jerusalem Conference of Acts 15.

The fact that, while the sending off of the collection in charge of Barnabas and Paul is mentioned in Acts 11:30, the return of these two from Jerusalem is not recorded until Acts 12:25, may give the impression that they arrived in Jerusalem before Agrippa's persecution of the church and remained there until after his death. But the phrase 'about that time' (κατ' ἐκεῖνον δὲ τὸν καιρόν) in Acts 12:1 indicates only a general synchronism, and we must conclude that the writer of Acts turns back in 12:1-24 to bring his history of the Christian community in Jerusalem down to the time when Barnabas and

Paul paid it this visit.[28] Before their arrival the persecution was over, Agrippa was dead, and the church had entered upon a new period of quiet growth and expansion. ' In these chapters ', writes Plooij,[29] ' Luke proceeds *synchronistisch* and not *akoluthistisch*, to use Wieseler's expression. What he means to say is not that Barnabas and Paul lived through all that is told in Chapter 12, but that what is recorded in Chapter 11:19-28 ran simultaneously with the happenings in Jerusalem recorded in Chapter 12:1-24.'

According to certain scholars the famine in the time of Claudius took place later than A D 46. In an article on this matter entitled ' Sabbathjahr und neutestamentliche Chronologie ',[30] J. Jeremias points out that Tiberius Alexander must have succeeded Cuspius Fadus as procurator of Judaea in A D 45(46) or 47 and that the famine thus belongs to the interval A D 45(46)-48. He then proceeds :

Of these years only the last two have to be considered, for in Acts 11:28 it is recorded that the whole world was visited by the same distress. Now Rome was affected by it according to Tacitus in winter A D 50/51, according to Orosius in A D 50, according to Eusebius in A D 50 or A D 49, and Greece according to Eusebius in A D 49 or A D 48. Accordingly we ought not to go back beyond A D 48 or A D 47. Finally, since the rabbinic literature and Josephus probably speak of several years of scarcity and since further A D 47 (autumn)-48 was a sabbatical year, the harvest must have failed in the summer of A D 47 and the sabbatical year A D 47/48 will have intensified the famine and prolonged it to the next harvest in the spring of A D 49.

[28] Cf. J. B. Lightfoot, *Biblical Essays*, p. 216. So in Acts 18:24-8 the record of events in Ephesus is brought down to the time of Paul's arrival there.

[29] *De chronologie van het leven van Paulus*, pp. 10 f.

[30] *ZNTW* XXVII (1928), pp. 98 ff. The reasoning of Jeremias is resumed by Dupont, ' Notes sur les Actes des Apôtres ', *Revue Biblique* lxii (1955), pp. 45-59, who puts the generosity of queen Helena in A D 48 or the winter A D 48-9. Benoit, ' La deuxième visite de saint Paul à Jérusalem ', *Biblica* xl (1959), pp. 778-92 writes, also in dependence on Jeremias, that the famine must have occurred in the years A D 46-8, indeed rather in A D 49.

But in considering the famines outside Palestine which may have given rise to the tradition of a world-wide famine in the reign of Claudius, there is no reason why attention should be confined to those which occurred in Greece and Italy in the period A D 48(49)–51. Those which occurred in the period A D 41–45(46) may equally well have contributed to its growth. Here, therefore, there is no ground on which to conclude that the famine in Judaea should be dated in or immediately before the former of these periods rather than be dated in or immediately after the latter. If the harvest failed in Judaea in the spring of A D 47 and a sabbatical year began in October of that year, then there were famine conditions in the land until the gathering in of the harvest of the spring of A D 49, and these conditions were at their worst immediately before that ingathering, therefore in the procuratorship of Cumanus and not, as Josephus indicates, in that of Tiberius Alexander. According to Ralph Marcus [31] the sabbatical year referred to in Josephus, *Ant.*, xii.378, was 163 (Oct)–162 B C, whence it would follow that A D 48 (Oct)–49, and not A D 47 (Oct)–48, was a sabbatical year. A sabbatical year commencing in October A D 48 would not have prolonged famine conditions resulting from a failure of the harvest in the spring of A D 47. That Josephus suggests several years of scarcity can be maintained only if ἐπὶ τούτοις is read in *Antiquities*, xx.101, and taken to mean ' in the time of these two [Cuspius Fadus and Tiberius Alexander] '; but ἐπὶ τούτου is undoubtedly the more satisfactory reading. Further it needs to be noted that, in his account of the famine in the time of Tiberius Alexander, Josephus nowhere makes any reference to a sabbatical year. Finally it is difficult to believe that, as Jeremias maintains lower down, the famine-relief visit did not take place at the beginning of the famine and may be put *c.* A D 48. As already indicated, the likelihood is that the Christians of Antioch sent help immediately they had word that famine conditions were beginning to obtain in Judaea, therefore in the winter before the spring in which the harvest failed.

[31] Edn., of the works of Josephus in the *Loeb Library*, VII.196, note a.

'It should be clearly understood', writes C. W. Emmet in *The Beginnings of Christianity* (I.ii.272 f), 'that there is nothing suspicious in the story of Acts 11 as it stands.' 'The objections', he continues, 'arise solely from the supposed difficulty of finding room for it in Galatians.' We turn now to the question whether or not this supposed difficulty is a real one.

The problem which the mention of the famine-relief visit in Acts occasions has its own occasion in the assumption that the narrative, Galatians 1:11–2:10, is uninterrupted autobiography, more particularly that throughout it Paul pursues a single purpose, and that a purpose of such a nature that he is under obligation to mention every visit paid by him to Jerusalem in the period covered by the narrative. Examination of the passage, however, hardly bears this out.

In Galatians 1:18 Paul writes ἔπειτα μετὰ τρία ἔτη ἀνῆλθον, and in Galatians 2:1 ἔπειτα διὰ δεκατεσσάρων ἐτῶν πάλιν ἀνέβην. In the latter verse πάλιν stands in some manuscripts after ἀνέβην. There is also some authority for its omission, and according to Lietzmann [32] it may possibly be an addition. If, as is generally agreed, it belongs to the original text, it does not necessarily indicate the first visit to Jerusalem after the one mentioned in 1:18; it stands alone and is not followed by δεύτερον, as in John 4:54, 21:16, or by ἐκ δευτέρου, as in Matthew 26:42, Acts 10:15, or by some other word or phrase defining it more closely. This πάλιν then does not exclude the possibility of one or more visits to Jerusalem between those of 1:18 and 2:1. Particularly noteworthy is the fact that in the first of these verses the preposition used is μετά, but in the second διά. This change indicates that here Paul does not think of his life since his conversion in terms of periods which follow immediately upon one another and are mutually exclusive: the fourteen years of which he speaks in 2:1 did not come immediately after the three years which he has already mentioned in 1:18, but include them and, like them, are reckoned from his conversion. The fact that he proceeds in this way suggests that it is the two visits to Jerusalem

[32] *An die Galater*, in *Handbuch zum Neuen Testament*, III.i, p. 233.

which he singles out that at the moment count with him and are, first the one and then the other, all his concern, and that the interval between them, with any visit to Jerusalem and indeed any other event or events that may have occurred within it, is wholly out of his sight.

In Galatians 1:11–24 Paul's purpose is to prove that no man put the Gospel into his hands or taught him what it meant (οὐδὲ γὰρ ἐγὼ παρὰ ἀνθρώπου παρέλαβον αὐτό, οὔτε ἐδιδάχθην). In pursuit of this purpose he states that after his conversion he remained in Damascus for three years and during that time was away from that city only on a sojourn in Arabia, that after these three years he paid a visit to Jerusalem where he stayed only a fortnight and saw none of the apostles save Cephas and James the Lord's brother, and that at the end of the fortnight he left for the regions of Syria and Cilicia. In referring to his going there his aim is to make it clear that even after the three years which he has mentioned he continued to be well away from Jerusalem and the apostles there; and his further words, 'I remained unknown' (ἤμην δὲ ἀγνοούμενος), and, 'They [Christ's congregations in Judaea] continued to hear' (ἀκούοντες ἦσαν) imply, and were doubtless intended to indicate, that he stayed in Syria and Cilicia for some time. He does not say for just how long he did so. But to do that was not necessary. Having brought his history since his conversion down to his stay in Syria and Cilicia and shown how extremely little contact he had with the apostles throughout this initial period of it, he has sufficiently proved that he received his Gospel not from any human authority but from God. In Galatians 2:1–10 his purpose is different, namely to assure his readers that his mission to the Gentiles met with the full approval of the apostles.[33] That necessitated his recording another visit to Jerusalem, a later visit, but not necessarily the first after the one he has recorded in Chapter 1.

[33] 'When', he writes, 'they perceived the grace that was given to me, James and Cephas and John ... gave to me and Barnabas the right hand of fellowship, that we should go to the Gentiles' (Galatians 2:9).

CHAPTER TEN

The First Missionary Journey

IT WAS SOON, but apparently not immediately, after their return from Jerusalem to Antioch (Acts 12:25), and probably therefore in the spring of A D 46, that Paul and Barnabas set out on what is commonly called the First Missionary Journey. In the course of it they laboured in the Gospel first in Cyprus and then, crossing to Asia Minor, at Pisidian Antioch and Iconium in Phrygia, at Lystra and Derbe in Lycaonia, and at Perga in Pamphylia. The account of this journey given in Acts 13 and 14 is in some of its parts little more than a sketch, and there are no precise notes of time.

I

According to a theory first advanced by Schwartz [1] there was no such missionary journey. Paul, it is declared, was never with Barnabas in Cyprus, and Barnabas was never with Paul in Asia Minor. The writer of Acts, it is maintained, had at his disposal two sources, in each of which particulars were given first about a visit to Jerusalem and then about a missionary journey in Asia Minor. Failing, however, to discern that these referred to one and the same Jerusalem visit and one and the same missionary journey, he has recorded two Jerusalem visits, Acts 11:27-30, 12:25, and Acts 15:1-29, and two missionary journeys, Acts 13:13-14:25 and Acts 15:40-16:4. Of these journeys the latter, which followed the Jerusalem Conference (held in winter AD 43-4), was the one actually made.

This theory has been described, not without good reason, as unduly revolutionary, as unnecessarily complicated, and as an arbitrary recasting of the tradition. As is pointed out in

---

[1] ' Zur Chronologie des Paulus ', *Nach.v.d.kgl.Gesellschaft d.Wissenschaften zu Göttingen* (1907), pp. 263-99.

another place,[2] it is very improbable that there can have been two accounts of the one visit to Jerusalem so altogether unlike one another that the writer of Acts, examining them, as he doubtless would have done, intelligently and critically, would have found himself obliged to conclude that they referred to different visits. If the Jerusalem visits mentioned in the sources which on this theory he had before him were different, then the missionary journeys mentioned after these visits were represented there as having been made at different times. That does not necessarily mean that these journeys were different: the authority behind one of the two sources may have assigned the one journey to a wrong time. But the journeys which on this theory are recorded in Acts 13:13–14:25 and Acts 15:40–16:4 in dependence on these two sources, while made in the same part of Asia Minor, differ from one another in several noteworthy respects. The missionary activity recorded in the first of these passages is a breaking of new ground for the Gospel; that recorded in the second passage does not have this pioneering character. The portion of missionary progress that is recorded in detail in the first passage takes place from west to east; the progress recorded in the second passage takes place in the opposite direction. The miracle wrought at Lystra and its extraordinary issues recorded in the first passage are not referred to in the second; and of the circumcision of Timothy, which has a prominent place in the second passage, there is no mention in the first. These differences sufficiently indicate that the missionary journeys mentioned in the two sources which the writer of Acts is assumed to have used were not identical and that there they were rightly assigned to different times.[3]

---

[2] Page 75, *infra*.
[3] On the present theory the mission to Cyprus (Acts 13:4–12) is a parallel to the mission referred to in Acts 15:39b. The story told is a fabrication which culminates in the legend of an encounter of Paul with a magician that led to the conversion of a Roman official of high rank. For a theory claiming kinship with that of Schwartz but even more complicated see Lake in *The Beginnings of Christianity*, I.v.467 ff.

II

Sailing from Seleucia, the missionaries landed in Cyprus at Salamis on the east coast. Later they traversed the island to New Paphos, the provincial capital, in the south-west. When they were there, the proconsul Sergius Paulus sent for them as he wanted to hear the word of God. He seems to have been impressed by what they said to him, for Bar-Jesus, a magician in his entourage, apparently afraid lest his services would be dispensed with, tried to turn him away from the faith. Rebuked by Paul, this magician became blind for a season, and Sergius Paulus, it is recorded, when he saw what had happened, believed, being astonished at the doctrine of the Lord.

The historicity of this incident has been questioned on the ground that the conflict of Paul with Bar-Jesus resembles that of Peter with Simon Magus recorded in Acts 8:18–24. But the circumstances are clearly different; and the fact that if the writer of Acts had fabricated the present story he would not have given the magician a name involving the sacred name of Jesus, proves that here he communicates information which he had himself received. There has also been much discussion as to the sense in which it is recorded that the proconsul 'believed' ($\dot{\epsilon}\pi\acute{\iota}\sigma\tau\epsilon\upsilon\sigma\epsilon\nu$).[4] But it is generally agreed that his name is correctly given, and that is important. The year when Sergius Paulus was proconsul of Cyprus would obviously furnish students of the Pauline chronology with a helpful date. It is, therefore, not surprising that much endeavour has been made to determine it.

It used to be thought that Pliny in his *Historia Naturalis* gave the name Sergius Paulus in the list of his authorities for Book II, and again in the list of his authorities for Book XVIII; it was also

---

[4] See Ramsay in *Expository Times*, XXIX.(1918).324–8, and in his book, *The Bearing of Recent Research on the Trustworthiness of the New Testament*, pp. 150 ff; J. Foster in *Expository Times*, LX.(1949).354. According to the *Acts of Barnabas* (not earlier than saec.v) Bar-Jesus continued in his opposition to Christianity—see *Acta Apostolorum Apocrypha*, ed., Lipsius and Bonnet, 11:2 (ed. Bonnet, 1903), pp. 298, 299 and 300.

noted that in both these books he seems to give special information about Cyprus; and so it was suggested that this Sergius Paulus and the proconsul of Acts 13:6-12 ought perhaps to be identified. But more recent study of the textual tradition of Pliny shows that in the one list it strongly supports the reading Sergius Plautus and in the other is divided between the readings Sergius Paulus and Sergius Plautus.

L. Sergius Paullus is one of the curators of the Tiber in the reign of Claudius whose names are given in the inscription *CIL*, vi.31545. This inscription was found at Rome in 1887, and its text is as follows:

> PAVLLVS FABIVS PERSI[cus
> C. EGGIVS MARVLL[us
> L. SERGIVS PAVLLVS
> C. OBELLIVS RV[fus
> L. SCRIBONIV[s Libo
> CVRATORE[s riparum
> ET ALV[ei Tiberis
>   EX AVCTORIT[ate
> TI. CLAVDI CAESARIS
>   AVG. GERMANIC[i
>   PRINCIPIS. S[ui
> RIPAM. CIPPIS POS[itis
> TERMINAVERUNT A.TR[ig]AR
> AD PONTEM AGRIPPA[e

Gatti, the first to publish this inscription, considered that the *cippus* or boundary stone on which it appears must have been set up when Claudius was censor, A D 47-48,[5] on the ground that boundary stones erected in the reign of Vespasian are dated A D 73/74, and it was from July A D 73 to July A D 74 that Vespasian was censor. Doubt as to the soundness of this argument has been expressed by Kornemann[6] and Zahn.[7] The

[5] Tacitus, *Ann.*, xi.13,25.
[6] In Pauly-Wissowa, *RE*, IV.1793.
[7] In *Prot. Real. Encykl.* XV.(3rd edn.).64.

latter points out that whereas the title censor is absent from the present inscription, it is entered in the similar inscriptions of the time of Vespasian. Plooij [8] grants that Gatti's reasoning may be sound. The care of the *opera publica*, he points out, was the responsibility of the censor; and since the works referred to in the inscription were of that order and were executed 'at the command of Ti. Claudius Caesar', Claudius may have been censor. He maintains, however, that so long as no dating can be deduced from any of the other names mentioned on the *cippus*, Gatti's hypothesis is 'absolutely uncertain and consequently cannot be relied upon'. Moreover it is not known that the L. Sergius Paullus mentioned here subsequently went to Cyprus as proconsul; and so long as that is not proved, there can be no assurance that he was the Sergius Paulus of Acts 13:6–12.

A dating 'in the proconsulship of Paulus' occurs in an inscription of Soloi in the north of Cyprus, discovered by General de Cesnola and published by him in his *Cyprus, its Cities, Tombs and Temples* (p. 425), but given more fully and accurately by D. G. Hogarth in his *Devia Cypria* (p. 114). This states that the monument on which it appears together with its enclosure was dedicated by a certain Apollonius to his father and mother according to their command. There follows a list of the offices which this Apollonius had held—those of clerk of the market, prefect, townclerk, high priest, and head of the record office. The date of the erection of the monument is then given—the 25th day of the month Demarchexousios in the year 13. Finally it is stated that Apollonius revised the senate by means of assessors in the proconsulship of Paulus. The following is the text of the inscription as restored by Hogarth:

Ἀπολλώνιος τῷ πατ[ρὶ τῷ δεῖνι τοῦ δεῖνος
καὶ τῇ μητρὶ Ἀρτ[εμιδώρᾳ τοῦ δεῖνος καθιερῶσε
τὸν περίβολον καὶ τὴν [στήλην? ταύτην κατὰ] τὰς
ὑμῶν αὐτῶν ἐντολὰς . . . .

---

[8] *De chronologie van het leven van Paulus*, p. 22.

5 ἑαυτοῦ τῆς Σολίων πόλεως, [ἀγορα]νο[μήσας, ἐ-
παρχήσας, γρα(μ)ματεύσας, ἀρχιε[ρασάμενος, ἐπὶ τοῦ
βυβλιοφυλακίου γενόμενος· Λιγ[·μηνὸς δημαρχε
              τιμητεύσας τὴν βουλ[ὴν δι-
ξουσίου κε΄.
           (ἀ) ἐξ(ετ)αστῶν ἐπὶ Παύλου [ἀνθυ-
πάτου.

The faulty alignment and a change in the lettering in the last two lines seem to indicate that they are a postscript.

Hogarth [9] thinks that a third letter in the number of the year is lost. He suggests ρ ($=100$), which makes the number 113; and assuming that the reckoning is from 'the establishment of the province', he gives A D 55 as the date of the inscription. If now Apollonius revised the senate in some year prior to A D 55, then it is possible that the Sergius Paulus of Acts 13:6–12 may have been the Paulus mentioned in this inscription. But the inscription provides us with no means of determining precisely how many years before A D 55 he was proconsul. Moreover, while Cyprus was annexed by the Romans in 58 B C,[10] there is no indication of its having been established as a province in that year, and a Cyprian era is much more likely to have begun in 27 B C, when, apparently along with Cilicia, the island became an imperial province,[11] or in 22 B C, when it was made a senatorial province.[12]

Accepting 13 as the number of the year, some think that the reckoning is from 22 B C and consequently that 10 B C is the date of the inscription. They further suggest that the proconsul Paulus mentioned in it ought perhaps to be identified with Paulus Fabius Maximus, who was consul in 11 B C and proconsul of Asia before 3 B C.[13] That at one time he held some office in Cyprus is inferred from the fact that, according to an inscription

---

[9] *Devia Cypria*, p. 115.
[10] Dion Cassius, xxxviii.30; Vellei. Paterc., ii.45.
[11] Dion Cassius, liii.12.
[12] Dion Cassius, liv.4.
[13] So Groag, in Pauly-Wissowa, *RE*, VI.1781 f.

which it bore, a monument was erected in Paphos by the senate and people to the honour of Marcia the daughter of Philip and wife of Paulus Fabius Maximus. The text of the inscription, *CIG* 2629, is as follows :

ΜΑΡΚΙΑ ΦΙΛΙΠΠΟΥ ΘΥΓΑΤΡΙ ΑΝΕΨΙΑΙ ΚΑΙΣΑΡΟΣ
ΘΕΟΥ ΣΕΒΑΣΤΟΥ ΓΥΝΑΙΚΙ ΠΑΥΛΟΥ ΦΑΒΙΟΥ
ΜΑΞΙΜΟΥ ΣΕΒΑΣΤΗΣ ΠΑΦΟΥ Η ΒΟΥΛΗ ΚΑΙ ΔΗΜΟΣ

But against this identification Plooij [14] rightly observes that had Paulus Fabius Maximus been proconsul, then (*a*) that would almost certainly have been mentioned in the Paphos inscription, and (*b*) he would not have been referred to in the Soloi inscription merely by his praenomen Paulus.

Others think that by the year 13 is meant the 13th year of the reign of Claudius, i.e. A D 53, on the ground that in some other inscriptions from Cyprus [15] the reckoning appears to be according to the tribunicial year of the reigning emperor. If now the year 13 in the Soloi inscription is A D 53, if further the visit of Paul and Barnabas to Cyprus is chronologically in its proper place in Acts so that the Sergius Paulus of Acts 13:6–12 was proconsul of Cyprus in some year before the arrival of Paul in Corinth early in A D 50,[16] and if yet further this Sergius Paulus is the same person as the proconsul Paulus mentioned in the Soloi inscription, then the concluding words of that inscription, ' having revised the senate by means of assessors in the proconsulship of Paulus ', must refer to a service which Apollonius rendered at some time prior to A D 50 and were apparently added by a later hand to make good an omission in the earlier part of the inscription.[17] But the inscription itself,

[14] *De chronologie van het leven van Paulus*, p. 24.
[15] E.g. *CIG* 2632 and 2634.
[16] Page 115, *infra*.
[17] Lake (*The Beginnings of Christianity*, I.v.457) thinks it likely that if the last two lines were added later, they must refer to a service that was rendered later, i.e. after 25 Demarchexousios of the year 13. Obviously, if this is assumed and year 13 is taken to be A D 53, the Paulus of Acts and the Paulus of the Soloi inscription cannot be identified.

on this interpretation of it, does not enable us to determine how long before A D 50 Apollonius rendered this service and thus to say precisely when Paulus was proconsul of Cyprus. The hope that has for long been entertained that inscriptions may one day throw light on this matter has not yet been fulfilled. From *CIG* 2632 it is known that Julius Cordus was proconsul of Cyprus in A D 51 and Lucius Annius Bassus in A D 52, and with regard to Sergius Paulus all that inscriptions enable us to say is that he was not proconsul in either of these years.

III

The time occupied by the First Missionary Journey has been variously estimated. Ramsay [18] puts it at two years and four months and maintains that this estimate is the lowest possible; Goguel [19] puts it at between two and five years; E. Meyer [20] at two and a half to three years; Jacquier [21] at three years; and Clemen [22] at not less than three years and perhaps in all four or five years. On the other hand, Haenchen [23] considers that a place can be found for all the recorded events between the spring and the autumn of a single year. There being no precise chronological notes in Acts 13 and 14, the duration of the journey cannot be determined with any absolute certainty. Attention must be paid to the few vague notes of time which occur in these chapters; heed must be given to the distances traversed; difficulties which the missionaries encountered or may have encountered must be thought of; and reasonable time must be allowed for the work which they are reported to have done. That we may reckon approximately how long they were away we proceed to follow in their steps.

---

[18] *The Church in the Roman Empire*, pp. 65–73.
[19] ' Essai sur la chronologie Paulinienne ', *Revue de l'Histoire des Religions*, LXV.(1912).285–339.
[20] *Ursprung u. Anfänge des Christentums*, III.204.
[21] *Les Actes des Apôtres*, p. 300.
[22] *Paulus : Sein Leben und Wirken*, I.349 ff.
[23] *Die Apostelgeschichte* (12th edn., 1959), p. 380.

F

From Seleucia to Salamis was a distance of about a hundred miles, and with a favourable wind Paul and Barnabas may have made the crossing in a few hours. The Jewish colony in Salamis, then the commercial capital of the island, was so considerable that there were at least two synagogues in the place. As the missionaries preached in these (Acts 13:5), their stay in the city may have been two or three weeks in duration. No information is given as to the route they followed in going from Salamis to Paphos. According to present-day oral tradition in the island they went on foot to Cition and then struck inland to Tamassos.[24] If they did so, they may then have completed their journey by continuing westwards through the central plain and entering Paphos by the road from Soloi. This tradition may have arisen out of the thought that Paul and Barnabas cannot have come to Cyprus without visiting Tamassos,[25] a town in the near neighbourhood of which there were some of the copper-mines which had been farmed out by Augustus to Herod the Great[26] and where presumably there was a large Jewish community. Nevertheless it is possible that this is the route which they followed. In the *Peutinger Table*[27] one of the roads connecting Salamis and Paphos runs by way of Cition, Threnitus, Tamassos and Soloi. It is, however, also possible, and indeed is very often assumed,[28] that they travelled by the slightly shorter road, also shown in the *Peutinger Table*, which kept close to the south coast and passed through Cition, Amathus, Karion and Old Paphos.

The journey, by whatever road they made it, appears to have been a missionary progress. The verb διέρχεσθαι used in Acts 13:6 may signify that, as they went, they halted at places on the way and preached the Gospel in them.[29] That it has this meaning

[24] Morton, *In the Steps of St. Paul*, p. 128.
[25] This once busy mining-centre lay in the neighbourhood of Politiko and Pera.
[26] Josephus, *Ant.*, xvi.128.
[27] See inset in Map of Cyprus, in Lewin, *The Life and Epistles of St. Paul*, I, facing p. 120.
[28] See e.g. H. Metzger, *Les routes de saint Paul*, fig. I, p. 13.
[29] Moulton and Milligan, *Vocabulary of the Greek Testament*, s.v.

here is made very probable by the fact that, there being many Jews in the island,[30] their synagogues in the larger towns afforded opportunities which Paul and Barnabas are not likely to have missed. Since the best manuscripts read ὅλην before τὴν νῆσον in Acts 13:6 and so mention a journey through the whole island, it is possible that whilst they kept for the most part to one of the main roads connecting Salamis and Paphos, they occasionally broke away from it to visit places of some size lying not far from it. If it was what he had heard of their work in Paphos that led Sergius Paulus to send for them, their stay there, as in Salamis, may have been of two or three weeks.

According to Pliny [31] there were, besides Salamis and Paphos, fifteen towns (*oppida*) in the island. That there were synagogues in them all or that Paul and Barnabas visited them all is improbable. The likelihood rather is that they confined most of their missionary activity to the principal towns lying on or near the road by which they journeyed westward. Their stay in these need not have lasted more than four months in all. If then they arrived in the island in the spring of A D 46, it may be concluded that they laboured there throughout the summer and sailed for Pamphylia early in the autumn of that year.

The statement of Acts 13:13 that when the missionaries loosed from Paphos they came to Perga, suggests that the vessel which they boarded in the harbour of Paphos made for the mouth of the Cestrus on the coast of Pamphylia and sailed up that river to the harbour of Perga on its western bank.[32] If, however, the vessel was westward bound, it is likely that it made for Attalia on the Pamphylian coast and that the missionaries disembarked there and thence made their way to Perga overland. The crossing whether to Perga or to Attalia may have occupied three

---

[30] This is clear from Josephus, *Ant.*, xiii.284, 287, and Philo., *Leg. ad Caium*, 282C.

[31] *H.N.*, v.35.

[32] According to Strabo 667 the harbour was sixty stadia (= seven miles) upstream. Perga itself lay five miles west from the Cestrus.

days. The journey of twelve miles from Attalia to Perga can easily have been completed in a single day.

Apparently without making any long stay in Perga or attempting any missionary work there,[33] Paul and Barnabas proceeded northwards and, crossing the Taurus, came to Pisidian Antioch. Whether they travelled by way of Lakes Ascania and Limnai (so Conybeare and Howson) or more directly through Adada (so Ramsay), the road was difficult and dangerous. The ordinary rate of travel, twenty miles a day,[34] may not have been maintained, and the journey may have occupied more than eight days. On the whole, however, it seems possible that, leaving Paphos in the beginning of August, Paul and Barnabas may have reached Pisidian Antioch soon after the middle of that month.

Since they were in Pisidian Antioch at least over two successive Sabbaths (Acts 13:14,44), their stay there can hardly have been less than ten days. But it appears to have been considerably longer. It may be, as Haenchen[35] suggests, that the envy of the Jews spoken of in Acts 13:45 did not begin to manifest itself until after the coming into being of a community of Christian believers that was independent of the synagogue. According to Acts 13:49 the Word of God was published throughout all the region. That need not necessarily mean that Paul and Barnabas themselves engaged in missionary work in the surrounding country. But it apparently took place before they were obliged to leave Antioch. Some time may also have elapsed before the Jews, with the help of certain women of standing, managed to enlist the leading men of the city on their side against Paul and Barnabas and so to get them expelled from the district.

From Pisidian Antioch the missionaries proceeded to Iconium.

---

[33] No entirely satisfactory answer has yet been given to the question: Why at this time did Paul and Barnabas proceed to the interior of Asia Minor without first preaching the Gospel in such centres of population as Perga, Sylleum and Aspendus?

[34] See p. 121, note 18, *infra*.

[35] *Die Apostelgeschichte* (12th edn., 1959), p. 356.

If, in doing so, they first crossed the Sultan Dagh to Philomelium, then travelled along the Eastern Trade Route as far as Laodicea, and finally went south from there to Iconium, the journey must have occupied several days. But if, as seems more likely, they remained south of the Sultan Dagh and at the outset kept for some distance to the Roman road that ran from Antioch via Neapolis to Lystra, the journey may have been completed in twenty-seven hours.[36]

In spite of Jewish opposition Paul and Barnabas remained in Iconium for a 'long time' ($ἱκανὸν\ χρόνον$). The phrase $ἱκανὰς\ ἡμέρας$ occurs in Acts 18:18. There, however, it denotes not the eighteen months during which Paul stayed in Corinth, but the time from the Gallio incident to Paul's departure from the city;[37] and that time, as Wieseler[38] indicates, cannot have been more than one or two months. Ramsay's inference that Paul and Barnabas remained in Iconium for some eight months is thus without foundation. But the narrative of Acts gives the impression that they did much effective work in the city, and it may perhaps be assumed that they came to it early in November A D 46 and remained throughout the rest of the winter on until the end of March A D 47.

Lystra, to which they fled, lay about twenty miles south-west of Iconium. At the end of March the journey there may have been one of considerable difficulty. But that need not have deterred them. They had been apprised of a plot against them in Iconium; if, because of rain or melting snow, the way to Lystra was heavy going, it was comparatively short; and that town promised them a new missionary opportunity and, so perhaps they thought, freedom from Jewish molestation.

It was a Roman colony; there were apparently few Jews resident in it, and no mention is made of a synagogue. The miracle wrought on the lame man deeply impressed the native population. But what may well have proved a very fruitful

[36] So Ramsay, *The Church in the Roman Empire*, p. 30.
[37] See p. 114, *infra*.
[38] *Chronologie des apostolischen Zeitalters*, p. 46.

mission was halted by the arrival of Jews from Antioch and Iconium, who won over the crowds, stoned Paul, and dragged him out of the city, thinking him dead (Acts 14:19). Ramsay's suggestion [39] that these Jews were ' brokers or middle-men, who were speculating on the approaching harvest ' is unacceptable. Such men have rarely been religious enthusiasts. Almost invariably their over-ruling concern has been material gain, and the beliefs confessed by those with whom they have driven hard bargains have meant nothing to them. The Jews who came from Antioch were doubtless extremists who, not content with having secured the expulsion of the missionaries from their own town, were now determined to drive them from Asia Minor. So also those who came from Iconium were doubtless extremists who, annoyed that their purpose to stone the missionaries had been foiled in their own town, were now resolved to achieve it in Lystra. Time must be allowed for a report of the activity of Paul and Barnabas in Lystra to be carried back to Iconium and Antioch, for parties of Jews to be organized in these two places, and for their journey to Lystra. But that time need not have been long. Iconium was only twenty miles away, and Antioch, about sixty miles distant from Lystra, was connected with it by an excellent Roman road. There is perhaps sufficient room within six weeks for all that is recorded as having taken place during the stay of the missionaries in Lystra. It may then be concluded that they left it in the middle of May.

The site of Derbe, the town to which they now proceeded, has recently been identified by M. Ballance [40] as Kerti Hüyük about sixty miles south-east of Lystra. No details are given of the work done there by Paul and Barnabas. It is noted, however, that they preached the Gospel to that city and taught many (Acts 14:21), also that they engaged in missionary work in the country round about Lystra and Derbe (Acts 14:6 f).

---

[39] *The Church in the Roman Empire*, p. 69.
[40] ' The Site of Derbe ; A New Inscription ', *Anatolian Studies*, VII. (1957).147–51.

Derbe was the limit of their journey eastwards. From it they might have returned to Syrian Antioch via the Cilician Gates. The fact that they did not do so suggests that when they were in Derbe, they saw that it would be possible for them to retrace their steps to Pisidian Antioch, thence to regain the Pamphylian coast and to reach Syrian Antioch by sea before the season of navigation closed. They may also have seen opportunities which this course would afford them. As it is actually the course which they pursued, we may perhaps conclude that they ended their stay in Derbe early in July, that they spent the next three months first in encouraging and organizing the Christian communities which they had founded in Lystra, Iconium and Antioch, and then, after descending to Pamphylia, in ' preaching the word in Perga ' (Acts 14:25), and finally that, sailing from Attalia, they arrived in Syrian Antioch in October after an absence of about eighteen months.[41]

That the First Missionary Journey was of no longer duration cannot be proved. But we have sought to show—and we claim no more than this—that within about eighteen months, the reckoning being from March/April, there is sufficient time for all the events recorded in Acts 13:4–14:26.

[41] So Turner, ' Chronology of the New Testament ', *HDB*, I.422a ; Rackham, *The Acts of the Apostles* (Westminster Commentary Series), p. lxvii ; Plooij, *De chronologie van het leven van Paulus*, p. 146.

CHAPTER ELEVEN

The Jerusalem Conference

PAUL AND Barnabas spent 'a considerable time' (χρόνον οὐκ ὀλίγον) with the disciples in Antioch (Acts 14:28). Then, probably early in A D 48, fourteen years after Paul's conversion (Gal. 2:1), they went up to Jerusalem and attended an assembly of the church there, usually referred to as the Jerusalem Conference or Council, the occasion, proceedings and issues of which are recorded in Acts 15:1–29. At least as early as the time of Tertullian [1] and Irenaeus [2] this Conference was identified with the one which Paul records in Galatians 2:1–10. That this identification is correct is still recognized by a very large number of New Testament scholars. As Schlier [3] has shown very fully and convincingly, the accounts are in essential agreement. Assuredly there are differences between them, but these are not irreconcilable contradictions and do not prove that the accounts are those of different conferences. Rather they must be put down to two facts—the one that in Galatians 2:1–10 Paul, writing in a somewhat agitated and controversial spirit so that at several points his meaning is not quite certain, has confined himself to those parts of the proceedings which were supremely important for him, the other that the report of the proceedings given in Acts 15:1–29 has been to a considerable extent freely composed by the writer in the interest of his own theology.[4]

(1) Some maintain that Paul and Barnabas attended this Conference when they went to Jerusalem with the famine-relief collection that had been made in the church at Antioch, and

---

[1] *Adv. Marc.*, v.2.
[2] *Adv. haer.*, III.XIII.3.
[3] *Der Brief an die Galater* (Meyer Com., 11th edn., 1951), pp. 66–77.
[4] Dibelius (' Das Apostelkonzil ', *Theologische Literaturzeitung*, LXXII. [1947].193–8) underlines the writer's ' literary and theological concern '.

they either carry the famine-relief visit down to the interval between Paul's First and Second Missionary Journeys or carry the Conference back to a time shortly before the First Missionary Journey. It is suggested that in Antioch the writer of Acts learned only about a visit paid by Paul and Barnabas to Jerusalem to deliver the collection, and in Jerusalem only about a visit they had paid to attend the Conference, and that, being unaware that his information from these two sources referred to one and the same visit, he made two visits of one, putting the first before and the second after Paul's First Missionary Journey.[5]

(2) Generally the view that the one visit was paid on the earlier of these two occasions is preferred. This view can be traced back to Spitta.[6] It seemed to him that in Acts 15:23 only a mission in Syria and Cilicia is assumed, and so he inferred that the Jerusalem Conference must have taken place before Paul's First Missionary Journey. Accordingly he concluded that the account of it originally followed Acts 12:24 and that subsequently a redactor transferred it to its present place. Acts 15:35, he held, resumes Acts 14:28, and he took that as indicating that all that now lies between these two verses is an insertion.

(3) Weizsäcker[7] and E. Meyer[8] conclude that the Jerusalem Conference was earlier than the First Missionary Journey because the latter is not referred to in Galatians 1:21.

(4) Since the publication in 1908 of Harnack's *Apostelgeschichte*[9] a considerable number of scholars have held that, in composing part of the first half of his work, the writer of Acts used a written Antiochean source, and from their study of it some of them have concluded that the Jerusalem Conference

[5] See e.g. A. C. McGiffert, *A History of Christianity in the Apostolic Age*, pp. 171 ff.
[6] *Die Apostelgeschichte, ihre Quellen und deren geschichtlicher Wert*, pp. 179 ff.
[7] *The Apostolic Age of the Christian Church* (E.T. of *Das apostolische Zeitalter der christlichen Kirche*), I.109.
[8] *Ursprung und Anfänge des Christentums*, III.170.
[9] E.T. *The Acts of th Apostles* (Crown Theological Library, Vol. XXVII).

was prior to the First Missionary Journey. Among these scholars there is fairly general agreement that this source begins at 6:1, but difference of opinion as to whether or not it extends beyond 15:35. Joachim Jeremias,[10] who thinks that it possibly runs on to the end of the book, assigns to it 6:1–8:4, 9:1–30, 11:19–30, 12:25–14:28, and 15:35 ff, and regards 8:5–40, 9:31–11:18, 12:1–24, and 15.1–33 as insertions in it. He considers that 15:1–33, which he identifies with Galatians 2:1–10, is a doublet of 11:27–30, 12:25, and so puts the Jerusalem Conference before the First Missionary Journey and passes immediately from 14:28 to 15:35.

(5) An indication that the setting of the Conference in Acts is too late is found by some in the fact that according to Acts 15:7 ff and Galatians 2:9 Peter (Cephas) [11] was present at the Conference, whereas in Acts 12:17 it is reported that, on his miraculous release from prison and after calling at the house of Mary, the mother of Mark, ' he departed and went into another place ' (ἐξελθὼν ἐπορεύθη εἰς ἕτερον τόπον), and it is nowhere stated between Acts 12:17 and 15:7 that he had returned to Jerusalem.

(6) Another argument in support of the earlier setting of the Jerusalem Conference is provided by those who maintain that at the time when Agrippa I beheaded James the apostle (Acts 12:2) he also beheaded John, the brother of James. Since according to Galatians 2:9 John was present at the Jerusalem Conference, it must have been held at a time prior to Agrippa's persecution of the church. Indeed it is suggested that the persecution did not follow the Conference by mere chance, but was occasioned by it. The agreement reached by the Conference that for salvation Gentile Christians did not need to be circumcised, gave much offence to the Jews ; it revealed to them what

---

[10] ' Untersuchungen zum Quellenproblem der Apostelgeschichte ', *ZNTW*, XXXVI.(1937).205–21.

[11] There is no good reason to think, as W. M. Smaltz (' Did Peter die in Jerusalem ? ', *JBL*, LXXI.[1952].211 ff) suggests, that the Simeon of Acts 15:14 is the Simeon called Niger of Acts 13:1.

a gulf there was between them and the members of the church, and it was at their instigation and to please them that Agrippa proceeded to persecute the church. It is, so it is held, by way of indicating this connection between the Conference and the persecution that the account of the latter and of Agrippa's sudden death, which followed soon afterwards and was regarded as a divine judgement upon him for his measures against the church, is placed between the departure of Paul and Barnabas for the Conference (Acts 11:30) and their return from it (Acts 12:25).

We proceed to consider the foregoing contentions in order.[12]

(1*) The assumption that the information which the writer of Acts obtained in Antioch was very different from that which he obtained in Jerusalem can hardly be allowed. It seems in fact unlikely that in Antioch there can have been a tradition which confined itself to a generosity which the church there had once shown and said nothing whatever about an important Conference held in Jerusalem at the time when the fruits of that generosity were conveyed to the elders there by the hands of Paul and Barnabas. So also it can hardly be that in the church at Jerusalem remembrance of the visit of Paul and Barnabas to attend the Conference can have become completely dissociated from thankful remembrance of the succour which they had brought it on that same occasion. Care is needed lest, in attempting to justify a rearrangement of the events recorded in this part of Acts, the church at Jerusalem be indirectly accused of ingratitude and the church at Antioch of glorying in its good works.

(2*) The proper inference to be drawn from Acts 15:23 is not that at the time of the Conference Paul's First Missionary Journey was still in the future, but that Antioch, Syria and Cilicia were the only places in which, so far as those attending the Conference were aware, there had been agitation on the subject with which the decree (Acts 15:23–9) formulated and issued by the Conference is concerned or that the churches in these places

---

[12] (I *) answers to (1), etc.

were the only ones that through representatives had sought guidance on this matter from the Conference.

According to a considerable number of scholars the decree was formulated not by the Jerusalem Conference but at another time and possibly in another place. The writer of Acts, it is suggested, took over an account of it which he found in one of his sources and worked it into his narrative of the proceedings of the Conference so as to form what he thought would be a fitting conclusion to it. On this view the churches named in Acts 15:23 are simply those to assist which the decree was formulated; and, there being no certainty as to the date of the decree, their names can be no sure guide as to the sequence of the events recorded in this part of Acts.

In favour of this view it is urged that in his epistles Paul nowhere refers explicitly to the decree—not even in discussing the subject of fornication in 1 Corinthians 6 or that of meats offered to idols in 1 Corinthians 8 and 10 and Romans 14, that in Acts 21:25 the requirements of the decree are mentioned in his hearing as though he had not previously heard of them, and that, as appears from Galatians 2:1–10, his insistence at the Conference upon the liberty of the believer in Christ was such that he would not have agreed to any requirement that in any way or to any extent might seem to restrict it.

But it is possible, as Schlier [13] suggests, that the requirements of the decree were in Paul's mind when he wrote; ' They who seemed to be somewhat in conference added nothing to me ' (Gal. 2:6). The words of Acts 21:25, in which verse the terms of the decree are reproduced, are formally addressed to Paul. But, as Haenchen [14] points out, they are meant for the reader and intended to remind him of these terms. In Acts 16:4 it is recorded that as Paul and his fellow missionaries passed through the cities (at least Derbe and Lystra and the others in their neighbourhood), they delivered them the decrees for to keep, that were ordained of the apostles and elders which were

---

[13] *Der Brief an die Galater*, p. 77.
[14] *Die Apostelgeschichte* (12th edn., 1959), p. 541.

at Jerusalem.[15] Indeed there are two verses, 15:19 and 21:25, in which the writer of Acts gives us the impression that the decree was intended for Gentile Christians everywhere. It is then by no means inconceivable that while the decree was not formally addressed to any churches other than those mentioned in Acts 15:23, an understanding may have been reached at the Conference that Paul, Barnabas and other missionaries to the Gentiles would make its requirements known so far as they found that necessary in the places where they laboured. That Paul may have viewed such an understanding with sympathy is not unthinkable. Galatians 2:1–10 leaves us in no doubt that at the Conference his attitude was firm and immovable as regards certain matters. But as regards other matters he may not have been unyielding. Ordinarily he was willing to be conciliatory provided fundamental principles were not compromised. Actually, as is known from the passages in 1 Corinthians and Romans that have been mentioned, he himself found it necessary to give his converts rules which breathe essentially the same spirit and in large part make practically the same demands as do the requirements of the decree. The fact that in these passages he does not mention the decree has a sufficient explanation in this, that he preferred ' to lead his disciples behind the rule to the principle '.[16] The formulation of the decree had in view the solution of a practical problem. Conformity to its requirements was called for simply to facilitate table-fellowship between Jewish and Gentile Christians, and it is to be assumed that this was made quite clear by the deputies who conveyed the decree to the churches in Antioch, Syria and Cilicia and by the missionaries who commended it to the churches farther afield.

---

[15] A. S. Geyser (' Paul, the Apostolic Decree and the Liberals in Corinth ', *Studia Paulina in honorem Johannis de Zwaan*, pp. 124–38) ventures the opinion that Acts 16:4 is a later addition by the simple process of transplanting Acts 15:41 (as it appears in Codex Bezae). But it is more likely that the words παραδιδοὺς τὰς ἐντολὰς τῶν πρεσβυτέρων in the Western text of Acts 15:41 are an addition based on Acts 15:23 and 16:4.

[16] R. J. Knowling, in *Expositor's Greek Testament* II, p. 336.

The transition from Acts 14:28 to 15:36 is certainly easy. But too much ought not to be made of that. Acts 15:1 follows quite naturally upon 14:28, as also does Acts 15:36 upon 15:35.

(3*) The inference drawn from Galatians 1:21 by Weizsäcker and E. Meyer cannot be accepted. As has been indicated above,[17] in that part of Galatians Paul is concerned solely with the two visits to Jerusalem which he mentions and not with the intervening events.

(4*) Those who predicate the use by the writer of Acts of an Antiochean source do not all consider, as Jeremias does, that 15:1-33 is no part of it. Harnack retains it. Indeed he holds, and indicates in some detail, that it is 'most important for the criticism of 15:1-35 that the Antiochean origin of this passage should be kept in view'.[18] Benoit [19] also, in a recent reconstruction of the Antiochean source, gives 15:3-33 a place in it immediately after 11:27-30. According to this scholar 15:3-33 continues the account of the visit to Jerusalem begun in 11:27-30, and this visit was paid after the First Missionary Journey, 13-14 being an insertion in the Antiochean source which ought to have been made between 11:26 and 11:27.[20]

It is by no means evident that, as Jeremias claims on four grounds, 15:1-33 itself provides evidence that it is an insertion.

(1) As has been already pointed out, it ought not to be inferred from 21:25 that Paul learned about the decree formulated by the Jerusalem Conference only on his return to Jerusalem at the close of his Third Missionary Journey. From that verse then one cannot conclude that in 15:1-33 Paul is wrongly associated with the formulation of that decree.

[17] Pages 56 f.
[18] *The Acts of the Apostles*, p. 199.
[19] 'La deuxième visite de saint Paul à Jérusalem', *Biblica*, XL.(1959). 778-92.
[20] To make good his own conclusion Benoit undoubtedly needs to give convincing reasons why the section Acts 13-14 occupies its present position and does not stand between Acts 11:26 and 11:27. This, it seems to us, he has failed to do.

(2) In 15:1–33 ἀπόστολος may not have the same meaning as it has in 14:4, 14. But it has the same meaning in 16:4.

(3) As has already been indicated, the fact that in 15:23 only Antioch, Syria and Cilicia are mentioned cannot be regarded as evidence that at the time of the Jerusalem Conference the First Missionary Journey was still in the future.

(4) It is true that Acts 15:33 (Silas returns to Jerusalem) may seem to contradict Acts 15:40 (Silas in Antioch). But this seeming contradiction is easily resolved. When he became aware that Barnabas was not to accompany him on another journey, Paul must have sent word to Silas asking him to rejoin him in Antioch. As is well known, there are points at which the writer of Acts shows no particular interest in the movements of Paul's fellow workers.

It needs to be added that whilst the theory that the writer of Acts used an Antiochean source has still its advocates, there has been, since the appearance of the School of Form Criticism, a growing tendency to prefer the view that in composing the first half of his work he used isolated portions of tradition, which existed in free circulation and were either oral or written.

(5*) There has been considerable discussion as to what is meant by the other place to which, according to Acts 12:17, Peter betook himself. D. F. Robinson [21] maintains that, taken literally, the story told in Acts 12:1–19 is difficult to believe, and that it makes good sense only when read as an allegory of Peter's death. The truth conveyed by its statements that an angel of the Lord released Peter from prison and that Peter then departed to another place is that he died in prison in Jerusalem and went to his appointed place of glory. He can then have been present at the Jerusalem Conference only if it took place before Agrippa's persecution of the church. But 1 Corinthians 9:5 is sufficient evidence that he was still alive at least as late as A D 50, when Paul made his first contact with Corinth.

Justin Martyr [22] records that the Simon Magus who was

[21] ' Where and when did Peter die ? ', *JBL*, LXIV.(1945).255–67.
[22] *Apol.*, i.26.

confuted by Peter in Samaria (Acts 8:20–4) proceeded to Rome in the reign of Claudius and there performed such mighty works of magic that he was honoured as a god, a statue being erected to him with the inscription *Simoni Deo Sancto*. Apparently some found it difficult to believe that such success could have attended Simon for long, and so they taught that ' during the reign of Claudius the all-good and gracious Providence, which watches over all things, ... led Peter ... to Rome against this great corrupter of life '. Eusebius [23] took this as history and in his *Chronicle* [24] puts the arrival of Peter in Rome in the second year of Claudius, i.e. A D 42. Now that is not an impossible date for Agrippa's persecution of the church,[25] and hence the conjecture that the other place to which Peter went was Rome. But it is now considered unlikely that the Simon mentioned in Acts 8 ever went to Rome. Also it is now generally supposed that Justin was mistaken in his understanding of the statue, for in the place where he says it was erected, an island in the Tiber known as *inter duos pontes*, there was unearthed in 1574 an altar with the inscription *Semoni Sanco Deo*, and Semo Sancus was a Sabine deity. As regards Peter himself, it is now widely agreed that the tradition that he went to Rome and suffered martyrdom there is to be accepted.[26] But his arrival in the city is generally dated considerably later than A D 42. H. Katzenmeyer [27] puts both his arrival and his martyrdom early in the reign of Nero.

[23] *H.E.*, II.xiv,6.
[24] Ed. Schoene, II.153. The note in the version of Jerome runs : *Petrus apostolus cum primus Antiochenam ecclesiam fundasset Romam mittitur. Vbi euangelium praedicans XXV annis eiusdem urbis episcopus perseuerat.*
[25] See p. 42, *supra*.
[26] Among scholars who maintain that Peter never was in Rome are Merrill, *Essays in Early Christian History*, pp. 267 ff, and Heussi, in several articles including ' Galater 2 und der Lebensausgang der jerusalemischen Urapostel ', *Theologische Literaturzeitung*, LXXVII.(1952).67 ff. The arguments of the former are refuted by Streeter, *The Four Gospels*, p. 490, and those of the latter by Aland, ' Wann starb Petrus ? ', *New Testament Studies*, II.(1956).267 ff.
[27] ' Entstehung und Schicksale der Kirche Gottes in Rom ', *Internationale kirchliche Zeitschrift*, XXXI.(1941).36–45.

According to Cullmann [28] he probably came to Rome towards the end of his life and worked there for a very short time and died as a martyr under Nero. F. H. Chase [29] considers it probable that at the time of Agrippa's persecution of the church Peter went to Syria and entered on work there in which he continued until he proceeded to Rome c. A D 61. During his stay in Syria his headquarters were in Antioch, and his visits to Jerusalem were few. But one of these was at the time of the Conference.

In recent times it has been suggested that after leaving Jerusalem (Acts 12:17) Peter made the Palestinian journey recorded in Acts 9:32–11:18. K. Lake [30] maintains that in Acts the famine in Judaea is placed before the death of Agrippa I in A D 44. But according to Josephus the famine occurred in the procuratorship of Tiberius Alexander and so not earlier than A D 46. Accordingly Lake suggests that Acts 11:27–30 should be read not before, but after Acts 12:1–24. Going further, he suggests that the sequel to the story of Peter's miraculous release from prison and his departure from Jerusalem is given in Acts 9:32–11:18. But, as already indicated,[31] in Acts 12:1–24 the writer brings his account of the church in Jerusalem down to the time when Paul and Barnabas arrived there on their relief mission and places the famine in Judaea *after* the death of Agrippa. Lake has thus failed to give a compelling reason why Acts 11:27–30 should be read after Acts 12:1–24. The question whether the more considerable change which he suggests in the order of events ought to be made, is assuredly one ' which is bound to rise in the mind of the investigator '. It is conceivable that the writer of Acts brought the account of Peter's Palestinian journey forward in order that, after completing it, he might give a fairly long account, unbroken apart from the necessary interlude, 12:1–24, of the church at Antioch, first of its beginnings 11:19–26) and then of events associated with it and in large

[28] *Peter : Disciple-Apostle-Martyr* (2nd edn., 1962), p. 187.
[29] ' Peter (Simon) ', *HDB*, III.779a.
[30] In Jackson and Lake, *The Beginnings of Christianity*, I.v.468 f.
[31] Pages 53 f, *supra*.

part consequent upon its early development (11:27–30, 12:25, 13:1–14:28).

But that Peter made his Palestinian journey soon after Paul's first return to Jerusalem after his conversion (A D 37 or 38), perhaps even soon after Paul's conversion (A D 34 or 35),[32] is not only suggested by the setting in Acts of the account of the journey, but is also confirmed by the statement attributed to Peter in Acts 15:7 that the conversion of Cornelius took place 'in the early days' (ἀφ' ἡμερῶν ἀρχαίων). There were apparently no Roman troops in Caesarea during the reign of Agrippa I (A D 41–4). Accordingly, unless the writer of Acts has carried back the circumstances of his own day to the time of the Cornelius episode, that episode must be dated, if it was thus early, before A D 41.

Even, however, if Peter's Palestinian journey is given the suggested later setting, that does not necessarily exclude the possibility of his having attended the Jerusalem Conference. According to Lake, Peter, after his journey, Joppa-Lydda-Caesarea, returned to Jerusalem and later went to Antioch. F. W. Beare [33] and J. N. Sanders,[34] who also find the sequel to Acts 12:17 in Acts 9:32–11:18, both hold that from Caesarea Peter found his way to Antioch; and although the former writes that nothing indicates that he ever returned to Jerusalem, the latter inclines to think that from Antioch he paid a visit to the capital and there attended a meeting at which he, Barnabas and James drew up the apostolic decree.

The statement of Acts 12:17 is very indefinite. The ἐξελθών may mean simply that Peter left the house [35] and not that he left Jerusalem. But it is very likely that, seeking safety, he betook himself well beyond the city walls. There is, however, no

---

[32] So Chase, 'Peter (Simon)', *HDB*, III.764b : 'These events took place in the months succeeding St. Paul's conversion.'
[33] 'The Sequence of Events in Acts 9–15 and the Career of Peter', *JBL*, LXII.(1943).295–306.
[34] 'Peter and Paul in the Acts', *New Testament Studies*, II.(1955).133–43.
[35] So *NEB*.

compelling reason to think that the place to which he went was so far removed from Jerusalem that he is unlikely to have been back there for the Conference. To object that his return is not mentioned is to forget that in Acts no chronicle of his daily movements has been attempted.

(6*) Much attention has been paid to the theory of an early martyrdom of John, the son of Zebedee, and critical opinion regarding it continues to be sharply divided.[36] We proceed to adduce and to consider briefly the evidence which is alleged to support it.

(1) *The evidence of the martyrologies*

In a manuscript dated A D 411/12 of a very early Syriac martyrology the commemoration of the birth of Christ is put on 25th December, and then the following commemorations are detailed:

26th December, the first martyr at Jerusalem, Stephen the apostle, the head of the martyrs.
27th December, John and James, the apostles, at Jerusalem.
28th December, in the town of Rome, Paul the apostle and Simon Cephas, the head of the apostles of our Lord.

So also it seems likely that in the martyrology of Carthage (A D 505) the commemoration of John and James the apostles was originally assigned to 27th December. Actually the names given there are John the Baptist and James the apostle ' whom Herod killed '. But John the Baptist appears to be a mistake for John the apostle, the commemoration of John the Baptist being also assigned in this martyrology to 24th June.

These assignations are taken as indicating that John the son of Zebedee as well as his brother James died an early martyr death. But it is possible that this association of Stephen, John, James, Paul and Peter is due not to a belief that each of them had suffered ' red ' martyrdom, but to the recognition that they

---

[36] The theory is strongly advocated by R. H. Charles, *Revelation* (Inter. Crit. Commentary), I.xlv ff.

had all been martyrs in the earliest and widest sense of the word, witnesses unto Christ. Evidence that it is not merely possible but very likely that it was as such martyrs that they were commemorated has been found by J. H. Bernard [37] in certain writings of the fourth century—the homily of Aphrahat *On Persecution*, the panegyric of Gregory of Nazianzus on Basil the Great and three sermons of Gregory of Nyssa.

(2) *The evidence of Scripture*

According to Mark 10:39 Jesus said to James and John, the sons of Zebedee : ' Ye shall indeed drink of the cup that I drink of, and with the baptism that I am baptized withal shall ye be baptized.' This is regarded by some as a prediction that these two would suffer martyrdom, and it is maintained that this prediction would not have been given a place in Mark had it not been fulfilled by the time that Gospel was written. But this is too narrow an interpretation of what Jesus said. ' Although ', writes V. Taylor, ' James was martyred, martyrdom is not exclusively meant, or even necessarily implied, for the New Testament does not use the imagery of baptism in this sense, and it is not found in Christian usage until the turn of the second century.' [38] Others maintain that the words of Jesus just quoted are a *vaticinium ex eventu*. To that W. F. Howard has effectively replied : ' Mark 9:1 is sufficient evidence that sayings of Jesus were preserved in the Gospel because they were remembered, not because they were framed afterwards to fit events in history.' [39]

(3) *The evidence of Papias*

This is found in (*a*) the *Codex Baroccianus* 142, an epitome made between 600 and 800 of the *Christian History* of Philippus

---

[37] In *Studia Sacra*, pp. 275 ff. Cf. J. Armitage Robinson, *The Historical Character of St. John's Gospel*, pp. 77 ff, where the relevant passages are quoted.

[38] *The Gospel according to St. Mark*, p. 441.

[39] *The Fourth Gospel in Recent Criticism and Interpretation* (1st edn., 1931), p. 249 ; (4th edn., 1955), p. 273.

Sidetes (c. 430), also in (b) the manuscript *Coistinianus* 305 of the *Chronicle* of Georgius Hamartolus (saec. ix). According to (a) Papias recorded in his second book (δευτέρῳ λόγῳ) that John the Divine (ὁ θεολόγος) and James his brother were killed by the Jews. But Papias is not likely to have used the title ὁ θεολόγος, which is in fact not found earlier than the fourth century. The sections of the work of Papias were not called λόγοι but βιβλία. Also James the brother of John was not killed by the Jews but by Agrippa I (Acts 12:2). He has apparently been confused here with James the brother of the Lord,[40] who according to the *Chronicle* of Eusebius [41] and also according to a story told by Hegesippus preserved in Eusebius, *H.E.*, II. xxiii, met his death at the hands of the Jews. In (b) it is stated that Papias in the second book of the Oracles of the Lord says that John was killed by the Jews, and this is followed by a reference to Mark 10:39. But this statement is found in no other manuscript of the work of Georgius Hamartolus. In all likelihood it was carried into the *Coistinianus* either from Philip's *History* or, and this is more probable, from the epitome of it. Philip's *History* is lost, but accounts of it that have come down to us indicate that its loss is 'not to be regretted on literary grounds' and that Philip's 'credit for veracity is so small that in him we should have a very untrustworthy guide'.[42] It is then by no means impossible that he has quoted Papias carelessly and incorrectly. That neither Irenaeus nor Eusebius, both of whom were acquainted with the writings of Papias, anywhere record that John died a martyr's death is a significant fact, one that merits far more attention than testimony that is of late date, indirect, and so vaguely worded that it is variously interpreted even by those who accept it.

It is surprising that the account given in Acts of the martyrdom

---

[40] This is shown in detail by Bernard in *Studia Sacra*, pp. 271 f; cf. his *Commentary on the Gospel according to St. John (I.C.C.)*, I.xli f.

[41] Ed. Schoene, II.154 and 155.

[42] Venables, 'Philippus of Side', *Dictionary of Christian Biography*, IV. 356.

of James, who had been one of the twelve disciples of the Lord, is so brief and that so little information is communicated about its occasion and circumstances. Disquieted not necessarily by the findings of the Jerusalem Conference but simply by the steady growth of the church, the Jews may have instigated Agrippa to act as he did. From Josephus [43] and the Mishnah [44] it is known that he studiously courted the favour of the Jews. It is therefore not unlikely that he would have responded to such instigation. But what the short narrative of Acts suggests is rather that some outspoken word of James had offended Agrippa or that an accusation of disloyalty on the part of James, arising possibly out of misunderstanding of his proclamation of the Messiahship of Jesus, had been brought to Agrippa, and that it was essentially for a personal reason that he had James beheaded. It was apparently only when he saw that by doing so he pleased the Jews, that he proceeded to have Peter arrested (Acts 12:3). Certainly it is possible to retain the order in which events stand in this part of Acts without being at a loss for an explanation of Agrippa's action.[45]

The dating of the Jerusalem Conference before Agrippa's persecution of the church involves a chronological difficulty that tells against it. Goguel,[46] who favours the rearrangement of events at present under consideration, puts the death of Herod Agrippa in March A D 44, Agrippa's persecution of the church in January or February A D 44, and the Jerusalem Conference in the opening months of A D 44 or the closing months of A D 43. Recognizing that if the fourteen years of Galatians 2:1 were subsequent to the three years of Galatians 1:18, he would have to assign the conversion of Paul to A D 26/27, which is much too early, he adopts the view that the fourteen years include the three and assigns the conversion of Paul to A D 29/30, and so to a time eighteen months after the crucifixion, for which his date

[43] *Ant.*, xix.292–6, 328–31.
[44] *Bikkurim* iii.4 ; *Sotah* vii.8.
[45] On Acts 12:1–24 see pp. 53 f., *supra*.
[46] *Introduction au Nouveau Testament*, IV.i.94–9.

is the spring of A D 28. But the much more likely date of the crucifixion is either A D 30 or A D 33; and even if the earlier of these is preferred, A D 29/30 is too early a date for Paul's conversion.

G. G. Findlay [47] points out that according to his own account in Galatians 2:1–10 Paul played a leading role in the proceedings of the Jerusalem Conference, not only acting as the responsible head of the Gentile mission but being also recognized as such by the leaders of the church. ' All that ', he writes, ' we can understand as taking place *after the first missionary tour* and the events of Acts 13–14, which brought Paul to the forefront and displayed in him powers fully comparable to those manifested in Peter's ministry.' That is undoubtedly a telling argument against the identification already discussed of the visit to Jerusalem of Galatians 2:1–10 with the famine-relief visit to that city, and also against the rearrangement of events recorded in Acts with which we have been concerned.

It has long been customary to divide Acts into two parts, of which the first ends with Chapter 12 and the second begins with Chapter 13. The first part is largely devoted to the activity of Peter. In the second part the writer confines himself almost exclusively to Paul's missionary work among the Gentiles; and it may be argued that the matters discussed at the Jerusalem Conference are likely to have been disposed of before he entered on that work, and consequently that historically the Conference has its right place immediately before he set out on his First Missionary Journey. But another division of the book seems preferable. The point of transition from its first to its second part lies, it may be claimed, not between Chapters 12 and 13 but in Chapter 15. That chapter appears to be its ' centre-piece ' or ' watershed '. Onwards from the 36th verse of that chapter Paul assumes command of the Gentile mission, and that mission is now directed and extended westward to Rome. By the time of the First Missionary Journey the church had established itself

[47] ' Paul the Apostle ', *HDB*, III.706a.

in places in which the Jewish element in the population preponderated or was at least considerable. Only in the course of that journey did it secure a footing in places where that element in the population was very small. Consequently it was not until that journey was over that it was in a position to deal realistically with problems which had already in some measure presented themselves or which could now be seen as likely to arise. P. H. Menoud,[48] who writes in support of this view of Acts, points out that it was only when Paul and Barnabas returned from the mission recorded in Acts 13–14 that the church comprised in its membership Jews, Samaritans, proselytes and idolatrous Gentiles, in short all the categories of men that, however far it might subsequently extend, it could possibly gather into its membership. That was precisely the occasion when it needed to put to itself and to answer the questions which came before the Jerusalem Conference.

[48] 'Le Plan des Actes des Apôtres', *New Testament Studies*, I.(1954). 41–51. Cf. Benoit who argues (in *Biblica*, XL.(1959).788) that it is necessary to put the First Missionary Journey before the Conference 'to explain the problem which occasioned the Conference'.

CHAPTER TWELVE

Paul's Collision with Peter
and
His Separation from Barnabas

IN GALATIANS 2:11–14 Paul records a collision that he had with the apostle Peter. He writes:

But when Cephas came to Antioch, I opposed him to his face, because he was clearly in the wrong. For until certain persons came from James he was taking his meals with gentile Christians; but when they came he drew back and began to hold aloof, because he was afraid of the advocates of circumcision. The other Jewish Christians showed the same lack of principle; even Barnabas was carried away and played false like the rest. But when I saw that their conduct did not square with the truth of the Gospel, I said to Cephas, before the whole congregation, 'If you, a Jew born and bred, live like a Gentile, and not like a Jew, how can you insist that Gentiles must live like Jews?'

It would appear that Paul's purpose in adducing this incident was to show that he was not in any respect inferior in authority to the chief apostles.

The collision is not dated expressly. But from the setting of the passage it has generally, and not unreasonably, been inferred that it took place after the meeting in Jerusalem recorded in Galatians 2:1–10. Wieseler [1] maintains that this meeting, which he distinguishes from the Jerusalem Conference, took place on the occasion of a visit which Paul paid to Jerusalem in the interval between his Second and Third Missionary Journeys, and he assigns the collision to the same interval: from Jerusalem, where the pillar apostles had concluded a gentleman's agreement with them, Paul and Barnabas proceeded to Antioch, and there

---

[1] *Chronologie des apostolischen Zeitalters*, pp. 179–208, 595.

Paul ' denounced Peter's lapse from his former freer manner of life '. John Knox [2] holds that the meeting in Jerusalem of Galatians 2, which he identifies with the Jerusalem Conference of Acts 15, took place on Paul's return to Syria recorded in Acts 18:18–22, and that his collision with Peter in Antioch took place soon after that meeting. And among the many scholars who identify the Jerusalem visit of Galatians 2 with that of Acts 15 and put it in the interval between Paul's First and Second Missionary Journeys, there are some [3] who carry down the collision to the interval between the Second and Third Journeys.

To this late dating of the collision there is, however, a decisive objection in the reference which Paul makes to Barnabas in his account of it. ' Even Barnabas ', he writes, ' was carried away.' At the time of the collision Barnabas was still intimately associated with Paul as his colleague and fellow traveller in missionary service. But in Acts onwards from 15:39 these two are never again found working alongside one another; in the Pauline epistles there is no indication, apart from the very questionable evidence of 1 Corinthians 9:6, that Barnabas had any part with Paul in his labours in Macedonia and Achaia in the course of his Second Missionary Journey; and even if it were true, notwithstanding this silence, that he accompanied Paul on this journey, it would be difficult to believe that after so long a partnership with him in work among Gentiles he can have yielded to the influence of Judaizers in Antioch and there

[2] ' " Fourteen Years Later ": a Note on the Pauline Chronology ', *The Journal of Religion*, xvi.(1936).341–9; ' The Pauline Chronology ', *JBL*, LXIII.(1939).15–29; and *Chapters in a Life of Paul* (1950). Cf. C. H. Buck, Jnr., ' The Date of Galatians ', *JBL*, LXX.(1951). 113–22; P. S. Minear, ' The Jerusalem Fund and Pauline Chronology ', *Anglican Theological Review*, XXV.(1943).389–96; D. W. Riddle, *Paul, Man of Conflict, A Modern Biographical Sketch*.

[3] E.g. A. Sabatier, *L'Apôtre Paul*, p. xiii, footnote 1; G. G. Findlay, ' Paul the Apostle ', *HDB*, III.709a; Bo Reicke, ' Der geschichtliche Hintergrund des Apostelkonzils und der Antiochia-Episode, Gal. 2:1–14 ', *Studia Paulina in honorem Johannis de Zwaan* (ed. J. N. Sevenster and W. C. van Unnik, 1953), p. 175.

have suffered himself to be carried away by them as he is reported to have done.

If the meeting in Jerusalem of Galatians 2 was the Jerusalem Conference of Acts 15 and the collision took place shortly after it and before the commencement of Paul's Second Missionary Journey, Peter's conduct in Antioch was very much in fault. He took a leading part in the proceedings of the Conference. Recalling the conversion of Cornelius and his friends, he declared that God, by the faith with which he had inspired them, had cleansed their hearts and had thereby done away all distinction between believing Gentile and believing Jew (Acts 15:9). On coming to Antioch he acted in the spirit of that declaration, having table fellowship with his Gentile brethren. But, we are informed, when certain persons came from James he withdrew himself from these brethren and ceased to eat with them.

From early times this conduct of Peter has occasioned difficulty, and various attempts have been made to save his credit. According to Eusebius, *H.E.*, I.xii.2, Clement of Alexandria in his *Hypotyposeis* maintained that the Cephas (Gal. 2:11) whom Paul withstood was not Peter the apostle, but one of the Seventy, a man who bore the same name.[4] This distinction has been favoured by others down to comparatively modern times;[5] but it would almost certainly never have been drawn but for the desire to exonerate the apostle. According to a theory first ventured by Origen, strongly advocated by Jerome and for a time much in favour, the scene in Antioch was concerted by Peter and Paul for the edification of the church. Augustine rightly insisted that this theory imputes dishonesty to both apostles, and such was the hurt that he did it by this assault upon it that it scarcely outlived his time.

In modern times the problem which Peter's conduct in Antioch occasions has been approached in another way. Paley

---

[4] On the Cephas-Peter problem see D. W. Riddle, ' The Cephas-Peter Problem and a possible Solution ', *JBL*, LIX.(1940).169–80.

[5] See Lagrange, *Épître aux Galates* (2nd edn., 1950), p. 41.

in his *Horae Paulinae* [6] writes: 'There is nothing to hinder us from supposing that the dispute at Antioch was prior to the consultation at Jerusalem.' The same assumption is made by Turner.[7] He considers that the meeting of Galatians 2:1-10 is the Jerusalem Conference of Acts 15:1-39, and suggests that Galatians 2:11-14 is chronologically out of its place and should be read immediately before Galatians 2:1-10. It is then possible to identify the persons who came from James to Antioch (Galatians 2:12) with those who came down there from Judaea (Acts 15:1; cf. 15:24) and to date the collision shortly before the Jerusalem Conference. H. -M. Féret in his study, *Pierre et Paul à Antioche et à Jérusalem. Le ' Conflit' des deux Apôtres* (Paris, 1955), likewise identifies the Jerusalem visits of Galatians 2 and Acts 15 and assigns the collision to the time Paul and Barnabas spent in Antioch after returning from the First Missionary Journey and before they went up to Jerusalem to attend the Conference there. The collision is also assigned to this time by most of the scholars referred to on pp. 45 ff above who identify the Jerusalem visit of Gal. 2:1-10 with the famine-relief visit of Acts 11:27-30, 12:25; and indeed they find a confirmation of the correctness of this identification in the fact that, without disturbing the recorded order of events in Galatians 2:1-14, they are able to give the collision this setting.

Generally it is claimed that when the collision is assumed to have taken place before the Jerusalem Conference, it is possible to put a more favourable construction on the conduct of Peter; and admittedly, if the incident belongs to that time, he may seem to have been somewhat less in the wrong. We proceed, however, to show (1) that the proposed inversion of Galatians 2:1-10 and 2:11-14 cannot be justified on grammatical or historical grounds, (2) that only when the collision is put later than the Jerusalem Conference can Paul's conduct in Antioch be adequately explained, and (3) that it is not inconceivable that

---

[6] Edn. of Binnie (1880) p. 109.
[7] ' Chronology of the New Testament ', *HDB*, I.424a.

after the Jerusalem Conference Peter's conduct in Antioch may have been such as it is reported to have been.

(1) Paul gives no indication that at Galatians 2:11 he breaks away from the chronological order to which, in his narrative of events, he has adhered up to this point. Turner's paraphrase, ' So far from submitting to them, I once publicly rebuked their chief', contains the word ' once ' for which there is no justification in the Greek. It is true that in Galatians 2:11 Paul no longer uses ἔπειτα as he has done in Galatians 1:18, 21; 2:1. But there need be no doubt that there, as e.g. in Matthew 9:25, 13:26; Acts 8:12; Galatians 1:15, 2:12, 4:4, ὅτε δέ denotes chronological sequence. While the stay of Paul and Barnabas in Antioch immediately after the Jerusalem Conference does not appear to have been so long [8] as their stay there immediately before it, no proof can be given that it was too short for the happenings recorded in Galatians 2:11-14. That Peter cannot have visited Antioch after the delimitation of his sphere of labour mentioned in Galatians 2:7 cannot be allowed. There were Jews in that city, and Peter, entrusted with the Gospel for Jews, was entitled to go there should he choose or find it necessary to do so.

(2) Let us consider Peter's conduct in Antioch as it is described in Galatians 2:11-14 on the assumption that it belongs to the time after the return of Paul and Barnabas from the First Missionary Journey and before they went up to the Jerusalem Conference. It certainly appears surprising. On coming to Antioch he ate with the Gentile Christians there. Later, yielding to certain Judaizers, he ceased to eat with them. He acted inconsistently. He did so in the sense that his conduct was not all of a piece. But it cannot be asserted with any confidence that he did so in the sense that he acted contrary to his convictions. His eating with Gentile Christians was an indication that he thought it not wrong to do so, but it was no proof that he was not open to correction in the matter. It is not known that he had by this time made any solemn open declaration as to where he stood,

---

[8] On its possible length see p. 112, *infra*.

and at this stage Paul cannot have known with any certainty whether Peter had already thought out all the practical implications of his experiences in the house of Simon the tanner and in the house of Cornelius and so was fully persuaded in his own mind. Consequently Paul can have had no sure ground for his conclusion that in yielding to the Judaizers Peter was not conforming his practice to his convictions and so was guilty of dissimulation (ὑπόκρισις). In these circumstances Paul is likely to have resorted to private conversations with Peter, and that in these he would have succeeded in winning him to conduct that squared with the truth of the Gospel need not be doubted. Only when it is assumed to belong to a time after the Jerusalem Conference does Peter's conduct in Antioch appear in glaring inconsistency with his declared convictions, and it is only then that both the severity with which Paul rebuked him and the fact that he rebuked him to the face, i.e. before the whole congregation,[9] are fully understandable.

(3) Many find it unbelievable that after his experience in Joppa as recorded in Acts 10:1–23 and his experience in Caesarea as recorded in Acts 10:24–48, Peter can have been guilty of the self-condemning behaviour attributed to him in Galatians 2:11–14. How, they ask, can the apostle who had been taught in so remarkable and memorable a way what his attitude ought to be towards his fellows of every race, ever afterwards have assumed another attitude and in this matter have hearkened to men and not to God? His conduct in Antioch, Bousset[10] maintains, is psychologically quite inconceivable at any time subsequent to the conversion of Cornelius, and we must conclude either that the conversion is unhistorical or that it took place at a time later than the collision in Antioch.

But the difficulty with which we are here concerned appears to

---

[9] According to Bonnard, *L'Epître de saint Paul aux Galates*, the words ' to the face ' (κατὰ πρόσωπον, Gal. 2:11) indicate that ' the confrontation took place in public, doubtless in the course of a meeting of the whole church '.

[10] In J. Weiss, *Die Schriften des Neuen Testaments* (2nd edn, 1908), II.45.

be due in large part to the writer of Acts. He obviously attached much importance to the Cornelius episode. He has recorded it at length, and there is good reason to conclude that, seeking to serve a theological end, he has made certain substantial additions to the original story.[11] What in fact came to pass was, it would seem, less extraordinary than it is represented as having been, and its message does not seem to have been at once fully apprehended or at once felt as a compelling power. There is no indication that Peter forthwith devoted himself to work among Gentiles or that ' the apostles and brethren that were in Judaea ' (Acts 11:1) forthwith organized a mission to Gentiles. When the incident was over, Peter had only what had actually happened to think upon, and its far-reaching significance does not appear to have come home to him until he had met Paul and Barnabas in Jerusalem and compared his own experience with the experience that they had had in the course of the First Missionary Journey.[12]

It is then in the light not of what is recorded in Acts 10:1–11:18 but of the part that he had in the proceedings of the Jerusalem Conference that the conduct of Peter in Antioch must be judged, and undoubtedly, when so judged, it cannot be described fairly as anything other than ὑπόκρισις. In Antioch he acted contrary to the principles which he had avowed at the Conference. His guilt lay in this, that, knowing the truth, he had not the courage to conform his practice to it.[13] But this, while the last-

[11] See e.g. Dibelius, ' Die Bekhrung des Cornelius ', *Coniectanea Neotestamentica xi in honorem Antonii Fridrichsen*, pp. 50–65 (= Dibelius, *Studies in the Acts of the Apostles*, pp. 109–22), and Trocmé, *Le ' Livre des Actes ' et l'Histoire* (1957), pp. 169–74.

[12] ' St. Luke plainly gives us to understand that St. Peter did not understand the *general intention* of the Divine vision vouchsafed to him, as related in the story of Cornelius ; and that it was necessary for the mission to be set on foot by others before he could be brought to a right way of thinking '—Harnack, *The Acts of the Apostles* (E.T. of *Die Apostelgeschichte, Beitr. zur Einl. in d.N.T.* iii), p. 190, note 1.

[13] According to Cullmann, *Peter : Disciple-Apostle-Martyr* (2nd edn., 1962), p. 53 : ' It must be said in extenuation that as the missionary leader dependent on the Jerusalem church, he [Peter] occupied in relation to the party of James *an infinitely more difficult position* than did the independent Paul.'

recorded, was by no means the first occasion on which Peter was guilty of conduct of the kind. His behaviour in Antioch, however unbelievable, consists with his character as it is disclosed to us in the gospels. ' We recognize in it ', writes Benjamin Jowett,[14] ' the lineaments of him who confessed Christ first, and first denied Him ; who began by refusing that Christ should wash his feet, and then said, " not my feet only, but my hands and my head "; who cut off the ear of the servant of the High Priest when they came to take Jesus, and then forsook Him and fled. Boldness and timidity, first boldness, then timidity, were the characteristics of his nature.'

The collision thus falls into the interval between the return of Paul and Barnabas from the Jerusalem Conference and their separation immediately prior to the Second Missionary Journey. According to Acts 15:36 ff they separated because they fell out over Mark. In some quarters, however, it is maintained that their separation was an issue of the collision, and that the story told in Acts 15:36 ff is an invention of the writer.

Paul, it is pointed out, does not say how the collision ended : he does not say that Peter, Barnabas and the other Jewish Christians in Antioch recognized the soundness of his contention and resumed table fellowship with their Gentile brethren. He says nothing of the kind, it is argued, because he was not in a position to do so. His authority was not recognized. On the contrary, ' in its immediate results the collision was for Paul a defeat, an apparently disastrous defeat. Not one of those on whom he had a right to count among the church leaders stood by him.'[15] ' The conflict ', writes Goguel,[16] ' affected the rest of Paul's career with the most dire consequences. It disturbed his relations with the church at Antioch and, what was more

---

[14] *The Epistles of St. Paul to the Thessalonians, Galatians, Romans*, I.297.
[15] B. W. Bacon, ' Peter's Triumph at Antioch ', *Journal of Religion* ix (1929), p. 206.
[16] *The Birth of Christianity* (E.T. of *La Naissance du Christianisme*), p. 304.

serious, with the church at Jerusalem. It left him an isolated individual right up to the time of his death.'

Now it is true that Paul is silent as to the issue of the collision. At Galatians 2:14 his report of his words to Peter merges into reflection and comment. But it is unbelievable that he would have adduced as proof of his apostolic authority an incident in which it was set at nought. He did not need to state expressly what, he must have been sure, his readers would assume, namely that his intervention in Antioch achieved its purpose.

It is also maintained that in all likelihood the writer of Acts knew about the collision, and that he has not only left it with all its grievous issue unmentioned, but has also sought to hide it out of sight by inventing another explanation of the separation of Paul and Barnabas. It needs to be noted, however, that this explanation is recorded in a straightforward, matter-of-fact manner, and that there is not the least indication that the writer is trying to conceal something from his readers. A difference between Paul and Barnabas about Mark is by no means impossible, and it is undoubtedly a sufficient reason for their separation. Moreover, those who have a first-hand acquaintance with the Church in the mission field of today are aware that when a matter, grievous and fraught, if not remedied, with disastrous consequences, has once been disposed of by a congregation, the decision is accepted without bitterness, whilst the incident is left to find its own level and is seldom mentioned. The silence of the writer of Acts about the collision, even if he knew about it—and that is not to be taken for granted—is quite understandable.[17] Some allowance needs perhaps to be made for the vehemence with which Paul records the collision, but it need not be doubted that Peter along with Barnabas and the others who

---

[17] Referring to the fact that the collision is not mentioned in Acts, F. Rendall, in *Expositor's Greek Testament*, III.161, writes : ' It bears out the impression which the Epistle [Galatians] itself conveys, that the collision was a transitory incident and had no lasting effect on Church history.' This judgement seems to us much nearer the mark than those of Bacon and Goguel quoted in the text.

had followed Peter's example humbly accepted correction and that, far from cherishing resentment, they gratefully accepted Paul's counsel and conformed their practice to it.

Before proceeding to the chronology of the Second Missionary Journey we shall investigate two dates which have a determinative bearing upon it—that of the edict of Claudius expelling all Jews from Rome and that of Gallio's proconsulship of Achaia.

CHAPTER THIRTEEN

Claudius's Expulsion of the Jews from Rome

ACCORDING to Acts 18:1 f when Paul came to Corinth in the course of his Second Missionary Journey, he fell in with a Jew named Aquila, a native of Pontus, and his wife Priscilla. They had recently arrived from Italy because Claudius had issued an edict that all Jews should leave Rome. The narrative indicates that all three had arrived in Corinth about the same time, Aquila and Priscilla perhaps a littler earlier than Paul, and that Claudius's edict of expulsion had been issued shortly before then.

Of the Roman emperors the first to take repressive measures against the Jews living in Rome was Tiberius. Influenced by his confidant Sejanus,[1] he had the able-bodied men among them deported to Sardinia to fight against the brigands there, and he ordered the rest of them to quit the city.[2] On the death of Sejanus he changed his attitude. That he actually revoked his edict of expulsion is not known with certainty, but Jews did begin to return to Rome.[3] Under Caligula there was much unrest among the Jews of Alexandria and also of Palestine.[4] In edicts issued in the beginning of his reign Claudius intimated his desire to pursue a favourable policy towards the Jews resident in Alexandria and towards Jews everywhere throughout the

---

[1] So Philo is known to have written in a part that has not survived of his *Leg. ad Gai.* Its substance is given in Eusebius, *H.E.*II.v.7 ; *Chron.* (ed. Schoene, II.150) ; Syncellus, *Chronographia* (ed. Dindorf, I.621).
[2] Josephus, *Ant.*, xviii.83 f.; Tacitus, *Ann.*, ii.85 ; Suetonius, *Tiber.*, 36.
[3] Dion Cassius, lx.6 : πλεονάσαντας αὖθις.
[4] On Caligula and the Jews see J. P. V. D. Balsdon, *The Emperor Gaius*, pp. 111–45.

99

empire.[5] But sooner or later he found it necessary to resort to repressive measures against the Jews in Rome. Their precise nature is, however, a matter of dispute. According to Dion Cassius [6] he refrained from ordering the Jews to leave the city, recognizing that since they were so many such an order might be difficult to carry into effect, and so merely prohibited them from assembling together. But Suetonius [7] and the writer of Acts speak of expulsion.

Dion Cassius deals with the matter in his account of A D 41. Most scholars point out that there he gives merely an introductory, general characterization of Claudius' reign and has not yet entered on a chronologically ordered account of its events. Because of that, they maintain, it cannot be assumed with any certainty that the occasions are different, i.e. that Dion Cassius refers to a repressive measure taken some years earlier than was the one referred to by Suetonius and the writer of Acts. Two possibilities are suggested. The one is that Dion Cassius mentions only the initial step taken by Claudius, and that when the Jews in Rome, in defiance of his instruction, continued to assemble together, he then ordered their expulsion from the city. The silence of Dion Cassius as to this later order may then be put down to the fact that in large part it also proved ineffective. The other possibility is that Claudius tried expulsion and then, finding it unworkable, fell back upon an order prohibiting the assemblies of the Jews. It may then be said of Suetonius and the writer of Acts that they have told only the beginning of the story.

---

[5] Josephus, *Ant.*, xix.280 ff, xix.287 ff. With the first of these edicts there needs to be associated a letter addressed by Claudius to the city of Alexandria, preserved in a Philadelphian papyrus and published with translation and notes in 1924 by H. I. Bell in his work, *Jews and Christians in Egypt*, pp. 23–37.

[6] lx. 6.

[7] *Claud.* 25 : ' The Jews, who by the instigation of one Chrestus were evermore tumultuous, he banished from Rome.' (*Judaeos impulsore Chresto assidue tumultuantes Roma expulit.*) The words *impulsore Chresto* have been much discussed.

It should be added, however, that some scholars now consider that in A D 41 Claudius did issue a decree forbidding the Jews in Rome from assembling together.[8] Momigliano [9] thinks that in that year the emperor's measures against these Jews would have been more drastic but for the fact that he was then under the influence of Agrippa I. He also thinks that at a later time, after the death of Agrippa, he may have ordered an expulsion of the Jews from the city as Suetonius and the writer of Acts relate, and that this may have been recorded by Dion Cassius in the now lost portion of his history dealing with the period after A D 46.

Lewin [10] holds that an order expelling the Jews from Rome was issued in A D 52, being occasioned by the receipt there of intelligence that Judaea was in a state of revolt. But that is little more than a possibility.[11] He also reasons,[12] but not convincingly, from certain statements made by Suetonius that the edict of expulsion referred to by him must have been issued in A D 52. Tacitus, *Ann.*, xii.52, states that a decree, stringent but ineffectual, was passed by the Senate in the consulship of Faustus Sulla and Salvius Otho (i.e. in A D 52) for the expulsion of the Mathematici from Italy, and Wieseler [13] maintains that the same edict applied also to the Jews resident in the country. The Mathematici were astrologers and magicians, and many Jews practised magic. In fact Jews and magicians are often mentioned together. But it does not necessarily follow that the Jews in Italy as well as the Mathematici there were named in this edict. In this chapter Tacitus may, for such reasons as

---

[8] H. J. Cadbury, *The Book of Acts in History*, p. 134, note 13, thinks that a good deal can be said for dating the expulsion in A D 41 ; cf. J. Knox, *Chapters in a Life of Paul*, pp. 82 f. Under that year, however, Dion Cassius refers not to an edict expelling the Jews from Rome, but to one that forbade them the right of assembly in the city.

[9] *Claudius : The Emperor and his Achievement* (trans. from the Italian by W. D. Hogarth, 1934), p. 31.

[10] *Fasti Sacri*, p. 295, no. 1773.

[11] According to Dion Cassius, lvi.23, Augustus expelled all Gauls and Celts from Rome on learning that Varus had lost his legions.

[12] *Fasti Sacri*, p. 296, no. 1774.

[13] *Chronologie der apostolischen Zeitalters*, pp. 125 ff.

Wieseler suggests, have underlined the expulsion of the Mathematici, but these reasons do not suffice to explain his failure to mention an expulsion of the Jews. In any case, as will be seen below, A D 52 is too late a date for the edict mentioned in Acts 18:2

The earliest to give a precise date for this edict is Orosius,[14] who writes: 'Josephus relates that the Jews were expelled from the city by Claudius in the ninth year of his reign, but I am influenced more by Suetonius, who speaks in this way: "The Jews, who by the instigation of one Chrestus were evermore tumultuous, Claudius banished from Rome".' [15]

Schürer [16] describes this statement as 'certainly incorrect with regard to authority and therefore probably unreliable with respect to matter.' But a much more favourable view of it is taken by Harnack in his article 'Chronologische Berechnung des "Tags von Damaskus"'.[17] He recognizes that there is no reference to the matter in any of the writings of Josephus that have come down to us; but that, he maintains, does not justify the rejection of the statement as worthless. For his account of the reign of Claudius, he holds, Orosius's principal source was not Josephus, to whom he makes only one reference,[18] but the *Chronicle* of Jerome. Of it, however, he used an exemplar which here and there had been enriched with particulars that someone had carried over from Julius Africanus. It is of course possible that Africanus may have found the date 'his ninth year' in a writing of Josephus that is now lost, but Harnack is unwilling to fall back upon that as a solution. He prefers to think that the person who transferred the date from Africanus to the *Chronicle* wrongly inferred that Africanus had found it in Josephus and so wrongly attributed it to Josephus in the *Chronicle*.

---

[14] *Historia ad. paganos*, vii.6, 15 (ed. Zangemeister, p. 451).
[15] '*Anno eiusdem* [Claudii] *nono expulsos per Claudium urbe Judaeos Josephus refert sed me magis Suetonius movet qui ait hoc modo : Claudius Judaeos impulsore Chresto assidue tumultuantes Roma expulit.*'
[16] *The Jewish People in the Time of Jesus Christ*, II.ɪɪ.237, note 69.
[17] See p. 28, *supra*.
[18] Even this reference appears to be repeated from Jerome's *Chronicle*.

While Harnack's observations impart a certain likelihood to the view that the date ' his ninth year ' stood in a work of Julius Africanus, they by no means provide a proof of that.[19] The fact that Orosius himself had no particular respect for this date indicates that it was not based on calculations of his own and attributed by him to Josephus by way of giving it some standing, but was taken over by him from a source. On the other hand, the fact that he preferred the statement of Suetonius, in which there is no indication as to when the edict of expulsion was issued, may suggest that he had doubts as to the correctness of this date. As we shall see,[20] Paul came to Corinth early in A D 50. The ninth year of Claudius' reign ran from 25th January A D 49 to 24th January A D 50 ; [21] and if the edict of expulsion was issued within that period, then, precisely as the writer of Acts indicates, Aquila and Priscilla and Paul all arrived in Corinth about the same time. The fact that the date given by Orosius thus harmonizes so satisfactorily with Acts cannot be taken without more ado as proof of its soundness ; but it is certainly remarkable.

[19] Deissmann, *Paul* (E.T. of *Paulus*), p. 258, suggests that the Josephus to whom Orosius refers may be another Josephus, and this other Josephus perhaps ' the Christian Josephus '. The date ' the eighth year of Claudius ' stands in his *Hypomnesticon* in a passage (ii.80) where it seems to be quite wrong.
[20] See p. 115, *infra*.
[21] In maintaining that the year is 50 and not 49, Ramsay, *St. Paul the Traveller and the Roman Citizen*, pp. 58 and 254, forgets that we have here to do not with Orosius but with his authority.

CHAPTER FOURTEEN

Gallio's Proconsulship of Achaia

AN INSCRIPTION discovered in the ruins of Delphi is of capital importance for the chronology of the life of Paul. It fixes the year of Gallio's proconsulship of Achaia with a high degree of probability, and, as will be indicated in the following chapter, this, taken with the narrative of Acts 18:1-17, enables us to determine with considerable likelihood when Paul arrived in Corinth in the course of his Second Missionary Journey.

The inscription consists of seven fragments. For convenience of reference they are divided into two groups—group A, which comprises four fragments (in the Museum at Delphi, Nos. 3883, 2271, 4001, 2178), and group B, which comprises the remaining three (Nos. 500, 2311, 728).[1] It is agreed that the four fragments of group A belong together, and likewise that the three fragments of group B belong together. There is, however, a difference of opinion among authorities as to whether those of group B are part of the same original as those of group A. But this is a matter that need not detain us. There is a lacuna between the two groups the extent of which cannot be determined, and the text of group B is itself so mutilated that any restoration of it would be far too tentative to throw any sure light on the text of group A.

One of the fragments of group A was published by A. Nikitsky in 1894/5 [2] in a work in Russian entitled ' Epigraphical Studies at Delphi '. The first to discuss in detail and to attempt a restoration of all the four fragments of this group was Émile Bourguet in a thesis which he submitted to the Faculté des lettres de Paris and

---

[1] A photograph of all seven fragments taken by Bourguet is reproduced in the *Revue Biblique*, N.S.10 (22) (1913), facing page 45, and a facsimile of group A faces the title page in Deissmann's book on Paul.

[2] For some years before this H. Pomtow had been acquainted with all the fragments.

published in 1905 under the title ' *De rebus Delphicis imperatoriae aetatis capita duo* ' ; and the first to call attention in writing to the bearing of this inscription upon the chronology of the life of Paul appears to have been A. J. de Reinach, who, in a review of Bourguet's work contributed to the *Revue des Études grecques*, XX.(1907).49, wrote : ' *Ce texte fixe définitivement à 52 le séjour de St. Paul à Corinthe.*' For some years after that there was a considerable output of literature on the subject. The titles down to 1917 are listed by D. Plooij in his book *De chronologie van het leven van Paulus* (1918), p. 28, note 4. He singles out as of particular importance Appendix I in Deissmann, *Paulus* (1911), pp. 159 ff (E.T. pp. 235 ff), F. Prat's contribution ' *La chronologie de l'âge apostolique* ' to the *Recherches des sciences religieuses* 1912), pp. 374 ff, and A. Brassac's article ' *Une inscription de Delphes et la chronologie de Saint Paul* ' in the *Revue Biblique internationale*, N.S.10 (22) (1913), pp. 36–53, 207–17. To these there ought now to be added Plooij's own well-informed and instructive chapter ' *Gallio's Proconsulaat van Achaie* ' in the book just mentioned, pp. 27 ff.

The text of group A is in twelve lines, and is here given as transcribed and restored by Dittenberger.[3]

There is difference of opinion as to how some of the parts now missing ought to be made good. On the ground that they do not belong to the recognized style of Claudius, Plooij thinks that μέγιστος in line 1 and τιμητής in line 2 ought to be omitted. Bourguet reckons that in line 1 there were 54 letters, but Deissmann, whilst recognizing that ἀρχιερεύς without μέγιστος may be the right reading, inserts ἀρχιερεὺς μέγιστος and so brings the number up to 71. In line 3 πάλιν or παλαιοτάτῃ has been suggested instead of πάλαι. Both Deissmann and Brassac think that in line 4 χησα is more probable than χης α and so read

εὐτύ-
χησα. Ἐπετήρη[σα κτλ.

But—to note what is so important for the chronology—the

[3] *Sylloge inscriptionum Graecarum* ii (3rd edn.), 1917, pp. 493 f.

ΤΙΒΕΡ[ιος Κλαύδιος Κ]ΑΙΣ[αρ Σεβαστ]ΟΣ Γ[ερμανικός ἀρχιερεὺς μέγιστος δημαρχικῆς ἐξου]

ΣΙΑΣ [τὸ ‹ιβ›' αὐτοκράτωρ τ]Ο ΚΙ' Π[ατηρ πα]ΤΡΙΔ[ος ὕπατος τὸ ἐ τιμητής Δελφῶν τῇ πόλει χαίρειν]

ΠΑΛ[αι μὲν] ΤΗΙ Π[ολει τ]ΩΝ ΔΕΛΦ[ων πρόθ]ΥΜΟ[ς ἐγενόμην... καὶ εὔνους ἐξ ἀρ]

ΧΗΣ ΑΕΙ [δ'] ΕΤΗΡΗ[σα τῆ]Ν ΘΡΗΣΚΕΙ[αν τ]ΟΥ ΑΠΟ[λλωνος τοῦ Πυθίου· ὅσα δὲ ...]

5 ΝΥΝ ΛΕΓΕΤΑΙ ΚΑΙ [πολ]ΕΙΤΩΝ ΕΡΙ[δες ε]ΚΕΙΝΑΙ Ω[ν μνήμην πεποίηται ? Λεύκιος 'Ιου]

ΝΙΟΣ ΓΑΛΛΙΩΝ Ο Φ[ιλος] ΜΟΥ Κ[αὶ ἀνθύ]ΠΑΤΟΣ [τῆς 'Αχαίας ....]

ΕΤΙ ΕΞΕΙΝ ΤΟΝ ΠΡ[ότερ]Ο[ν ὁρισμὸν ? ΠΕ[... τῶν ἄλ]

ΛΩΝ ΠΟΛΕΩΝ ΚΑ.......

ΑΥΤΟΙΣ ΕΠΙΤΡΕ[π ..... Δελ]

10 ΦΩΝ ΩΣ ΠΟΛΕ[μίων ὄντων

ΤΑΙ ΜΕΤΩΚΙ[σ .....

[το]ΥΤΟΥ.......

number KE (= 26) in line 2 is above all doubt; so also is the name $\Gamma A \Lambda \Lambda I \Omega N$ in line 6; all who have studied the inscription are agreed that $K\lambda\alpha\acute{v}\delta\iota o\varsigma$ is correctly supplied in line 1, and also that in line 6 $\alpha\nu\theta\upsilon$ and not υ is to be supplied before $\Pi A T O \Sigma$.

The text of lines 1–7 [4] as given above may be translated as follows:

Tiberius Claudius Caesar Augustus Germanicus, pontifex maximus, in the 12th year of his tribunicial power, acclaimed emperor for the 26th time, father of his country, consul for the 5th time, censor, sends greetings to the city of Delphi. I have for long been zealous for the city of Delphi and well-disposed to it from the beginning, and always I have observed the worship of the Pythian Apollo; but with regard to the present stories and those disputes of the citizens of which a report has been made by Lucius Junius Gallio, my friend and proconsul of Achaia... will still maintain the boundaries as formerly marked out.

It is possible that, as at an earlier time,[5] the inhabitants of certain villages near Delphi had taken possession of lands and houses [6] belonging to the temple of the Pythian Apollo. Certainly disputes about boundaries had arisen. Gallio the proconsul had investigated the situation and prepared a report of it which he had forwarded to Claudius. The inscription is the emperor's rescript or reply. It is addressed to the citizens of Delphi. In it, after conveying to them his greetings, he speaks of his earlier and still continuing favourable attitude towards both their city and the cult of the Pythian Apollo; and then, referring to the disputes about which he has been informed by Gallio the proconsul, he intimates his decision that the boundaries hitherto marked out be retained.

It may be assumed that the people of Delphi, well satisfied with this rescript, proceeded to give it all possible publicity and

---

[4] Little remains of lines 8–12, and nothing can be gathered from them with any certainty: see Brassac, *op. cit.*, p. 50.

[5] In 191 and 190 B C. The particulars as gathered from Dittenberger are given by Plooij, *De chronologie van het leven van Paulus*, pp. 31 ff.

[6] Brassac, *Revue Biblique internationale*, N.S.10 (22), p. 50, suggests that $TO\Pi OY\Sigma$ in group B may refer to out-houses of the temple.

so had it inscribed on a slab of whitish grey limestone from the neighbouring quarries at Hagios Elias. It is very likely that this slab was then set up on an outer wall of the temple of Apollo at Delphi, and it may well be that it is back to it that we ought to carry the fragments with which we are here concerned.

The rescript was written after Claudius had been acclaimed *imperator* for the twenty-sixth time and before he was so acclaimed for the twenty-seventh time.[7] The twenty-sixth acclamation is mentioned in several other inscriptions, but only one of these provides information which enables something to be said about its date. It comes from the city of Kys in Caria and is as follows:[8]

ΤΙΒΕΡΙΟΝ ΚΛΑΥΔΙΟΝ ΚΑΙΣΑΡΑ ΓΕΡΜΑΝΙΚΟΝ ΑΥΤΟ
ΚΡΑΤΟΡΑ ΘΕΟΝ ΣΕΒΑΣΤΟΝ ΑΡΧΙΕΡΕΑ ΜΕΓΙΣΤΟΝ
ΔΗΜΑΡΧΙΚΗΣ ΕΞΟΥΣΙΑΣ ΤΟ ΔΩΔΕΚΑΤΟΝ ΥΠΑΤΟΝ
   ΤΟ ΠΕΜ
ΠΤΟΝ ΑΥΤΟΚΡΑΤΟΡΑ ΤΟ ΕΙΚΟΣΤΟΝ ΚΑΙ ΕΚΤΟΝ
ΠΑΤΕΡΑ ΠΑΤΡΙ
ΔΟΣ κτλ.

From this it is clear that at some time in Claudius's twelfth tribunicial year, 52 (25th January)–53, he had already been acclaimed imperator twenty-six times. But there is here no indication as to whether the acclamation was made after or before 25th January 52. For further help we turn to inscriptions in which acclamations earlier and later than the twenty-sixth are mentioned.

(1) Earlier acclamations.

Claudius's twenty-second acclamation is mentioned in the inscription *CIL*, iii.476:

TI. CLAUDIUS CAESAR AUG.
GERMANICUS PONT. MAX.
POT. XI IMP. XXII P.P. COS. V
AB EPH eso

---

[7] The number of the imperatorial acclamations went up by a unit every time the emperor or one of his lieutenants obtained a victory.
[8] *Bulletin de correspondance hellénique*, XI.(1887).305–7.

and his twenty-fourth acclamation in the inscription *CIL*, iii. 1977 :

(Ti.) CLAUDIO DRUS(i) F.
CAESARI AUG. (g)ERM. PONT. MAX.
TRIB. (p.) XI IMP. X(X)IIII COS. V
CENSORI P. P. P. ANTEIO LEG.
PRO PR.

Since the eleventh year of Claudius's tribunicial power ran from 51 (25th January) to 52, it follows that he must have been acclaimed imperator for at least the twenty-third and twenty-fourth times within that interval.

His twenty-fifth acclamation is mentioned on a fragment of marble on which only the name CLAUDIUS and the number XXV can be read (*CIL*, xi.824).

(2) Later acclamations.

Claudius's twenty-seventh acclamation appears to have been his last. It is mentioned in an inscription on an arch of the Aqua Claudia (*CIL*, vi.1256) :

TI.CLAUDIUS DRUSI F.CAISAR AUGUSTUS GERMANICUS PONTIF.
MAXIM.TRIBUNICIA POTESTATE XII COS.V IMPERATOR XXVII PATER
PATRIAE AQUAS CLAUDIAM EX FONTIBUS QUI VOCABANTUR CAERULEUS
ET CURTIUS A MILLIARIO XXXXV ITEM ANIENEM NOVAM A MILLIARIO
LXII SUA IMPENSA IN URBEM PERDUCENDAS CURAVIT.

Now it is known from Frontinus, *De aquaeductu*, 13,2 [9] that the Aqua Claudia was consecrated on 1st August A D 52. Accordingly Claudius must have been acclaimed *imperator* for the twenty-seventh time at some time prior to that date.

It follows that he must certainly have been acclaimed for the twenty-third, twenty-fourth, twenty-fifth, twenty-sixth and twenty-seventh times in the interval 25th January 51–1st August 52. As he is not likely to have been so all five times in 51, it is very probable that his twenty-sixth acclamation took place in the

[9] Ed. Grimal, p. 11.

first half of A D 52. The military history of those times tends to support this. According to what Tacitus writes in the last paragraph of *Ann.*, xii.40, it is possible that the second campaign against the Silures was not completed until A D 52. In that same year peace was restored in Palestine by Quadratus the governor of Syria, and the Cietae of Cilicia Aspera, then in a state of revolt, were dispersed and pacified by Antiochus of Commagene. Clearly there may have been two imperatorial acclamations in the year 52—one (the twenty-sixth) in the spring, and one (the twenty-seventh) somewhat later but before 1st August.[10] We are thus able to conclude with a considerable measure of confidence that Claudius wrote his letter to the people of Delphi at some time in the first half of A D 52.

Gallio was then proconsul of Achaia; and since he had already acquainted himself with the boundary question at Delphi and had prepared a report of it and since also time must be allowed for the transmission of his report to Rome and for study of it there, it is to be concluded that by the time the terms of the reply were finally determined he was in the second half of his year of office.

Very occasionally the governor of a senatorial province continued in office for a second year.[11] But for more than one reason it is altogether unlikely that Gallio did so. No special circumstances are known such as would have made a departure from the normal procedure desirable or necessary. Again, Achaia, which had been a senatorial province from 27 B C to A D 15, had again been transferred to the Senate in A D 44,[12] and a departure from the normal procedure so soon after that is unlikely. Yet again, Gallio does not appear to have been very robust. According to Pliny[13] he went *post consulatum* on a voyage to Egypt for his health; and his brother Seneca the

---

[10] Cf. Groag, ' Claudius ', Pauly-Wissowa, *RE*, III.2813, who concludes that Claudius assumed the title *imperator* two or three times in A D 52.
[11] Dion Cassius, lx.25.
[12] Ibid. 24.
[13] *HN*, xxxi, 33.

philosopher,[14] referring apparently to an earlier occasion, tells us that when he was in Achaia he caught a fever and immediately went on a voyage, ' declaring loudly that the cause of his illness was not in his body but in the soil ' (*clamitans non corporis esse sed loci morbum*). It may be assumed that in a province the climate of which suited him so little he did not stay longer than was strictly necessary.

At the end of their term of office governors of senatorial provinces were required to remain in them until their successors arrived. As some of the men appointed to these provinces delayed their departure from Rome and so did not arrive timeously in them, a regulation in regard to this matter became a necessity. In A D 25 Tiberius decreed that departures should take place within the period of the new moon of June.[15] In A D 42 Claudius fixed the day before that of the new moon of April,[16] and in A D 43 the middle of April [17] as the extreme date of departure. Mommsen [18] thought it likely that normally the change of office took place on 1st July, and in the more remote provinces that was possibly the case. But leaving Rome by the middle of April, governors appointed to provinces that were less remote must have arrived earlier. Travelling by land to one of the seaports of the south of Italy and sailing from there, Gallio can quite well have arrived in Achaia in the beginning of May. Accordingly we conclude that he was proconsul there from May 51 to May 52.

[14] *Ep. mor.*, civ.1.
[15] Dion Cassius, lvii.14: ἐντὸς τῆς τοῦ 'Ιουνίου νουμηνίας.
[16] Ibid., lx.11 : πρὸ τῆς τοῦ 'Απριλίου νουμηνίας.
[17] Ibid., 17: πρὶν μεσοῦν τὸν 'Απρίλιον.
[18] *Röm. Staatrecht*, II.256 : French trans., *Manuel des antiquites romaines* III.294.

CHAPTER FIFTEEN

The Second Missionary Journey

ON RETURNING to Syrian Antioch from the Jerusalem Conference, Paul and Barnabas stayed there, teaching and preaching the Word of the Lord. But 'after some days' (μετὰ δέ τινας ἡμέρας) Paul proposed to his colleague that they should return and visit the churches which they had founded on their former journey (Acts 15:36). Barnabas, it may be assumed, readily acceded to this proposal. He suggested, however, that they should take Mark with them. Failing to agree on this matter, they separated: Barnabas with Mark proceeded to Cyprus, whilst Paul set out on his Second Missionary Journey with Silas, one of two deputies who had been sent to Antioch to intimate to the church there the decree that had been formulated by the Conference.

The interval between the return from Jerusalem and the commencement of this new journey cannot be determined precisely. The 'time' (χρόνον—Acts 15:33) which the two deputies spent in Antioch is not known, but we cannot assume that it was quite short and need not be taken into account. The 'some days' of Acts 15:36 may be reckoned from the return of Paul and Barnabas from the Conference to Antioch, but it is possible that they ought to be reckoned from the departure of the deputies from Antioch for Jerusalem. Further, if the Silas of Acts 15:40 is the Silas who has been mentioned in earlier verses and if also Acts 15:34 is rejected as an insertion in the Western text, time must be allowed after the separation of Paul and Barnabas for Paul to send to Jerusalem for Silas and for Silas to join him in Antioch. It is thus fairly obvious that the interval between Paul's return to Antioch and his setting out on his Second Journey may have been several weeks, perhaps not less than eight. If the Conference took place in the middle of

April, and it may not have done so much earlier in the year, the Second Missionary Journey may have commenced towards the end of June.

Paul and Silas travelled first through Syria and Cilicia, bringing new strength to the congregations. They then went on to Derbe and Lystra. It may be assumed that in doing so they crossed the Taurus by the famous pass known as the Cilician Gates.[1] If two months are allowed for the journey through Syria and Cilicia, and that seems a sufficient allowance, the missionaries will have passed through these Gates towards the end of August and can quite well have been in Lystra by mid-autumn A D 48.

From Lystra or perhaps Pisidian Antioch [2] Paul with Silas and Timothy, a young man whom he had added to his company in Lystra, travelled north and then west in Asia Minor to Troas. Crossing thence to Europe, he travelled south along the west Aegean seaboard to Corinth. It may be convenient at this stage to consider his stay in that city (Acts 18:1–18).

On coming to it he fell in with Aquila and Priscilla and began to work with them as a tent-maker. As he was thus employed throughout the week, his missionary activity was confined to the Sabbath, when he spoke in the synagogue. After a time Silas and Timothy arrived from Macedonia. They brought him heartening news about the churches there (1 Thess. 3:6 ff). As appears from 2 Corinthians 11:8 f, they also brought him a gift of money. This set him free from the necessity of working for a living, and enabled him to devote himself entirely to missionary work among the Jews. But their opposition was so bitter that he separated his disciples from them, found a new meeting-place, and now addressed himself to the Gentiles. Many believed and were baptized, and in a vision by night the Lord strengthened Paul, bidding him remain in the city and

---

[1] Reached by a road from Tarsus. The view of Wieseler, *Chronologie des apostolischen Zeitalters*, p. 25, that Paul and Silas crossed the Taurus by a pass that lay somewhat west of the Cilician Gates and was reached by a road from Soli or Pompeiopolis, is generally considered less likely.
[2] See p. 115, *infra*.

assuring him that He had many people in it. Here the writer of Acts proceeds: 'So he settled down for eighteen months, teaching the word of God among them' ('Εκάθισεν δὲ ἐνιαυτὸν καὶ μῆνας ἓξ διδάσκων ἐν αὐτοῖς τὸν λόγον τοῦ θεοῦ—verse 11), and then he passes immediately to the Gallio incident.

Setting upon Paul, the Jews brought him before the proconsul's judgement seat and accused him of inducing the people to worship God in ways contrary to the law. They found, however, that they had miscalculated. Gallio at once perceived that it was not a question of crime or grave misdemeanour, but a dispute among the Jews about their religion. Accordingly he refused to handle the case and had them ejected from the court.

Proceeding, the writer of Acts records that after this Paul stayed on 'for some time' (ἡμέρας ἱκανάς) and then set sail for Syria (verse 18). The expression ἡμέραι ἱκαναί is 'a singularly vague note of time'.[3] In Acts it occurs in 9:23, where it is far from certain that it denotes the period of at least two full years mentioned in Galatians 1:18; [4] also in 9:43 and 27:7, but while in these two verses it appears to mean 'many days', in neither of them nor in the contexts is there any indication of their exact number. A study of the expression in these other places thus affords no help. The fact, however, that the period of verse 18 is indicated vaguely whilst that of verse 11 is given exactly, makes upon us the impression that the former is much the smaller: it may denote a whole month, in all probability less than a couple of months.[5]

There has been much discussion as to whether the period 'many days' of verse 18 is included in the period 'a year and six months' of verse 11 or is to be considered as having followed upon it and so as being additional to it. Following Anger, Wieseler [6] maintains that it is included, and several authorities

---

[3] Lake and Cadbury, in Jackson and Lake, *The Beginnings of Christianity*, I.IV.105.
[4] See p. 15, *supra*.
[5] So Wieseler, *Chronologie des apostolischen Zeitalters*, p. 46.
[6] Op. cit., p. 46.

accept this view. That, however, is not the inference that one naturally makes on reading through the passage; and the view expressed by Lewin [7] in the following terms is to be preferred:

It is much more probable that the year and six months are meant by Luke to mark the duration of Paul's undisturbed ministry up to the arrival of Gallio, which immediately follows the mention of the year and six months, and that Luke, after relating the scene before Gallio, intends a further period, when he writes that Paul tarried (or more literally ' stayed on ', προσμείνας, Acts 18:18, as in Josephus, *Vit.*, 12, 44, 49, 58) a good many days. Indeed, the word ' stayed on ' imports an addition to the interval of a year and six months previously mentioned.

Paul was brought before Gallio when the latter was proconsul of Achaia. The Greek is Γαλλίωνος δὲ ἀνθυπάτου ὄντος (when Gallio was proconsul) and not Γαλλίωνος δὲ ἀνθυπάτου γενομένου (when Gallio became proconsul). The incident cannot then be put right at the beginning of Gallio's term of office. The Jews apparently waited until, from what they had got to know about him, it seemed to them likely that he would hear them and give a decision against Paul. But it is also to be assumed that they sought to take advantage of his inexperience and are not likely to have delayed their appeal to him for more than a couple of months after his arrival. Now we have already concluded that Gallio arrived in Achaia early in May A D 51. Paul's appearance before him is then to be dated in the end of June or the beginning of July A D 51 and his arrival in Corinth, eighteen months earlier, in the early days of A D 50.

We proceed now to show that there is sufficient time between autumn A D 48 and the early days of A D 50 for all that took place from Paul's departure from Lystra onwards to his arrival in Corinth.

It is not expressly recorded that Paul and his colleagues visited Iconium and Pisidian Antioch. But in view of Acts 15:36 there need be no doubt that they did so. By that time Paul had

[7] *The Life and Epistles of St. Paul* I.296, note 267.

begun to entertain the thought of proceeding to Asia to preach the word there (Acts 16:6). It is likely that by Asia is meant here, as in the Revelation of St. John, not the Roman province of Asia but the Greek cities on and near the east coast of the Aegean Sea. To reach these Paul no doubt intended to go to Apollonia and to travel thence by way of Apamea and Laodicea down the Lycus and Meander valleys. Forbidden of the Holy Spirit to do this, he and his companions passed through τὴν Φρυγίαν καὶ Γαλατικὴν χώραν. These Greek words have occasioned much discussion. Happily, peculiarly little of it needs now to be repeated. Φρυγίαν cannot here be an adjective, for (1) in late Greek the adjective Φρύγιος has only two terminations, (2) Φρυγίαν is clearly a noun in Acts 18:23 : τὴν Γαλατικὴν χώραν καὶ Φρυγίαν, and (3) the parallel expression τῆς Ἰτουραίας καὶ Τραχωνίτιδος χώρας (Luke 3:1) shows that the article does not need to be repeated.[8] It is then to be understood that the missionaries passed through two territories, first through Phrygia and then through the Galatian country, i.e. the country in the heart of Asia Minor which since the time of Attalus 1 had been occupied by three Gallic tribes—the Trocmi, the Tectosages and the Tolistobogii. After travelling for a time in this country, they recrossed the boundary and came to a place in Phrygia, perhaps Dorylaion or Kotiaion, immediately south of Bithynia and over against Mysia, i.e. east of Mount Olympus. They were now minded to go into Bithynia, no doubt thinking that its larger towns on the shore of the Black Sea would afford them excellent spheres of work. But the Spirit of Jesus did not permit them (Acts 16:7). Accordingly they turned west, traversed [9] Mysia, and came to Troas. There in a vision Paul saw a man of Macedonia, who appealed to him saying : ' Come over and help us.' Taking this as the guiding hand of God, he and his party sailed immediately for Europe.

[8] See Haenchen, *Die Apostelgeschichte* (12th edn., 1959), p. 423, and Lake, in Jackson and Lake, *The Beginnings of Christianity*, I.v.231 ff.
[9] On this rendering of παρελθόντες see Haenchen, *Die Apostelgeschichte*, p. 424, note 4.

THE SECOND MISSIONARY JOURNEY 117

According to Ramsay [10] τὴν Φρυγίαν καὶ Γαλατικὴν χώραν is the *regio Phrygia Galatica*, in which Pisidian Antioch, Iconium, Lystra and Derbe were situated. That, however, is altogether unlikely, for (a) while there may have been a *regio* of that name (cf. *Pontus Galaticus*) known to Roman administrators, it is nowhere mentioned in ancient writings, (b) the correct rendering in Greek of *regio Phrygia Galatica* is ἡ Γαλατικὴ Φρυγία and (c) on passing through this *regio* the missionaries would not have emerged over against Mysia.

The account that is given of the journey through Phrygia and the Galatian country and then across Mysia is extremely meagre. Not until Troas is reached are we given the name of any town through which the missionaries passed, and not until then, apart from the interventions of the Holy Spirit, is any incident or experience of the way recorded. From this the reader may conclude that the journey was a hurried one; [11] throughout this journey, so it may seem to the reader, the divine voice that prompted the missionaries gave them no rest until they found themselves on European soil. Further, the reader may conclude that in the course of the journey no missionary work was done. These conclusions are, however, both without foundation. This brief account may be, as Haenchen [12] suggests,

---

[10] *St. Paul the Traveller and the Roman Citizen*, p. 102, and later works. According to the South Galatian Theory, strongly advocated by Ramsay, Paul did no missionary work in the ancient ethnic kingdom of Galatia in the northern part of the Roman Province of Galatia, but the churches which he founded in Pisidian Antioch, Iconium, Lystra and Derbe, being in the southern part of that Province, were Galatian churches, and it is to them that he addressed the Epistle to the Galatians.

[11] ' The impression is that the journey to Troas was pursued as directly and quickly as possible '—Lampe in *Peake's Commentary on the Bible*, ed. 1962, p. 910.

[12] *Die Apostelgeschichte*, p. 425. Others who think that a source has been abridged are J. Weiss and M. Goguel. According to Dibelius, *Studies in the Acts of the Apostles* (E.T. of *Aufsätze zur Apostelgeschichte*, ed. Greeven), p. 201, the brevity of each of the sections, Acts 16:6–10 and Acts 20:1–3, is ' not due to lack of information but to intentional selection from material available in the source '. The brevity of the writer's account of Paul's work in Phrygia and the Galatian country is

an abbreviation made by the writer of Acts of one that was much fuller. The voice that directed Paul and his party away from the road which they were minded to take did not do so continuously, but only at times and notably on three ocasions—when their visit to the churches of Derbe, Lystra, and doubtless also Iconium and Antioch was completed, again when they had completed their journey through Phrygia and the Galatian country, and yet again when they had completed their crossing of Mysia. When visiting the churches of Derbe, Lystra, etc., they were certainly not in a hurry, nor were they then inactive in Christ's service (Acts 16:1-4); and the mere absence of place-names and other details of the kind is no proof that they were so either when in Phrygia and the Galatian country or when in Mysia. For the part of the journey that lay through Phrygia and the Galatian country the verb used in Acts 16:6 is διέρχεσθαι which, as already stated,[13] may denote a journey in the course of which missionary work was done, and that it has that meaning here is made likely by the words ' having been forbidden *to speak the word* in Asia '. That such work was done in Phrygia and the Galatian country and proved fruitful is clear from Acts 18:23. It is precarious to infer from the fact that no detailed account of a mission in a particular area is given in Acts that there was no mission there. Acts records no mission in Galilee, but in Acts 9:31 we read that the church throughout Judaea, Galilee and Samaria was left in peace to build up its strength. In Acts there is no detailed report of a founding of churches in Syria and Cilicia, yet their existence is assumed in Acts 15:41.

We conclude then that the journey from Pisidian Antioch to Troas was in large part a missionary progress, that Paul and his party came into Phrygia in the late autumn A D 48, that they remained there and in the Galatian country until the spring

further discussed on pp. 133 f, *infra*. Findlay in *HDB*, III.707b writes that the clause ' all the disciples ' in Acts 18:23 implies ' that on the ground so lightly passed over in 16:6 considerable time had been spent and many souls won for Christ '.

[13] Page 66, *supra*.

of A D 49, and that, going on then to Troas, they arrived there in the end of March or early in April of that year.

Sailing from Troas, Paul and his party reached Samothrace the same day and, anchoring there for the night, made the crossing to Neapolis on the following day. Leaving Neapolis almost immediately, they proceeded to Philippi. Their way lay at first through a defile over a spur of Mount Pangaeus, but the distance was only about ten miles and the journey was doubtless completed in a single day.

In the account given in Acts 16:12–40 of their labours in Philippi it is nowhere stated expressly for how long these continued. The statement of verse 12, ' We were in that city abiding certain days ', may give the impression that their stay was quite brief. But from verse 13 it is clear that the reference there is to the time between the day of their arrival and the next ensuing Sabbath. The other indications which the passage affords point to a stay of some duration. The imperfect ἤκουεν in verse 14 indicates that it was only after several meetings with the missionaries that Lydia became a believer; and after that a week or two may have passed before her house became the headquarters of the mission. It was as they went to the place of prayer (verse 16) that a pythoness first began to follow the missionaries, crying out : ' These men are the servants of the most high God which show unto us the way of salvation.' It is added that she did this many days, from which we gather that it was only some time afterwards that Paul, unable any longer to bear her shouting, turned and, in the name of Jesus Christ, commanded the spirit to come out of her.[14] This is confirmed by the sequel. Resolved to avenge themselves, the woman's masters attempted to provoke a rising against Paul and Silas. Dragging them before the magistrates, they cried out against them that they were advocating customs which it was illegal for the citizens of Philippi, being Romans, to accept or

[14] Justice must be done to the statement : ' And this did she many days ' (Acts 16:18). Many have given reasons for Paul's expulsion of the python which leave us wondering why he did not expel it immediately.

follow. This attempt proved successful. Convinced that this charge was sound, the multitude of the citizens together with their magistrates rose against the missionaries. Paul and Silas were scourged; they were imprisoned for the night; the next morning they were expelled from the city. From this incident it is clear that prior to it Paul and his party had been engaged in missionary propaganda in the city for some time, and that the success of their mission had become not only a matter of general comment but also an occasion of general concern and irritation.

Paul and Silas [15] proceeded from Philippi to Thessalonica. On the way they passed through Amphipolis, *c.* 30 miles west-south-west of Philippi, and then through Apollonia, *c.* 30 miles west-south-west of Amphipolis and *c.* 35 miles east of Thessalonica. From the mention of these two places some [16] have inferred that the missionaries must have made a stay in them and have preached the Gospel there. Support for this is sought in the words ' all the brethren which are in all Macedonia ' in 1 Thessalonians 4:10 and in the reference to ' the churches of Macedonia ' in 2 Corinthians 8:1. But while the former passage may indicate that by the time 1 Thessalonians was written there were many Christians throughout Macedonia besides those in Philippi, Thessalonica and Beroea, it affords no proof either that by that time there were Christians in Amphipolis and Apollonia or, if there were, that some of them had been won for Christ when Paul and his party were in these towns; and the plural in the latter passage would have been sufficiently justified even if at a later time there had been churches in Macedonia only at Philippi, Thessalonica and Beroea. Moreover the express statement of Acts 17:1 that there was a synagogue of the Jews in Thessalonica seems to indicate that there was no synagogue either in Amphipolis or in Apollonia, and that the missionaries

---

[15] Timothy probably left Philippi along with Paul and Silas. If he left it later, he certainly joined them before Paul left Beroea for Athens (Acts 17:14).

[16] E.g. E. von Dobschütz, *Die Thessalonicherbriefe*, p. 9.

pressed on to the larger opportunity that awaited them in Thessalonica.

From the statement that the missionaries passed through Amphipolis and Apollonia others [17] have inferred that they may have made the journey in three stages. But their rate of progress on foot is hardly likely to have exceeded twenty miles a day.[18] Unless then they did part of the journey on horseback, they must have made it in at least five stages and cannot have completed it until, at the earliest, the afternoon of the fifth day. Since Apollonia was $c.$ 60 ($= 3 \times 20$) miles from Philippi, it is just possible that, travelling on foot at the rate just mentioned, they may have spent the third night there, and indeed a halt there seems to be suggested in Codex D, which reads: ' They came to Apollonia and thence went on to Thessalonica.' But it may well be that Amphipolis and Apollonia are mentioned not as places where the missionaries halted or rested on the way, but simply as indicating by what road they travelled.[19]

According to Acts 17:2 Paul, on coming to Thessalonica, attended the meetings of the Jews and for three Sabbaths reasoned with them out of the Scriptures. The two or three weeks thus indicated must be understood as the period during which, at the outset, Paul gave himself almost exclusively to work among the Jews, the period at the end of which he left the synagogue and, turning to the Gentiles in the city, began to make the winning of them for Christ his main concern. To take these weeks as the length of time he spent in Thessalonica is undoubtedly wrong. Acts 17:1–10 and 1 Thessalonians, *passim*, provide unmistakable evidence that the mission in Thessalonica was attended with much good success. If only a few Jews responded, a great multitude of God-fearing Greeks and a good many influential women became believers; of Gentiles a still

---

[17] E.g. Lake and Cadbury, in Jackson and Lake, *The Beginnings of Christianity*, I.IV.202. They suggest that horses may have been hired.
[18] See Ramsay, *The Church in the Roman Empire*, p. 65, also ' Roads and Travel (in the New Testament) ', *HDB*, extra vol., p. 386.
[19] So Haenchen, *Die Apostelgeschichte*, p. 445, note 2.

greater number turned to God from idols and became by far the major portion of the membership of the church at Thessalonica.[20] This good success points to a missionary campaign of some duration. Before Paul left Thessalonica, the converts there had been gathered into a well-ordered community and had attained a certain degree of Christian knowledge, all which presupposes a fairly long period of organization and instruction. Had Paul not lived with these converts for some months, he and they would not have got to know one another so intimately and to esteem one another so highly as they obviously did. Further, had his stay in Thessalonica not been protracted, it would hardly have seemed to him worth while to settle down, as he did when there (1 Thess. 2:9), to his own trade. Here reference needs also to be made to Philippians 4:16. During his stay in Thessalonica Paul received help from the Christians of Philippi on at least two occasions.[21] When one notes that Philippi was c. 100 miles away and that these gifts are hardly likely to have followed on the heels of one another, it again becomes evident that Paul's stay in Thessalonica must have been considerably longer than the two or three weeks of Acts 17:2.[22]

Eventually the unbelieving Jews in Thessalonica created a considerable disturbance. The situation that resulted was such that the members of the congregation thought it good that the missionaries should leave the city. Accordingly Paul and his party departed from Beroea. They may have gone there by a road that ran almost directly westwards, or they may have followed the Via Egnatia to a point on beyond Pella and then have

[20] There is an indication of this in the fact that while in 1 and 2 Thessalonians there are Old Testament words and expressions, there is not a single direct quotation from the Old Testament. See also the commentators on 1 Thessalonians 1:9.
[21] Haenchen, *Die Apostelgeschichte*, p. 449, maintains that in Philippians 4:16 καὶ ἅπαξ καὶ δίς means not 'twice' but 'repeatedly'. That, however, is disputed, see G. G. Findlay's note on 1 Thessalonians 2:18 in his Commentary on the Epistles to the Thessalonians in the *Cambridge Greek Testament for Schools and Colleges*.
[22] Cf. Dupont in Cerfaux and Dupont, *Les Actes des Apôtres* (2nd edn, 1958), p. 152.

turned south. The former route was the less frequented and somewhat the shorter of the two, and may have been the one that was chosen. Beroea being c. 50 miles west of Thessalonica, the journey, if made on foot, will have occupied about three days.

The Jews of Beroea were more liberal-minded than those of Thessalonica. There is no mention of an expulsion of the missionaries from the synagogue or of a turning on their part from the Jews to the Gentiles. But there was a mission also among the Gentiles. Many converts were made, Jews and Greeks and among them men and women of standing. All would apparently have continued to go well had not the Jews in Thessalonica heard of this spread of the Gospel in Beroea and sent certain of their number to attempt a repetition there of the tactics which they had employed in their own city. Happily some of the Christians in Beroea, sharing a general concern for Paul's safety, formed themselves into an escort party and immediately took him down to the sea-coast, probably to Dium,[23] and thence accompanied him to Athens. Leaving him there, they returned home with an urgent message from him to Silas and Timothy, who had both stayed behind in Beroea, to join him in Athens with all speed.

Since the mission in Beroea resulted in the winning of many converts, it is likely to have been one of some duration. Time must also be allowed for a report about the spread of the Gospel in Beroea to be carried back to Thessalonica, for the Jews there to decide on a plan of action and to choose the men whom they considered best fitted to carry it out, and for those chosen to travel to Beroea and there indicate with what intention they had come. Nothing is known about the nature of the hindrances referred to in 1 Thessalonians 2:17 f or as to when they occurred.

---

[23] Dium was about 16 miles away, and there was a direct road to it from Beroea. According to H. V. Morton, *In the Steps of St. Paul*, p. 254, there is a strong tradition in Verria (the Beroea of today) that, on leaving Beroea, Paul was taken first to Aeginion and then to Methone and from there sailed for Athens. Methone (on which see Strabo, pp. 374, 375 and 436) was on the Macedonian coast north of Dium.

Accordingly these two verses provide no information that can be turned to chronological account.

According to Acts 17:14, in which the best manuscripts read ἕως ἐπὶ τὴν θάλασσαν, the brethren in Beroea sent Paul off to go 'right as far as the sea' or 'down to the coast'. The ἕως may seem to be superfluous and is omitted in D S *gig* sa, but its use with a preposition seems to be a characteristic of the Lucan writings (see Lk. 24:50, Acts 21:5 and 26:11). If ὡς is read instead of ἕως as in the Antiochean text, the meaning is altered only very slightly, 'The brethren sent Paul off to go in the direction of the sea', and there is no need to assume a feigned movement on the part of the escort as is suggested in the rendering of the A V. It is possible that the escort may have gone some distance along the road leading to the coast and then have turned to the right and proceeded overland to Athens. But of the readings ἕως ἐπί and ὡς ἐπί the former is undoubtedly to be preferred. Again it is possible that, on reaching the coast, the escort may have found reason to take the overland route to Athens, and in support of the view that that is how they proceeded it is urged (*a*) that the writer of Acts usually mentions the port of embarkation, and (*b*) that had Paul sailed from the coast of Macedonia, the members of the escort, after seeing him safely on board, would have returned to Beroea and not have brought (ἤγαγον) him to Athens. But the writer of Acts may on this occasion have failed to conform to his custom, and Paul's physical condition at this time may have made it necessary that the escort should not only accompany him to the coast, but also sail with him to his destination and see him settled there before returning to its home town. Against a journey overland it may be urged that it would have taken a considerably longer time and have proved much more fatiguing. The brethren in Beroea, aware that the Jews of Thessalonica would continue to persecute Paul so long as they found that possible, must have recognized that the most effective way to secure his safety was to get him away by sea; and it may be assumed that the members of the escort, instructed accordingly, did in fact find places for him and themselves in a ship bound for Athens.[24] It is likely that they sailed only in the day-time and that the voyage occupied about a week.

We have concluded that Paul's stay in each of the towns, Philippi, Thessalonica and Beroea, was one of some duration. Adequate provision needs to be made for that conclusion. We are thus led to put Paul's arrival in Athens towards the end of October and to make the following allocations: about two months (April, May) to Philippi; about three months (June, July, August) to Thessalonica; and about seven weeks (September and part of October) to Beroea. Paul's physical condition has already been suggested as a possible reason why the escort accompanied him all the way to Athens; and it may well be that, after arriving there, he rested for some days in the hope of recovering his strength and did not enter immediately on a missionary campaign in the city. On leaving for home the members of the escort received from him instructions for Silas and Timothy to rejoin him with all speed (Acts 17:15). It is likely, therefore, that they returned by sea; and since according to Vegetius [25] the seas were closed to shipping onwards from 11th November, they must have completed their voyage by that date.

Whilst he awaited the arrival of Silas and Timothy, Paul resumed his missionary labours. He reasoned in the synagogue with those who worshipped there. He argued daily in the city square with casual passers by. He also addressed the Council of the Areopagus. The immediate results were, however, extremely meagre. Converts were few, and no church was founded.

From 1 Thessalonians 3:1 it appears that Timothy joined Paul in Athens. The distance overland from Beroea to that city was

---

[24] In the present connection no use can be made of the Western text of Acts 17:14 f. That text is a complete rewriting of the original text of these two verses due to a failure to understand their meaning, namely that Paul went to Athens by sea.

[25] *De re militari* iv.39.

about 300 miles, and the weather may not have been good. But travelling with all speed, Timothy may have reached Athens about the end of November. By this time Paul's concern for the converts whom he had left in Thessalonica was such that he sent Timothy back to encourage them to stand fast for the faith and, under all their hardships, not to be shaken.[26] He himself continued in Athens. But, it would seem, he became increasingly convinced that for the time being the conditions necessary for a fruitful mission did not exist in that city. Perhaps also he found it necessary to move to a commercial centre where he would have a fuller opportunity of working at his trade and providing for his ordinary needs.[27] Whatever his reasons, he left Athens for Corinth and arrived there in the early days of January A D 50.

[26] It is possible that Silas also joined Paul in Athens and was sent back on a similar mission to Philippi. Later both he and Timothy joined Paul in Corinth (Acts 18:5). But the problem of the movements at this time of Paul's missionary companions is one to which there is no generally accepted solution.

[27] As Goguel, *Intro. au Nouveau Testament* IV. i, 287, points out, it is significant that in the account of Paul's stay in Corinth (Acts 18:1 ff) it is first noted that there he carried on business as a tentmaker with Aquila and Priscilla.

CHAPTER SIXTEEN

Paul's Return to Syria, Acts 18:18–23

IN ACTS the story of Paul's return to Syrian Antioch at the close of his Second Missionary Journey is told in six verses, 18:18–23. After the Gallio incident he stayed on in Corinth for some time and then set sail for Syria. The ship called at Ephesus where it remained for a short time. There Paul took leave of Aquila and Priscilla, who had been among his fellow-passengers from Corinth. He then visited the synagogue where he held a discussion with the Jews. They invited him to stay longer, but he declined, promising, however, that he would come again. Resuming the voyage, he landed at Caesarea and went up and paid his respects to the church. He then went down to Antioch and spent some time there before setting out on his Third Journey. This brief narrative occasions several questions, of which two need particularly to be considered here : (1) Did Paul actually pay this visit to Syria ? and (2) If he did, what was his reason for doing so ?

(1) At two points the narrative is of doubtful historical value. It seems strange, particularly in view of Acts 18:26, that, on landing in Ephesus, Paul should take leave of Aquila and Priscilla and then proceed alone to the synagogue there. In Corinth, Aquila and his wife had shown him much kindness, and they are likely to have been the last persons to whom he said farewell before going on board again in the harbour at Ephesus. It is probable then that the words $\epsilon i\sigma\epsilon\lambda\theta\grave{\omega}\nu$ $\epsilon i s$ $\tau\grave{\eta}\nu$ $\sigma\upsilon\nu\alpha\gamma\omega\gamma\grave{\eta}\nu$ ... $\tau o\hat{\upsilon}$ $\theta\epsilon o\hat{\upsilon}$ $\theta\acute{\epsilon}\lambda o\nu\tau os$ (verses 19b–21a) [1] are an insertion made by the writer of Acts with a view to securing for Paul the distinction

---

[1] In the RV the passage beginning, ' but he himself entered into the synagogue ', and ending, ' if God will '.

of having been the first to preach the Gospel in Ephesus.² The church referred to in verse 22 may be the one in Caesarea, but the context, in particular the use of ἀναβαίνειν and καταβαίνειν ('went up' and 'went down' in verse 22), suggests that by it the writer of Acts intended the church at Jerusalem.³ It seems probable that he has taken advantage of Paul's landing at Caesarea, which may have been due to the prevalence of a north-easterly wind,⁴ to work in a visit of Paul to the mother-church at Jerusalem.⁵ But at this time it was not necessary and perhaps also not advisable that he should go there.

Certain scholars, however, go much farther. Denying the historicity of this whole narrative, they maintain that Paul did not pay this visit to Syria. According to some of them the story is a fabrication designed to get Paul away from Corinth before the arrival there of Apollos. Loisy ⁶ holds that the statement of verse 19 that Paul left Aquila and Priscilla in Ephesus implies that he went on into another country without them. That other country, he considers, was Galatia, where, because of the activities of the Judaizers, there was urgent need of his presence; and the story of his return to Syria was fabricated, he maintains, to conceal this painful fact by making it appear that he came into Galatia in due course when on a third missionary journey. These reasons for an invention of the story seem far-fetched and are not impressive. Weizsäcker ⁷ considers that Acts 18:18–23 is 'destitute of historical value' because there is no trace of it in Paul's epistles. But the apostle may have paid this visit although he himself nowhere mentions it and although its

---

² So Haenchen, *Die Apostelgeschichte* (12th edn., 1959), p. 483; Goguel, *Intro. au Nouveau Testament*, III.277 f.
³ Cf. Haenchen, op. cit. p. 484.
⁴ This explanation is suggested by Lake and Cadbury, in Jackson and Lake, *The Beginnings of Christianity*, I.IV.231.
⁵ Weizsäcker, *Apostolic Age* (E.T. of *Das apostolische Zeitalter der christlichen Kirche*), I.249: 'The author cannot conceive that Paul should have been so near Jerusalem without visiting the Church there.'
⁶ *Les Actes des Apôtres*, pp. 709 f.
⁷ Op. cit. I.248 f, II.11.

assumption may not be necessary to the understanding of any passage in his writings. Weizsäcker also maintains that since at the time when he wrote 1 and 2 Corinthians and Romans, Paul was preparing for the last visit which he paid to Jerusalem as for an extraordinary event, he cannot have been there a short time previously. But the interval between his departure from Corinth recorded in Acts 18:18 and his last return to Jerusalem (the interval to which these three epistles belong) was longer than Weizsäcker's premises allow: his date for the Jerusalem Conference is A D 52, but actually Paul had by then completed his Second Missionary Journey. Moreover this objection is pointless if on this return to Syria Paul paid no visit to Jerusalem. It has also been suggested that the return recorded in Acts 18:18–23 may be a doublet of the return recorded in Acts 20:3–21:16. In support of this Lake [8] points out that 'into Syria' occurs both in Acts 18:18 and in Acts 20:3, and also that the sombre note struck in 'if God will' (Acts 18:21) may be heard again in 'the will of the Lord be done' (Acts 21:14). Nevertheless he rejects this hypothesis for the sound reason that 'the suggestion of " doublets " in this place makes more difficulties than it solves'.

We conclude that Paul did pay this visit to Syria, but that during the call at Ephesus he made no contact with the Jews there and that neither on landing at Caesarea nor at any later time in the interval between then and the commencement of his Third Journey did he go up to Jerusalem. This return to Syria was more specifically a return to Antioch.

(2) For what reason did Paul return to Syria?

According to an insertion in the Western and Antiochean text of verse 21 he returned that he might keep an approaching feast in Jerusalem. But that insertion obviously owes its inspiration to Acts 20:16b and can afford us no sure help. Consideration of the vow mentioned in verse 18 helps us just as little. It ought

[8] In Jackson and Lake, *The Beginnings of Christianity*, I.IV.229.

perhaps to be referred to Paul rather than to Aquila. But it cannot have been a strictly Nazirite vow, the fulfilment of which, including the shearing of the head, had to be made in the Temple (Num. 6:13). Moreover there is no satisfactory evidence that a Jew could make a modified Nazirite vow outside Palestine, shearing his head there and later bringing the hair to Jerusalem and offering it up in the Temple.[9]

It may be thought that Paul's departure from Corinth was due to the Gallio incident, just as his departure from Ephesus (Acts 20:1) was due to the riot there. But the situations that obtained after these two events are not parallel. The opposition to the apostle shown in Ephesus had behind it the whole corporation of silversmiths and a vast multitude of sympathizers, and in it concern for material interests went hand in hand with pagan religious devotion. The riot was stayed by the town clerk, but after it an even greater danger threatened Paul so long as he remained in the city,[10] and his only wisdom was to leave it.

But in Corinth the demand that he should be tried by the proconsul was made only by the Jews; it was bluntly refused; and a similar demand in the near future was unlikely. Paul must have seen that, for after the incident he remained in the city for some time. Moreover, even if it were true that he left Corinth because of this incident, that would not explain his going to Syria.

After about twenty months' work in Corinth Paul may have judged that the church there could be left to the care of its elders. But, again, while that might account for his departure from Corinth, it would not account for his setting sail for Syria. He might have returned to Macedonia to strengthen the churches there. He might have penetrated farther into the Peloponnesus have crossed the Aegean to the cities of Asia and Bithynia, in which he had earlier been minded to preach the Gospel, or have sailed for Rome. There were many open doors; and it is inconceivable that, except for a particularly compelling reason, he would have decided not to enter in through any of them but

[9] See D. Eaton, ' Nazirite ', *HDB*, III.500b.
[10] See pp. 135 f.

to return to Syria. The view entertained by Wieseler [11] and more recently by John Knox [12] that Paul paid this visit to Syria that he might attend the meeting in Jerusalem referred to in Galatians 2:1-10 is quite unacceptable.[13] But behind it there lies the recognition that this visit requires to be given a large explanation and that Paul can have made it only because to do so was for him a pressing necessity.

It is conceivable that Paul returned to Antioch that he might attend personally to a domestic matter and that, important as it was, he quickly disposed of it and very soon resumed his missionary task. That, however, is mere conjecture, and a reason for his return to which his own epistles and the record of Acts impart some likelihood, is undoubtedly to be preferred. David Smith [14] attributes it to a breakdown in the apostle's health. That, we submit, may be its true explanation. He had not been well in Galatia. He had suffered injury and outrage in Philippi. It was probably because of his physical condition that the escort from Beroea accompanied him all the way to Athens. The fact that in 1 Thessalonians 3:1 he writes not $\mu\acute{\epsilon}\nu\epsilon\iota\nu$ (to remain) but $\kappa\alpha\tau\alpha\lambda\epsilon\iota\phi\theta\hat{\eta}\nu\alpha\iota\ \acute{\epsilon}\nu\ \text{'}A\theta\acute{\eta}\nu\alpha\iota s\ \mu\acute{o}\nu o\iota$ (to be left at Athens alone) suggests that, when he was in Athens, he had sent Timothy to Macedonia at a time when he was much in need of him, probably therefore at a time when he was ill.[15] Also the word $\dot{\alpha}\sigma\theta\acute{\epsilon}\nu\epsilon\iota\alpha$ in 1 Corinthians 2:3 may mean bodily weakness,[16] in which case we learn from the verse that when Paul came to Corinth his health was not good. That after twenty months' strenuous labour there it was so seriously impaired that a period of rest became an

---

[11] See p. 89, *supra*.

[12] See p. 90, *supra*.

[13] As indicated on p. 90, *supra*, a principal objection to it is the presence of Barnabas with Paul (Gal. 2:1, 9). For a brief statement of Wieseler's arguments and a refutation of his contention see Conybeare and Howson, *The Life and Epistles of St. Paul* (new edn., 1898), pp. 822 f.

[14] *The Life and Letters of Saint Paul*, pp. 188 f.

[15] So Goguel, *Intro, au Nouveau Testament*, IV.1.132.

[16] The word without the addition of $\tau\hat{\eta}s\ \sigma\alpha\rho\kappa\acute{o}s$ has this meaning in some of the papyri; see Moulton and Milligan, *The Vocabulary of the Greek New Testament*, s.v.

imperative necessity, is far from unlikely; and nowhere perhaps could he hope to make a better recovery than in Antioch, a city with which he had happy associations and in which he had good friends.

It is usually assumed that Aquila and Priscilla crossed to Ephesus in the pursuit of their business. But if it was bad health that obliged Paul to return to Syria, they may have chosen to cross at this particular time in order that they might assist him on the first stage of his journey. Further, this reason for Paul's return may explain why the account of it is so meagre. The incidents of his voyage to Syria and of his stay in Antioch belonged, on this view, to his private life, and for the most part the writer of Acts passes over such incidents in silence.[17]

Paul set sail for Syria within a couple of months after the Gallio incident,[18] therefore in the autumn of A D 51. It is hardly likely that in a single winter he made a full recovery from an illness that had obliged him to rest from his missionary task and withdraw to Antioch, and the phrase $\chi\rho\acute{o}\nu o\nu$ $\tau\iota\nu\acute{a}$ in Acts 18:23 may mean 'some length of time' as it seems to do in 1 Corinthians 16:7. Accordingly we assume that he continued in Antioch throughout A D 52 and did not set out on his Third Missionary Journey until A D 53.

---

[17] Those who consider that Luke was the writer of Acts may attribute his silence regarding Paul's illness to the fact that he was a doctor. Part of the Hippocratic oath ran : ' Whatsoever I shall see or hear in the course of my profession, as well as outside my profession in my intercourse with men, if it be what should not be published abroad, I will never divulge, holding such things to be holy secrets ' (trans. of W. H. C. Jones in edition of the works of Hippocrates in the *Loeb Library* (I.301).

[18] Page 114, *supra*.

CHAPTER SEVENTEEN

The Third Missionary Journey

SETTING out on his Third Missionary Journey, Paul passed through the Cilician Gates, possibly in June A D 53. Proceeding thence to the Galatian country and Phrygia (τὴν Γαλατικὴν χώραν καὶ Φρυγίαν), he travelled through (διερχόμενος) these two territories in order (καθεξῆς), bringing new strength to all the converts (Acts 18:23). In this statement several points call for comment.

(1) The word καθεξῆς shows that, as maintained above,[1] ' the Galatian country ' and ' Phrygia ' designate two distinct territories.

(2) In Acts 16:6, the only other verse in which these two are named together, Phrygia is mentioned first and then the Galatian country. Here, however, the two are mentioned in the reverse order : Paul made his way through the Galatian country and then on through Phrygia. This indicates that soon after passing through the Cilician Gates, he broke away from the road which he had pursued when on his Second Journey and proceeded north through the Kingdom of Antiochus of Commagene and then, perhaps by way of Tyana, Nazianzus and Archelais Colonia or by way of Tyana and Caesarea, through Cappadocia until he reached the southern border of the Galatian country. The distance traversed from the Cilician Gates must have been well over 200 miles and the journey can hardly have been completed in less than a fortnight.

(3) The account given of Paul's missionary activity in the Galatian country and in Phrygia both in the present verse and in 16:6 is very meagre. That hardly seems to be adequately

---

[1] Page 116.

explained by saying that the writer had no detailed knowledge of it or that he was in a hurry to pass on in the one place to Paul's work in Ephesus and in the other to his work in Europe. It indicates rather that he was reluctant, by giving an extended account of their beginnings, to bring to remembrance churches which by their inconsistency and apostacy occasioned Paul much anxiety and sorrow, or perhaps that he judged it unwise to make more than a brief reference to work which, by the time he wrote, had proved largely labour lost. J. N. Sanders [2] notes that we cannot tell whether Paul's purpose in writing his Epistle to the Galatians was achieved. ' It is by no means unlikely ', he writes, ' that the Galatian churches were unmoved by his appeal.'

(4) The verb $\delta\iota\epsilon\rho\chi\delta\mu\epsilon\nu\sigma$ together with the statement that Paul brought new strength to all the converts shows that, as he went through these territories, he engaged in a considerable amount of missionary work. He won new converts; he instructed the members of the churches which he had already founded; he was at particular pains to confirm them in the faith and generally to consolidate the gains he had made on his earlier visit. This work with the journeys which it involved must have occupied many months. Accordingly it may be assumed that he did not proceed to Ephesus until the autumn of A D 54.

The narrative of Paul's Third Journey is resumed in Acts 19:1: passing through ($\delta\iota\epsilon\lambda\theta\delta\nu\tau\alpha$) the upper country ($\tau\dot{\alpha}$ $\dot{\alpha}\nu\omega\tau\epsilon\rho\iota\kappa\dot{\alpha}$ $\mu\dot{\epsilon}\rho\eta$), he came to Ephesus. There is here a retrospective reference to the missionary progress mentioned in 18:23, the upper country being the high-lying parts of Asia Minor, i.e. the Galatian country and Phrygia.[3] Neither the point at which Paul crossed the boundary of Phrygia when he had completed his work in that territory nor the road by which he travelled from

---

[2] ' Galatians ', *Peake's Commentary on the Bible* (edn., 1962), p. 974.
[3] The interpretation of ' the upper country ' given by Ramsay, ' Roads and Travel (in the New Testament) ', *HDB*, extra vol., p. 390b is bound up with the South Galatian Theory and the assumption that Paul journeyed to Ephesus directly from Pisidian Antioch.

THE THIRD MISSIONARY JOURNEY 135

there across the Province of Asia to Ephesus, can be determined.[4]
A fairly long account of Paul's stay in Ephesus is given in Acts 19:1-41. Actually, however, only verses 1-20 are devoted to his ministry there, the remaining verses containing first a statement of a great journey from Ephesus by way of Macedonia and Achaia to Jerusalem and thence to Rome which, he was persuaded,[5] God was calling him to undertake (verses 21-2) and then an account of the riot in Ephesus which immediately preceded his departure from that city (verses 23-41). From 1 and 2 Corinthians it is clear that his ministry in Ephesus was considerably more crowded and arduous than the account of it given in Acts indicates. He suffered much at the hands of opponents,[6] and he had painful dealings with the church at Corinth, which involved the writing of three epistles [7] and at one stage a visit to that city.[8] According to Acts 20:31 he ministered in Ephesus for the space of three years ($\tau\rho\iota\epsilon\tau\acute{\iota}\alpha\nu$).[9] For the first three months of that time he devoted himself to work among the Jews (Acts 19:8) ; for the next two years he taught in the school of Tyrannus (Acts 19:10) ; and the remainder is the season ($\chi\rho\acute{o}\nu o\nu$) mentioned in Acts 19:22.

The writer of Acts appears to minimize, perhaps he even attempts to conceal, the extent to which the riot was the occasion of Paul's departure from Ephesus. From what the apostle himself writes [10] it is apparent that on several occasions his position in that city was fraught with much danger. One of these

---

[4] Wieseler, *Chronologie des apostolischen Zeitalters*, p. 52, thinks it likely that Paul came to Ephesus by way of Sardis. Cf. H. Metzger, *Les Routes de Saint Paul*, p. 40.
[5] In Acts 19:21 $\dot{\epsilon}\nu\ \tau\hat{\omega}\ \pi\nu\epsilon\acute{u}\mu\alpha\tau\iota$ and $\delta\epsilon\hat{\iota}$ are significant.
[6] 1 Cor 15:32 ; 2 Cor 1:8.
[7] The first is referred to in 1 Cor 5:9. The second is the canonical 1 Cor. The third is referred to in 2 Cor 2:3, 9 ; 7:8, 12.
[8] 2 Cor 12:14 ; 13:1-3.
[9] $\tau\rho\iota\epsilon\tau\acute{\iota}\alpha$ may mean three years less a few months.
[10] 1 Cor 15:32 : 2 Cor 1:8. According to some Paul alludes in the latter passage to the riot in Ephesus, and while he writes in general terms, he discloses to us more clearly than does the writer of Acts the gravity of the situation in which he then found himself.

occasions was assuredly when a vast crowd, roused by the appeal of Demetrius, surged through the streets crying, 'Great is Diana of the Ephesians', and thronged into the theatre. The town clerk succeeded, it is true, in dispersing the multitude. Paul, however, was not out of danger. On the contrary, he was now exposed to a graver danger. The feelings which Demetrius had roused were of the kind that once roused are not easily allayed; and there was now a very great likelihood that in a way much less open and far swifter, before disciples or asiarchs could come to the rescue or the town clerk could intervene, Paul's opponents would work their will upon him. There need be no doubt that the riot brought about a tense and perilous situation from which it was imperative that Paul should deliver himself by forthwith proceeding elsewhere.

It follows that if the date of the riot could be determined, we would then be able to say when Paul left Ephesus.

(1) Some [11] have thought it possible that the riot took place during the Artemisia,[12] a festival in honour of Artemis (Diana) held in Ephesus annually in the month Artemisios.[13] During the time of it the city was crowded with people who had come from all quarters. This gave Paul a splendid opportunity for missionary work; and it is assumed that a very great measure of good success attended him, that in consequence there was a marked fall in the material gains which Demetrius harvested at this season, and that, exasperated on this account, he took the steps which according to the record in Acts led to the riot. Ordinarily those who adopt this view also assume that Paul's departure, precipitated by the riot, took place shortly before Pentecost (1 Cor 16:8).

Authorities are not agreed as to the month in our calendar to which the month Artemisios in the Ephesian calendar corres-

[11] G. S. Duncan, *St. Paul's Ephesian Ministry*, p. 140 : ' It is tempting to believe that the outburst may have been connected with the celebration of the great Ephesian festival of the Artemisia.'
[12] Also called *Ephesia*, Thucydides, iii.104.
[13] In the inscription referred to below, this month is called *Artemision* (see Ginzel, *Handbuch d. math. u. tech. Chronologie*, II.336).

ponded. Lewin [14] gives May, Ideler [15] April, Lersch [16] 25th April to 24th May, Ginzel [17] 24th March to 22nd April. In each of the years A D 52 to 58 and in A D 60 Pentecost fell on a day in May and in A D 59 on a day in June. Originally the Artemisia was celebrated only for some days in the month Artemisios, but according to an inscription [18] discovered by Chandler and generally assigned to about the middle of the first century of our era, it was enacted that the period of the festival should be extended to cover the entire month. In view of these particulars it is certainly possible that the riot, if it took place at the time of the Artemisia, may have done so shortly before Pentecost. It is, however, very likely that Paul did not go to Corinth as he promised in 1 Corinthians 16:5-8, but that, owing to unhappy conditions in the church there, he paid the city a short visit, going and returning by sea. Moreover, there is in Acts 19:23-41 no indication that at the time of the riot the Artemisian festival was in progress. Indeed it may be argued that Demetrius did not wait until then, but that having suffered heavy losses during the festival in the first two years of Paul's stay in Ephesus, he was resolved to have him expelled from the city before the next festival season came round. If, as E. L. Hicks [19] has suggested, ποιῶν ναούς (Acts 19:24) is due to a misunderstanding of νεωποιός, then Demetrius was a warden of the temple, and the possibility of a real concern on his part for the worship there needs to be taken into account. In part his purpose in seeking the expulsion of Paul may have been to prevent him doing that worship the same hurt that he had already done it on the two previous occasions. The presence in Ephesus for the Artemisia of many from all parts of the Province of Asia undoubtedly gave

---

[14] *Fasti Sacri*, p. 309, no. 1837.
[15] *Handbuch der math. u, techn. Chronologie* i, p. 419.
[16] *Einleitung in die Chronologie* I.65.
[17] *Handbuch d. math. u. tech. Chronologie*, III.20.
[18] Text given by Boeckh, *Corp. Inscr.*, 2954, is quoted by Lewin, *Fasti Sacri*, p. 309, no. 1837, trans. in Lewin, *The Life and Epistles of St. Paul*, I.405 f.
[19] In *Expositor*, 4th ser., I.(1890).401 ff.

Paul a large opportunity to spread abroad the Gospel message. But he may not have had that season in mind when he wrote: ' A great door and effectual is opened unto me ' (1 Cor 16:9). In Ephesus such a door was open to him daily practically all the year round.

(2) Some have thought that a chronological datum is to be found in the words of the town clerk, ἀγοραῖοι ἄγονται καὶ ἀνθύπατοί εἰσιν (Acts 19:38). They take ἀγοραῖοι ἄγονται to mean ' assizes are being held at this very time in Ephesus ', and so conclude that the riot took place at a time when one of the stated sessions of the assizes was being held in the city. So also they take ἀνθύπατοί εἰσιν to mean ' there are at present proconsuls ', and conclude that the riot took place at a time when there was more than one proconsul of Asia. From Tacitus, *Ann.*, xiii.1, and Dion Cassius, lxi.6, it is known that, at the instigation of Agrippina and shortly after the accession of Nero on 13th October A D 54, Publius Celer, a Roman knight, and Helius, a freedman, poisoned Junius Silanus, the then proconsul of Asia. Accordingly it is suggested that for a few years thereafter these two together discharged the duties of the proconsular office in Asia, and that the riot took place at some time in the course of these years.[20] But the words of the town clerk need to be interpreted in the light of their context. He does not refer to assizes actually in session or to proconsuls actually in office, but speaks in a colloquial way and in effect says: ' Well, as you are aware, assizes are held and there are such people as proconsuls.'

There being no other reliable data, we are obliged to combine our conclusion that Paul probably arrived in Ephesus in the autumn of A D 54 with his statement that he had ministered there ' by the space of three years ' and so to assign his departure to the late summer of A D 57 and his arrival in Troas to the autumn of that year.

---

[20] From Tacitus, *Ann.*, xiii.33, it appears that Publius Celer remained in Asia until A D 57.

Some time before the riot Paul had sent Titus to Corinth to help the church there to rid itself of its disorders and had instructed him to come back not directly by sea but by land. Accordingly after the riot he went north to Troas, intending to await Titus' arrival there on his return journey. Whilst he thus waited in Troas, he engaged in missionary work and apparently built up a community of converts in the city. So much may be inferred from his words, ' Taking my leave of them ', in 2 Corinthians 2:13 ; and although the founding of a church in Troas is not recorded in Acts, the existence of one there is assumed in Acts 20:7. It is likely then that Paul spent some time in this place. But he was ill-at-ease because Titus did not come, and he was full of anxiety about the church at Corinth. Accordingly he proceeded to Macedonia (2 Cor 2:13), making the crossing possibly early in the new year, A D 58. There he met Titus and received from him news about the church at Corinth that very much heartened him (2 Cor 7:5–7). Relieved of anxiety, he continued on his way towards Corinth, evangelizing in Macedonia [21] and possibly carrying the Gospel as far west as Illyricum (Rom. 15:19).[22] Arriving in Greece, he spent three months there (Acts 20:3), as appears from Acts 20:6 the months of winter, A D 58–9 ; and he planned to sail, no doubt from Corinth, in the following spring, that of A D 59, for Syria.

For some years before this, one of Paul's main concerns had been the organizing in the Gentile churches which he had founded of a collection for the mother-church in Jerusalem.[23] It was arranged apparently that representatives of the contributing churches with their contributions should assemble in Corinth so that they might all sail together with Paul directly

---

[21] Acts 20:2 : When he had gone through (διελθών) these parts.
[22] This is denied by E. Meyer, *Ursprung u. Anfänge des Christentums*, III.130 f ; see also Sanday and Headlam, *The Epistle to the Romans*, p. 409.
[23] In Acts there is only one clear reference to this matter (24:17). What seems a likely reason for this almost complete silence is suggested by E. B. Allo, ' La portée de la collecté pour Jérusalem dans les plans de saint Paul ', *Revue Biblique*, XLV.(1936).529–37.

from there to Syria. But news of a Jewish plot against Paul obliged them to change their course. From Corinth they went to Macedonia.[24] After the days of unleavened bread (Acts 20:6) they crossed from there to Troas. Thence they proceeded by way of Assos, Mitylene, Chios, Samos, Miletus, Cos and Rhodes to Patara, thence to Tyre, and thence by way of Ptolemais and Caesarea to Jerusalem, where they arrived presumably in time for Pentecost A D 59.

Several scholars [25] have attempted to determine the year of this last visit of Paul to Jerusalem by making use of the following statements : (1) that Paul and his fellow-travellers sailed away from Philippi after the days of unleavened bread (Acts 20:6) ; (2) that they came to Troas in five days (Acts 20:6) ; (3) that they abode in Troas seven days (Acts 20:6) ; (4) that Paul preached in Troas on the first day of the week, ready to depart on the morrow (Acts 20:7) ; and (5) that Paul hasted, if it were possible for him, to be at Jerusalem the day of Pentecost (Acts 20:16).

It will suffice to summarize the arguments of two of these scholars.

Plooij [26] maintains that Paul and his party left Troas on a Monday, that they arrived there on the Tuesday of the preceding week (the day of departure and the day of arrival being included in the seven days), that they left Philippi on the Friday preceding that Tuesday (the day of departure and the day of arrival being included in the five days), and that since Paul hasted to be in Jerusalem, they must have left Philippi on the

[24] Those who went ahead and waited for the rest of them in Troas (Acts 20:5) were probably Tychicus and Trophimus : cf. Lake, in Jackson and Lake, *The Beginnings of Christianity*, I.iv.253.

[25] Among them, in addition to Plooij and Gerhardt who are mentioned in the text, are Wieseler, *Chronologie des apostolischen Zeitalters*, pp. 113 ff ; Lewin, *Fasti Sacri*, pp. 313 f, no. 1857 ; Ramsay, ' A Fixed Date in the Life of St. Paul ', *Expositor* 5th ser., III.(1896).336–45, *Paul the Traveller and the Roman Citizen*, pp. xiv ff and p. 289 ; *Pauline and Other Studies*, pp. 352 ff ; W. B. Bacon, ' A Criticism of the New Chronology of Paul, ' *Expositor*, 5th ser., X.(1899).83–5.

[26] *De chronologie van het leven van Paulus*, pp. 83–5.

day immediately following the last day of unleavened bread, and so on 22nd Nisan; the 22nd Nisan, and therefore 1st Nisan, in that year was thus a Friday and calculation shows that of the years A D 52–60, A D 54 and A D 57 are the only ones in which that was the case. Rejecting A D 54 as too early, Plooij concludes that Paul returned to Jerusalem for the last time in A D 57.

O. Gerhardt [27] adopts the exegesis given by Zahn of the relevant verses of Acts. Paul preached in Troas on a Sunday evening, the service continuing until early in the Monday morning, when Paul and his party took their departure. The stay of seven days in Troas must then have begun on a Monday, and the journey of five days from Philippi to Troas must have begun on a Wednesday morning. Since Paul left Philippi immediately after the feast of unleavened bread was over, that Wednesday must have been 22nd Nisan, and calculation shows that the possible years are A D 55, 58, and 59.

As regards A D 59 Gerhardt points out that only if the new moon was first seen after conjunction in the evening of 3rd April after the appearing of the stars, would 4th April have been sanctified as 1st Nisan and 22nd Nisan have been 25th April, a Wednesday. But that the new moon was seen in these circumstances is, he adds, extremely unlikely. He rejects A D 55 on the ground that between the time, as fixed by the Gallio inscription, of Paul's first visit to Corinth and that year there is not room enough for all the events of the Third Missionary Journey. Accordingly he concludes that Paul's arrest in Jerusalem when he returned there for the last time took place in A D 58.

In making their calculations, Plooij and Gerhardt proceed in essentially the same way: both list the times of astronomical new moon for the Greenwich meridian given by Ginzel in his *Handbuch der mathematische und technische Chronologie*, II.548 f; both deduce from these the times of astronomical new moon for the Jerusalem meridian; and both assume that the new moon

---

[27] 'In welchen Jahr wurde der Apostel Paulus in Jerusalem gefangen gesetzt.' *NKZ*, XXXIII.89 ff.

AD	PLOOIJ	GERHARDT	AD
52	Tuesday, 21st March Wednesday, 19th April		52
53	Monday, 9th April	Sunday, 11th March Monday, 9th April Tuesday, 10th April	53
54	**Friday**, 29th March	Friday, 29th March	54
55	Tuesday, 18th March Thursday, 17th April	**Wednesday**, 19th March Thursday, 20th March Friday, 18th April	55
56	Monday, 5th April	Monday, 5th April Tuesday, 6th April	56
57	**Friday**, 25th March	Friday, 25th March Saturday, 26th March Sunday, 24th April Monday, 25th April	57
58	Tuesday, 14th March Thursday, 13th April	**Wednesday**, 15th March Thursday, 13th April Friday, 14th April	58
59	Saturday, 4th March Monday, 2nd April	Tuesday, 3rd April **Wednesday**, 4th April	59
60	Saturday, 22nd March	Sunday, 23rd March Sunday, 21st April	60

was visible for the first time thirty-six hours after conjunction. Their dates for 1st Nisan in the years A D 52 to A D 60 are shown in the table given on this page. The day of the week for 1st Nisan being that also for 22nd Nisan, it has been possible to show in **heavy** type the Fridays which according to Plooij and the

Wednesdays which according to Gerhardt determine the possible years of Paul's return to Jerusalem.

Gerhardt's investigation is the more detailed of the two, and the fact that often he gives alternative dates for 1st Nisan indicates his desire to explore all the possibilities. More reliable dates for 1st Nisan would be obtained if the intervals between conjunction and phase were calculated according to either of the formulae used by Fotheringham [28] in determining the year of the crucifixion. But however dependable these might be, they would not enable us to determine with any certainty the year of Paul's last return to Jerusalem. There are in fact sound reasons for dismissing as altogether inconclusive the argument pursued by Plooij, Gerhardt, and others on the basis of the statements in Acts listed above.

(1) There is no agreement among authorities as to how the five days and the seven days mentioned in Acts 20:6 ought to be reckoned.

(2) While the first day of the week on the night of which Paul preached in Troas (Acts 20:7) was assuredly a Sunday, there is uncertainty as to whether that night was Saturday or Sunday night, and so as to whether the departure from Troas took place on Sunday or on Monday. 'The night in question', writes Haenchen,[29] ' was the one from Saturday to Sunday or the one following.' Among those who have accepted the view that it was the one from Saturday to Sunday are Conybeare and Howson,[30] Rackham [31] and Lumby.[32] A. Robertson [33] regards the assumption that it was Sunday and not Saturday night as ' a very dubious point in view of the Jewish phraseology used to denote the day '. In his article ' Numbers, Hours and Years ' (in *HDB*, extra

---

[28] ' The Evidence of Astronomy and Technical Chronology for the Date of the Crucifixion ', *JTS*, XXXV.(1934).158 ff.
[29] *Die Apostelgeschichte* (12th edn., 1959), p. 517, note 1.
[30] *The Life and Epistles of St. Paul* (new edn., 1898), p. 545.
[31] *The Acts of the Apostles* (14th edn., 1951), p. 377.
[32] *The Acts of the Apostles* (Cambridge Greek Testament for Schools and Colleges), p. 354.
[33] ' 1 Corinthians ', *HDB*, I.485b.

volume, p. 477a), Ramsay states that 'in the Jewish and the Greek usage the Day was reckoned from sunset to sunset', and yet in his discussions of the matter now before us, assuming apparently that the day was regarded as beginning at dawn, he speaks of the night in question as a Sunday night. Among others who consider it probable that it was a Sunday night are Lake,[34] Bruce,[35] and Lampe.[36]

(3) If Paul and his party left Philippi on the morning of 22nd Nisan, they can have reached Neapolis, its harbour, in the afternoon of the same day. But we cannot assume with certainty that they then found a ship bound for Troas and were able to set sail before darkness fell. They may have been delayed for some days either because no ship was going in the direction of Troas or because of weather conditions. The suggestion that the five days mentioned in Acts 20:6 may include any delay of the kind, pays insufficient attention to the statement of the same verse, 'we set sail' ($\dot{\epsilon}\xi\epsilon\pi\lambda\epsilon\dot{\nu}\sigma\alpha\mu\epsilon\nu$).

(4) According to Acts 20:16 Paul hasted, if it were possible for him, to be in Jerusalem the day of Pentecost. This is noted in explanation of the fact that he had decided to sail by Ephesus and so avoid having to spend time in the Province of Asia. When was it that he made that decision? It need not have been before his departure from Philippi. From the end of the days of unleavened bread to Pentecost was a period of six weeks, and, conditions being normal, that was ample time for a journey to Jerusalem with a call at Ephesus in addition to the calls that were to be expected. As to that there need be no doubt, for although Paul spent seven days in Troas (Acts 20:6), seven days in Tyre (Acts 21:4) and many days (($\dot{\eta}\mu\dot{\epsilon}\rho\alpha s$ $\pi\lambda\epsilon\dot{\iota}ovs$) in Caesarea (Acts 21:10), he appears nevertheless to have reached Jerusalem in time for Pentecost. Turner [37] has pointed out that the journey between Troas and Tyre appears to have occupied no more than a fort-

---
[34] In Jackson and Lake, *The Beginnings of Christianity*, I.IV.255.
[35] *The Acts of the Apostles*, p. 372.
[36] In *Peake's Commentary on the Bible*, (edn. of 1962) p. 918.
[37] 'Chronology of the New Testament', *HDB*, I.423a.

night; and that is in fact what Chrysostom in his *Hom. in acta apostolorum*, *XLV*, allows for it—from Troas to Miletus six days, from Miletus to Patara three days, and from Patara to Tyre five days.[38]

It may be assumed that Paul left Philippi fairly soon after 21st Nisan. But as he had ample time in hand, it was not essential that he should leave on 22nd Nisan and not some days later; and at this stage nothing obliged him to decide, by way of saving time, to sail by Ephesus. But the crossing to Troas, apparently slowed down by adverse wind, took much longer than usual; in Troas also, apparently because weather conditions were unfavourable or because a ship was not available, Paul was delayed much longer than he had anticipated; and it was then in all likelihood that he became concerned as to whether he would reach Jerusalem in time for Pentecost and determined to sail past Ephesus. In view of this possibility that the need to save time referred to in Acts 20:16 was not felt by him until after he had crossed to Troas, that verse cannot be used as proof that he must have set sail from Neapolis on 22nd Nisan.

In some quarters this 'calendar' method, as W. B. Bacon has called it, of determining the year in which Paul finished his Third Missionary Journey has been much over-rated. As has been indicated, it has inherent weaknesses, and because of them it cannot of itself lead to a reliable conclusion or be used with any confidence to confirm a conclusion that has been reached in some other way.

[38] Migne, *PG*, lx.316 f.

CHAPTER EIGHTEEN

The Date of Festus's Entrance on Office as Procurator of Judaea

(I) THE ANTEDATED CHRONOLOGY

AFTER HIS return to Jerusalem at the close of his Third Missionary Journey Paul was seen one day in the temple by Jews from the Province of Asia. They had previously seen him in the city with Trophimus a Gentile Ephesian and assumed that he had brought him into the temple. Accordingly they now cried out against him, declaring that he had attacked the law and profaned the sanctuary. A riot ensued, and Paul would almost certainly have been slain had not Lysias, the captain of the Roman garrison, rescued him and taken him into custody (Acts 21:27–22:29). Next day there was a trial, which proved inconclusive, at a full meeting of the Sanhedrin. Learning that more than forty Jews had taken an oath to kill Paul, Lysias had him transferred to Felix the procurator at Caesarea (Acts 22:30–23:35). Another trial ordered by Felix took place there. It too proved inconclusive. Felix continued to keep Paul under open arrest; and when he returned to Rome, he left him in custody (Acts 24). A further trial took place some days after Festus, the new procurator, had assumed office. To his question, ' Are you willing to go up to Jerusalem and stand trial before me there ? ', Paul replied by appealing to Caesar, and not long afterwards, in the charge of a centurion, he was on board a ship on the first stage of his voyage to Rome (Acts 25:1–27:2).

From this it is clear that the date on which Festus succeeded Felix as procurator of Judaea is of considerable importance for the chronology of the later part of Paul's life. If only we knew it, we would be able to say by what year his Third Missionary Journey was over and also what were the two years of his imprisonment in Rome (Acts 28:30). In regard, however, to this date critical opinion is sharply divided. Those who adhere to the traditional chronology put it c. A D 60, whilst according to what is known as the antedated chronology it is A D 55 or 56. In the present chapter we set out and examine the grounds on which this earlier date is preferred.

I

The antedated chronology owes the favour which it now enjoys largely to the presentations of it that have been made by comparatively recent scholars, notably Kellner, Harnack and Schwartz.[1] But it is found already [2] in the *De Doctrina Temporum* (Paris, 1627) of the great Catholic theologian Dionysius Petavius. He observes that the two years (διετία) referred to in Acts 24:27 may be the period throughout which Paul was detained as a prisoner in Caesarea or the period for which Felix served as procurator of Judaea, and he adds, ' We prefer the latter view ' (' *Nos posteriorem rationem magis amplectimur* '). If this is the correct interpretation of the διετία, then it is possible that there was no long imprisonment of Paul in Caesarea and that his return to Jerusalem from his Third Journey, his transference to Caesarea, the recall of Felix and the entrance of Festus in his room all took place in quite a short space of time. According to

---

[1] H. Kellner in Wetzer and Welte's *Kirchenlexicon* (2nd edn, 1886), IV.1311 ff; A. von Harnack, *Geschichte d. altchristlichen Literatur bis Eusebius*, II.1; *Die Chronologie d. altchristlichen Literatur bis Irenaeus* (1897), pp. 233 ff; E. Schwartz, ' Zur Chronologie des Paulus ', *Göttinger Nachrichten* (1907), pp. 263 ff.
Add: Holtzmann, *Neut. Zeitgeschichte* (1st edn., 1895), pp. 125 ff; Fr. Blass, *Acta apostolorum* (1895), pp. 21 ff; H. von Soden, in *Encycl. Biblica* (1899–1903), I.817 ff; A. Loisy, *Actes des Apôtres* (1920), pp. 868 ff; K. Lake, in Jackson and Lake, *The Beginnings of Christianity* (1920–33), I.v.445 ff.

[2] Still earlier Baronius had taken the διετία of Acts 24:27 to mean the first two years of the reign of Nero (A D 55, 56): *Porro hoc biennium intelligendum est de Neronis imperio, ad quod usque tempus Felix eam administravit provinciam* (*Annales ecclesiastici*, ed. Theiner, I.543a).

Petavius [3] the date of Paul's arrest in Jerusalem is A D 55 and that of the beginning of Festus's procuratorship A D 56. According to Baronius [3] the date of both these events is A D 56, and according to Weber [3] and Haenchen [4] A D 55.

The view that Felix was procurator of Judaea only for two years conflicts, it may be urged, with these words which according to Acts 24:10 Paul addressed to Felix : ' Knowing as I do that for many years you have administered justice in this province.' But, it is maintained, there is evidence that Felix had a hand in Judaean affairs for some time before he entered on his two-years' procuratorship. What Tacitus writes in *Ann.*, xii.23 and 54, is taken as suggesting that in A D 49 Claudius ventured on a new way of governing Palestine : he put Judaea in the narrow sense under the direct rule of the governor of Syria and appointed Cumanus procurator of Galilee and Felix procurator of Samaria.[5] The experiment did not prove a success ; and when Cumanus was deprived of his office, Felix became procurator of the whole country. The fact noted in Josephus *Ant.*, xx.162, that Jonathan the high priest desired Caesar to send Felix as procurator of Judaea, is also regarded as evidence that before that time he had been known there. On these assumptions he had, at the time when Paul addressed him, administered justice in the country not for two but for six or seven years, A D 49–55(56).[6]

According to the statement of Tacitus in *Ann.*, xii.23, ' Ituraea and Judaea, on the death of their kings, Sohaemus and Agrippa, were annexed to the province of Syria '. But there Judaea is naturally understood not of Judaea in the narrow sense, but of all

---

[3] See the comparative chronological tables in Wieseler, Hoennicke and Plooij.

[4] *Die Apostelgeschichte* (12th edn., 1959), p. 64.

[5] From Tacitus *Ann.*, xii.54, some gather that Cumanus became procurator of Galilee and Felix of Samaria *and Judaea*.

[6] No use can be made in the present connection of the statement of Suetonius, *Claud.*, 28, that Claudius ordained Felix ' captain over the cohorts and cornets of horsemen, yea, and ruler of the province of Judaea ', for it is not stated where Felix held this military command ; and if he held it in Judaea, it is not clear whether he did so before or whilst he was procurator there.

the territory over which Agrippa had ruled. Although the statement occurs in the account of the events of A D 49, it records what, so far as Judaea is concerned, was done on the death of Agrippa in A D 44. Judaea in the wide sense was then annexed to Syria in that, while it was given a procurator of its own, it was put under the general supervision of the legate of Syria.[7] Josephus records that Cumanus came as successor to Tiberius Alexander (*Ant.*, xx.103), which obviously means that he came as procurator of the whole country. Whilst the years of the first two procurators, Cuspius Fadus and Tiberius Alexander, had not been free from trouble, there had been in them no outstanding disturbances such as might have brought home to Claudius the need of a change in the way of governing the country. In his account of the administration of Cumanus, Josephus refers to him simply as the procurator, and nowhere as the procurator of Galilee. Moreover it is not until he has recorded the banishment of Cumanus that he introduces Felix, describing him as the brother of Pallas and stating that Claudius sent him to take care of the affairs of Judaea (*Ant.*, xx.137). Josephus thus knows nothing of such a separation of Galilee and Samaria for administrative purposes as Tacitus mentions in *Ann.*, xii.54. The accounts of these two historians here contradict one another, and of the two that of Josephus is undoubtedly to be regarded as the better informed.[8] It may be that here Tacitus follows a tradition which, in its hatred of Felix, was not content to list the enormities of his own administration, but sought also to involve him in responsibility for the misdoings of his predecessor.[9]

---

[7] On the view of Bormann, *De Syriae provinciae Romanae partibus*, p. 4, that the subordination of Judaea to Syria did not take place until A D 49, see Marquardt, *Organisation de l'Empire Romain*, II.358, note 9, and Schürer, *The Jewish People in the Time of Jesus Christ*, I.ii.165, note 48.

[8] Cf. Furneaux, *Annals of Tacitus*, II.129 : Josephus ' should certainly have been the better informed as to events which took place when he was fifteen years old and living in Jerusalem '.

[9] Cf. E. Meyer, *Ursprung u. Anfänge d. Christentums*, III.48.

Jonathan the high priest went to Rome with certain eminent persons whom Quadratus the governor of Syria sent there to answer for the part they had had in the grievous collisions between Jews and Samaritans that marked the closing period of Cumanus's procuratorship, and it was apparently then that he desired Claudius to send Felix as procurator to Judaea. From the fact that he did so it does not necessarily follow that Felix had previously been procurator of part of the country. Lewin [10] suggests that he may have been sent with the emperor's replies to inquiries that Cumanus had made on the outbreak of the collisions, and that he may then have taken opportunity to ingratiate himself with the Jews. But since at the time Pallas the brother of Felix was a great power in the imperial court, it is possible that his influence with Claudius, the latter's acquittal of the Jews, and the request of Jonathan were inter-related and that Felix had not previously been in Judaea.

For these reasons this way of reconciling Acts 24:27 ($\delta\iota\epsilon\tau\iota\alpha$ being referred to the procuratorship of Felix) and Acts 24:10 seems to us unsatisfactory.

A reconciliation of these two verses is attempted in another way. It is maintained that the speech in Acts 24:10–21 resembles speeches in classical historians : it is not a *verbatim* report of what Paul said, but a free composition of the author of Acts which he has put into the mouth of Paul. Paul himself in addressing Felix may not have referred to him as one who ' for many years ' ($\dot{\epsilon}\kappa$ $\pi o\lambda\lambda\hat{\omega}\nu$ $\dot{\epsilon}\tau\hat{\omega}\nu$) had administered justice in the country. The word $\pi o\lambda\acute{u}s$, it is pointed out, occurs frequently in the opening paragraphs of ancient speeches and treatises.[11] This use of the word, it is urged, is conventional, and the word itself ought not to be taken strictly. That, however, is by no means always apparent. For instance the writer of the Third Gospel tells us in his proem that many accounts of the life of Jesus were in circulation ; and since, as he indicates, it was the

---

[10] *Fasti Sacri*, p. 297, no. 1777.

[11] Several examples are given by Schwartz, *Göttinger Nachrichten* (1907), p. 29, note 2.

existence of this multiplicity of accounts that had brought home to him the need of a strictly reliable one, it is clear that by many he means many. If in 24:27 the writer of Acts gave his readers to understand that Felix was procurator for two years, he is not likely seventeen verses earlier to have put into Paul's mouth words from which, as he must have seen, they might quite well draw a very different conclusion. Some have considered it unlikely that Paul can have been kept a prisoner for any considerable time. But for Felix Paul's case was by no means a simple one, and, knowing that he was a Roman citizen, he must have realized what need there was of caution. It is better then to interpret the διετία in Acts 24:27 as the period of Paul's imprisonment in Caesarea and to gather from Acts 24:10 that, in addressing Felix, Paul did in fact, at the outset and by way of compliment, refer to his having been procurator for many years. For this interpretation of the διετία excellent reasons have been given. Thus Wieseler [12] notes that if the word had referred to the procuratorship of Felix, Luke would have written διετίαν πληρώσας, also that whereas it would have been a departure from Luke's manner to give the duration of the procuratorship, it was to his interest to give the duration of Paul's imprisonment; and J. Weiss [13] writes : ' The author who has spoken of " deferring " (verse 22), of " being kept in charge " (verse 23), of a " convenient season " (verse 25), and of frequent interviews, was decidedly taking pains to explain why Felix neither condemned the prisoner nor set him free. In short, the author has so plainly pictured a long lasting situation that it is impossible to refrain from referring the two years to this.'

II

The antedated chronology is sometimes also called the Eusebian chronology because some find its principal basis in the *Chronicle* of Eusebius as preserved in the Latin translation of it by Jerome.

[12] *Chronologie des apostolischen Zeitalters*, p. 61, note 2.
[13] *History of Primitive Christianity* (E.T. of *Das apostolische Zeitalter der christlichen Kirche*), I.377, note 115.

In it over against the year 2072 from Abraham, the 2nd year of Nero, and the 12th year of Agrippa II there is entered the note: 'Festus succeeds Felix, before whom and in the presence of king Agrippa the apostle Paul expounds the doctrine of his own religion and is sent as a prisoner to Rome.'[14] Since the 1st year of Nero was A D 55 and the 1st year of Agrippa II was according to the synchronistic system of the canon A D 45, the year indicated is A D 56.

In the Armenian version of the *Chronicle* of Eusebius a note to the same effect[15] stands over against the year 2070 from Abraham, the 14th year of Claudius and the 10th year of Agrippa II, i.e. A D 54, the last year of the reign of Claudius. This cannot have been the place in which Eusebius himself put it. In his *HE*, II.xxii.1 he writes: 'Festus was sent to be Felix's successor by Nero. Under him Paul, having made his defence, was sent bound to Rome.' In the Syrian epitome of the *Chronicle* of Eusebius the coming of Festus in the room of Felix is put in A D 56 (or 57).[16] Syncellus,[17] who had the Greek text of the work of Eusebius before him, says: 'Festus, the successor of Felix, was sent by Nero.' Josephus also (*Ant.*, xx.160 ff) assigns at least part of the activity of Felix to the reign of Nero, and in *Ant.*, xx.182, he records that Porcius Festus was sent as successor to Felix by Nero.

Plooij[18] attempts, nevertheless, to speak a good word on behalf of one of the dates, namely the 10th year of Agrippa II, given in the Armenian version for the commencement of Festus's procuratorship. He thinks it likely that this date was derived by Eusebius from Justus of Tiberias.[19] Agrippa I died

---

[14] Ed. Schoene, II.155 : *Festus succedit Felici, aput quem praesente Agrippar ege Paulus Apostolus religionis suae rationem exponens uinctus Romam mittitur.*
[15] Ed. Schoene, ii.152.
[16] *Evsebi Chronicorum Libri Dvo*, ed. Schoene, II.212.
[17] *Chronographia* 636.16 (ed. Dindorf).
[18] *De chronologie van het leven van Paulus*, pp. 58 ff.
[19] A contemporary of Josephus. He wrote a Chronicle of the Jewish kings from Moses to Agrippa II.

in A D 44. His brother Herod king of Chalcis, whom Agrippa II succeeded, died in A D 48 (Josephus, *Ant.*, xx.104). But since according to Josephus (*Bell. Jud.*, ii.284) the 12th year of the reign of Nero was the 17th year of the reign of Agrippa II, the 1st year of the latter's reign was not the 5th year of the reign of Claudius, i.e. A D 45, as in the *Chronicle* of Eusebius, but the 10th year of that reign, i.e. A D 50.[20] Plooij maintains that according to Justus of Tiberias the year in which Festus succeeded Felix was the 10th year of the reign of Agrippa II reckoned in this way, and so A D 59.

The following table may help to elucidate the three foregoing paragraphs.

	Chronicle OF EUSEBIUS			Justus of Tiberias (?)
		Jerome's Version	Armenian Version	
A D 45	CLAUDIUS 5	AGRIPPA II 1	AGRIPPA II 1	
50	10			AGRIPPA II 1
54	14		10 Festus succeeds Felix	
55	NERO 1			
56	2	12 Festus succeeds Felix		
59				10 Festus succeds Felix
66	12			17

Plooij's argument is intriguing, but there can be no assurance of its soundness. When the reasoning which he employs is applied to other dates in years of Agrippa II given in the Armenian version, some of the conclusions to which we are led

[20] Cf. Erbes, 'Die Todestage der Apostel Paulus und Petrus', *TU*, n.f.IV.i, 1899, pp. 26 f.

are quite impossible. Thus Felix was appointed procurator of Judaea in the 7th year of Agrippa II, which means A D 56, Albinus succeeded Festus in his 16th year, which means A D 65, and the Jewish War began in his 26th year, which means A D 75.

The correctness of the date A D 56 given for the commencement of the procuratorship of Festus in Jerome's version of the *Chronicle*, has been vigorously championed by Harnack.[21] He maintains that this date was taken over by Eusebius from Julius Africanus and so rests on a trustworthy tradition. Schürer,[22] however, has made a detailed study of all the notes bearing on Jewish affairs which appear in Jerome's version for the period extending from the death of Herod the Great to the outbreak of the Jewish War (except those referring to Jews in Alexandria, for which Philo is given as the authority). In this study he shows that, as regards the vast majority of these, Eusebius obtained the dates which he gives over against them from Josephus, and that he can quite well have arrived by conjecture at the dates he gives for the rest of them. Nothing justifies the assumption that for any one of them he turned to a source other than Josephus.[23] He did not find in Josephus the date of the coming of Festus in room of Felix. But finding in *Ant.*, xx.158, a reference to the first year of the reign of Nero and noting that the account of what happened when Festus succeeded Felix began at *Ant.*, xx.182, he allowed a year for the events recorded in Ant., xx.158–181 and so put the coming of Festus in the second year of Nero.[24] That date has thus no value whatever other than that of a mere estimate.

[21] Op. cit. (note 1, *supra*), II.1.233–8.
[22] 'Zur Chronologie des Lebens Pauli', *Zeit. f. wissenschaftliche Theologie*, XLI.(1892).21–42.
[23] For this reason Schürer also rejects the view of Blass (*Acta apost.*, p. 22) that the ultimate source of the date A D 56 for the coming of Festus was Justus of Tiberias.
[24] C. H. Turner ('Chronology of the New Testament' *HDB*, I.419a) suggests that Eusebius may have arrived at the date A D 56 by striking a mean between the date of the coming of Felix, the immediate predecessor of Festus, and that of the coming of Albinus, his immediate successor.

THE ANTEDATED CHRONOLOGY 155

Since Julius Africanus appears to have spent part of his life at Emmaus (Nicopolis) in Palestine, he may well have had special opportunities of collecting and verifying information. But Hoennicke [25] maintains that ' the impression that what we know about him makes upon us is not one of great historical accuracy ', and consequently that, even if it were true that the date A D 56 for the commencement of Festus's procuratorship was taken over from him, that would not guarantee its correctness.

III

Some find the principal basis of the antedated chronology in Josephus, *Ant.*, xx.182, taken together with Tacitus, *Ann.*, xiii.14. In the former passage it is stated that ' when Porcius Festus was sent as successor to Felix by Nero, the principal of the Jewish inhabitants of Caesarea went up to Rome to accuse Felix ; and he had certainly been brought to punishment for his misdeeds towards the Jews, unless Nero had yielded to the importunate solicitations of his brother Pallas, who was at that time had in the highest honour by him (μάλιστα δὴ τότε διὰ τιμῆς ἔχων ἐκεῖνον)'. In the latter passage, which belongs to the historian's account of A D 55, it is recorded that Nero ' removed Pallas from the charge of the business with which he had been entrusted by Claudius, and in which he acted, so to say, as the controller of the throne '. It is accordingly concluded that the beginning of Festus's procuratorship cannot be put later than A D 55.

The date of the removal of Pallas from office can be determined somewhat more closely. In Tacitus the account of it is followed by the story of the poisoning, death, and burial of Britannicus at some time between 1st January A D 55 and the day on which he would have completed his 14th year. Now according to Suetonius (*Claud.*, 27) Britannicus was born on 13th February A D 41, and so would have been fourteen years old on 13th February A D 55. The removal of Pallas thus took place in A D 55 and before 13th February of that year.

[25] *Die Chronologie des Lebens des Apostels Paulus*, p. 17.

Two difficulties here present themselves.

(a) If the appointment of Felix as procurator of Judaea lapsed on the death of Claudius, it must have been renewed at once. Certainly it is clear from Josephus *Ant.*, xx.160 ff, that Felix continued in office for some time after the accession of Nero (13th October A D 54). When Nero decided to terminate the appointment, he must have sent Felix a message instructing him to return home. Time must be allowed for the transmission of this message to Caesarea. On receipt of it and after due preparations Felix must have set out for Rome. He may not have journeyed by sea, the dangerous season for navigation commencing on 14th September and the seas being closed on 11th November.[26] But however he made his way, he can only have done so slowly since it was the winter season; and he is not likely to have reached Rome in time to find his brother Pallas still in a position to plead on his behalf.

(b) Felix must have left Judaea and Festus must have succeeded him there either towards the end of A D 54 or quite early in A D 55. But as is shown below [27] Festus must have entered on his office in summer.

These difficulties would both disappear if the death of Britannicus took place in A D 55 after 17th December, the date of the commencement of the *Saturnalia*, at the time of which feast Britannicus was alive in the year of his murder.[28] The events with which we are here concerned would then be dated as follows.

A D 54, 13th October	Nero's Accession	
55	Felix continues as procurator	
Pentecost		Paul arrives in Jerusalem (Acts 21:17)
Summer	Festus becomes procurator	Paul leaves for Rome (Acts 27:2)
	Pallas removed.	

[26] Vegetius, *De re militari*, iv.39. [27] Page 171.
[28] Tacitus, *Ann.*, xiii.15.

THE ANTEDATED CHRONOLOGY 157

    17th December
                      Murder of Britannicus
    31st December
56
    13th February

This dating of events involves, however, two assumptions, neither of which can be allowed.

(i) It is assumed either that at the time when Britannicus was put to death he was approaching his fifteenth birthday or that he was born in A D 42.[29] But in the place (*Ann.*, xiii.15) where he states that the day was near when Britannicus would complete his fourteenth year Tacitus is about to tell the sombre story of the murder of that young man; and that, as Turner [30] notes, was ' far too crucial an event to be likely to be misdated '. The date of the birth of Britannicus is given by Suetonius in these words: ' His son Britannicus, whom Messalina bore to him on the twentieth day after he came to the empire (*vicesimo imperii die*) and in his second consulship (*inque secundo consulatu*), . . . he recommended etc.' (*Claud.*, 27). According to Haenchen [31] *vicesimo imperii die* (= 13th February) gives only Britannicus's birthday, while *in secundo consulatu* (= A D 42) gives the year of his birth. But Suetonius clearly means that Britannicus was born on the twentieth day after Claudius's accession, therefore on 13th February, A D 41, and his added words *inque secundo consulatu* undoubtedly seem to be out of accord with that, their most obvious meaning being A D 42. Attempts have been made to secure agreement.[32] These, however, have not succeeded, and the possibility remains that here Suetonius contradicts himself. But if Britannicus was actually born on the twentieth day after Claudius became

[29] $41 + 15 = 42 + 14 = 56$.
[30] *H.D.B.*, I, p. 419b. Turner here rejects the view of Harnack that Tacitus wrongly assigned the downfall of Pallas to A D 55 and referred to Britannicus's 14th birthday whereas he ought to have referred to his 15th.
[31] *Die Apostelgeschichte*, p. 63, note 3.
[32] See Lewin, *Fasti Sacri*, p. 270, no. 1616.

emperor, that is likely to have impressed itself on the popular mind and to have been long remembered. The fact that Suetonius gives the date in this way and not, as is his normal practice in dating births, in the terms of the Roman calendar, is significant. It suggests that here he is reproducing a reliable tradition. If then we must choose for the birth of Britannicus either A D 41 or A D 42, we must undoubtedly prefer the earlier of these years.

(ii) The dating of events now before us also involves the assumption that the murder of Britannicus took place between 17th and 31st December A D 55. Now Tacitus concludes his account of the events of that year with a short statement (*Ann.*, xiii.24) of what took place *fine anni*. His use of that phrase confirms what is otherwise likely, that on the whole his record of the happenings of the year is chronologically ordered. But the account of the murder of Britannicus stands not in *Ann.*, xiii.24, but in *Ann.*, xiii.16–17 and so near to *Ann.*, xiii.11, where the account of the year begins. This means that the commencement of Festus's procuratorship must be dated after the accession of Nero on 13th October A D 54 and not later than 13th February A D 55. But it means also that the two considerable difficulties (*a*) and (*b*) mentioned above still confront us, and they tell decisively against the view that Festus assumed office in this interval.

It has often been maintained that, after being dismissed from court, Pallas continued to exercise a considerable influence in state affairs. Some have even suggested that in time he became as influential as ever he had been. This would open up the possibility of a later date for the commencement of Festus's procuratorship. But it is very unlikely. In the passage from Josephus now before us reference is made to the high honour in which Pallas was had by the emperor. It is, however, very much open to question whether onwards from the time of his accession Nero ever held Pallas in any honour at all. Before the end of A D 54 his attitude to him was already one of disgust (*taedium*, Tacitus *Ann.*, xiii.2), and there is no evidence that it ever changed for the better. Pallas's stipulation on leaving his office ' that he should not be questioned for anything he had done in the past, and that his accounts with the state were to be considered as balanced ', can hardly have been regarded by Nero as other than one more sample of that freedman's arrogance. The fact that when accused of treason Pallas was acquitted, need not have changed in the least the emperor's attitude towards him. It is true that Pallas was wealthy, and it is doubtless also true that he exercised the power of wealth. But had he been powerful enough to save his brother Felix from the punishment he deserved, he would also have been powerful enough to prevent his recall from Judaea. The statement of Josephus that at the time of Felix's recall Pallas was had in the highest honour by the emperor is not a mere exaggeration ; it is a misrepresentation ; and it may well be, as Erbes [33] suggests, that we have here to do with a story fabricated by the Jews of Caesarea to explain why, when they went to Rome to accuse Felix, they failed to secure his condemnation. It follows that no help in fixing the date of the commencement of Festus's procuratorship can be expected with any confidence from a study in conjunction of the two passages, the one from Josephus and the other from Tacitus, that have been before us.

If Festus succeeded Felix in A D 55 or A D 56 and the $\delta\iota\epsilon\tau\iota\alpha$ in Acts 24:27a is regarded as the period of Paul's imprisonment in Caesarea, then the Third Missionary Journey, which cannot have begun earlier than autumn A D 51, must have ended in A D 53 or A D 54. But the Ephesian ministry itself lasted for the space of three years (Acts 20:31). Accordingly, if the generally accepted interpretation of Acts 24:27a is retained, the antedated chronology is impossible.

[33] Op. cit. (note 20, *supra*), p. 17.

CHAPTER NINETEEN

The Date of Festus's Entrance on Office as Procurator of Judaea

(II) THE TRADITIONAL CHRONOLOGY

JOSEPHUS in *Ant.*, xx.137 f writes: 'So Claudius sent Felix, the brother of Pallas, to take care of the affairs of Judaea; and, when he had already completed the 12th year of his reign, he had bestowed upon Agrippa the tetrarchy of Philip.' Since Claudius, who began to reign on 25th January A D 41, completed his 12th year on 24th January A D 53, it follows that Felix was appointed in A D 52 or early in A D 53. A D 52 is to be preferred since in Tacitus *Ann.*, xii.54, the deposition of Cumanus is assigned to that year. Festus died in office and was followed by Albinus. The date of the latter's arrival in Judaea is gathered from Josephus, *Bell. Jud.*, vi.300 ff. Albinus as procurator was in Jerusalem at the time of a feast of Tabernacles when a man Jesus, a plebeian and an husbandman, caused much indignation by his oft-repeated cry: 'A voice from the four winds, a voice against Jerusalem and the holy house.' It was the Tabernacles 'four years before the war began', therefore the Tabernacles of A D 62. Also it was 'at a time when the city was in very great peace and prosperity', and in the period of Albinus's procuratorship such a condition obtained only for a brief season at its commencement. Albinus then assumed office shortly before Tabernacles A D 62.

The procuratorships of Felix and Festus thus covered a period of about ten years. On four grounds it can be regarded as very likely that by far the greater portion of that period fell to Felix.

(1) In the *Antiquities* Josephus gives a fairly long account of the procuratorship of Felix (xx.160–81); the account which he gives of the procuratorship of Festus (xx.182–96) is shorter, and

160

a considerable part of it (xx.189-96) is devoted to one incident. In the *Jewish War* the difference in the lengths of these two accounts (ii.253-70, ii.171) is still more marked, the period of the procuratorship of Festus being disposed of in two sentences. This admittedly does not prove, but it does suggest that Felix was in office for a considerably longer time than Festus. The harsh rule of Felix stirred, not simply in certain quarters but throughout the whole country, feelings such as, once aroused, are not easily allayed. From the brief account given by Josephus it is sufficiently clear that the grievous disorders that marked the period when Felix was procurator did not come to an end with his removal, and that the measures taken by Festus, prompt and severe as they were, failed to stay them. Throughout the above-mentioned ten years much undoubtedly happened that was well worth recording, and in view of the fact that the recorded incidents of the period of Festus's administration are few it certainly appears likely that he was in office only for a very short time.

(2) In his *Vita*, 13, Josephus writes : ' when I had completed the twenty-sixth year of my age, it happened that I took a voyage to Rome '. He then proceeds to state that his purpose in making this visit to Rome was to secure the release of certain priests who had been sent there as prisoners by Felix. Now he was born in the first year of Caligula (*Vita*, 5) i.e. between 16th March A D 37 and 15th March A D 38, and he completed his *Antiquities* in the thirteenth year of Domitian (14th September A D 93-13th September A D 94) when he was in his fifty-sixth year (*Ant.*, xx.267). It follows that he entered on his twenty-seventh year between 14th September A D 63 and 15th March A D 64. In all likelihood then he made this journey to Rome in summer A D 64.[1] In the matter of these priests he may have taken no action for a time, believing that, since Felix had been recalled, their case would be heard and a decision given in their favour. He may not have decided to visit Rome until it became apparent

---

[1] Cf. Wieseler, *Chronologie des apostolischen Zeitalters*, pp. 97 f.

to him that only through personal intervention were they likely to be set at liberty. But it is to be assumed that, on this becoming apparent to him, he proceeded on his journey as soon as he possibly could. It follows that Felix must have been recalled only a few years before A D 64.

(3) In the period of Paul's imprisonment in Caesarea a bitter conflict about citizen rights developed in that city between its Jewish and Syrian inhabitants, and it was apparently Felix's mishandling of this situation that was the immediate cause of his recall. He had referred the matter to Nero, and the latter's rescript regarding it was apparently delivered in Caesarea soon after Festus became procurator.[2] It very much embittered the feelings of the Jewish inhabitants and occasioned disturbances which Josephus[3] interprets as the beginning of the great storm that burst on the country in A D 66. That interpretation of them is the more easily understood the nearer the deliverance of the rescript, and consequently the beginning of Festus's procuratorship, is brought to AD 66.

(4) Two years before Felix was removed Paul addressed him as one who for many years had administered justice in the country (Acts 24:10). The procurators who had immediately preceded him had held office for short periods : Fadus for two years, Tiberius Alexander for two years, Cumanus for four years. In view of this, Paul, it is maintained by some, may have meant by many years no more than five years. There is, however, no good reason to think that Paul's statement was based on such comparisons. We ought rather to assume that he used the word 'many' quite simply, and in consequence we ought to make the period of Felix's administration as long as we can reasonably make it.

Felix must have returned to Rome in A D 61 at the latest ; and we proceed to show (i) that the recorded events of his procuratorship may have occupied the period A D 52–61, (ii) that those of the procuratorship of Festus can be accommodated within the

---

[2] Josephus, *Ant.*, xx.184.
[3] *Ant.*, xx.184 ; *Bell. Jud.*, ii.284.

year A D 61 (summer)–62, and that there is no sound reason why they should not be so.

I

Josephus in *Ant.*, xx.158–9, mentions certain events of the first year of Nero (A D 55). He then commences a fairly detailed account of Felix's procuratorship, which he introduces with the observation: ' Now, as for the affairs of the Jews, they grew worse and worse continually.' He mentions first the steps that Felix took to suppress the Zealots, with whom, he says, the country was again filled. The measures taken by Quadratus the legate of Syria, the deposition of Cumanus, and the coming of a new procurator in the person of Felix had restored order, if at all, only for a short time. During the years A D 52–5 there had been a marked return, instigated and furthered by fanatical Zealots, to a condition of widespread lawlessness. That during these years Felix had already made attacks upon the Zealots is very likely, but there need be no doubt that the events recorded in Josephus *Ant.*, xx.160–81 (= *Bell. Jud.*, ii.253–70) took place onwards from the end of A D 55 and that, while there may be some overlapping, the order in which these events are given is chronological.

By treacherous means Felix succeeded in capturing Eleazar, a notorious ring-leader of the Zealots, whom he then bound and sent to Rome. As regards the Zealots whom he crucified and the citizens who were found to have had commerce with them, whom he brought to punishment, they were, Josephus writes, ' a multitude not to be enumerated '. The steps which Felix took were effective, and yet they were quite unsuccessful. The country was purged of the Zealots, but another order of them sprang up known as the Sicarii, who, particularly at the festivals, ' mingled themselves among the multitude, and concealed daggers under their garments, with which they stabbed those that were their enemies; and when they fell down dead, the murderers became a part of those that were indignant thereat, by which means they appeared persons of such reputation that they could by no means be discovered'. Their first victim was Jonathan the high priest; and as his murder, which had been desired and paid for by Felix, went unavenged, they increased in number and boldness, killing their political opponents and causing such suspicion among the people that a man could not trust his own friends. In the period of Felix's procuratorship there was yet ' another body of wicked men gotten together, not so impure in their actions but more wicked in their intentions '. These were men who, giving out that they were divinely inspired, led multitudes of people into the wilderness, where, they assured them, God would show them ' the signals of liberty '. Felix construed this as the beginning of a revolt and sent troops who destroyed a great number of them. The most celebrated of these religious fanatics was an Egyptian Jew. He claimed to be a prophet and drew a great multitude of people about him to the mount of Olives on the pretence that at his command the walls of Jerusalem would fall down, whereupon they would enter the city and secure the government. But Felix, immediately on hearing this, ordered an attack to be made on him. Some of his followers were slain, others were captured, whilst he himself and the rest of them fled and disappeared.

Since the task of purging the country ($\kappa\alpha\theta\alpha\rho\theta\epsilon\iota\sigma\eta\varsigma$ $\tau\hat{\eta}\varsigma$ $\chi\omega\rho\alpha\varsigma$) of the Zealots may itself have involved two campaigns, all these happenings, from the capture of Eleazar to the escape of the Egyptian, may well have occupied three years (A D 56, 57, and 58). The Egyptian and his doings are referred to in Acts 21:38. When Lysias arrested Paul, he noted that he spoke Greek, and at once he inquired of him, ' So you speak Greek do you ? [4] Then you are not the Egyptian who started a revolt some time ago ($\pi\rho\grave{o}$ $\tau o\acute{u}\tau\omega\nu$ $\tau\hat{\omega}\nu$ $\dot{\eta}\mu\epsilon\rho\hat{\omega}\nu$) and led a force of four thousand [5] out into the wilds ? ' Now Paul was arrested about the time of Pentecost ; and if it was earlier in the same year that the Egyptian was defeated and obliged to flee, the possibility that he had

[4] Lysias was apparently unaware that the Egyptian Jews spoke Greek.
[5] The number in Josephus is 30,000. Commentators suggest that the signs $\triangle$ and $\wedge$ have been confused.

already returned and shown himself in the temple was so remote that the thought of it is hardly likely to have occurred to Lysias. Bearing this in mind and, more especially, making what seems adequate allowance for the interval referred to in the phrase ' some time ago ', we may conclude that the flight of the Egyptian took place in one year and the arrest of Paul about the Pentecost of the year following,[6] therefore the Pentecost of A D 59. The recall of Felix, two years later, must then be dated A D 61.

II

In the *Antiquities* Josephus devotes three paragraphs to the procuratorship of Festus. In the first, xx.182-4, he relates that eminent Jewish inhabitants of Caesarea went to Rome to accuse Felix, but failed to have him brought to punishment; he also explains by what means the Syrian inhabitants of Caesarea obtained an imperial rescript which declared them to be the lords of the city and took away from the Jews resident there the equality with them in citizen rights which they had previously enjoyed. In the second, xx.185-8, he refers to the growing menace of the Sicarii and to the suppression by Festus of yet another religous fanatic. In the remaining paragraph. xx.189-96, which he introduces with the words 'about the same time' (κατὰ τὸν καιρὸν τοῦτον), Josephus records a dispute which arose between Agrippa II and Festus on the one hand and the chief men of Jerusalem on the other. Agrippa had a story added to the palace of the Hasmonaeans in Jerusalem, from which he had an excellent view of the city, of the temple, and of the priests as they went about their duties there. But the chief citizens thought it not fitting that the priests should thus be spied upon. Accordingly they raised a wall in the temple area which intercepted Agrippa's view. But it also cut off the view of the interior of the temple from one of the stations of the Roman guard.

[6] Wieseler, *Chronologie des apostolischen Zeitalters*, p. 79, gives reasons for thinking that the Egyptian made his attempt to head a revolt at the time of a feast of Passover, the Passover, he then maintains, of the year preceding the year at the Pentecost of which Paul was arrested.

Ordered by Agrippa and Festus to remove the wall, the Jews refused to do so; and when they asked to be allowed to send a deputation to Rome to lay the matter before Nero, Festus granted them permission. The deputation found a friend in Poppaea, Nero's wife. To gratify her Nero instructed that the wall should stand.

Festus entered on his office in summer;[7] and the fact that his successor arrived in Judaea shortly before Tabernacles A D 62,[8] indicates that he must have died in summer, perhaps early in July, of that year, for a period of about three months must be allowed for the report of his death to reach Rome, for a new appointment to be made, and for the journey of the new procurator from Rome to Judaea.

It will be allowed that all the happenings recorded in the paragraphs of Josephus, *Ant.*, xx.182-4 and xx.185-8 may have taken place in the space of a single year. The building operations mentioned in the paragraph xx.189-96 may have been finished by April A D 62, for if the deputation left then for Rome, it would have been in the city shortly after the marriage of Nero and Poppaea, which took place about the beginning of May;[9] and it cannot be said with confidence that the new story to the

---

[7] Page 171, *infra*.

[8] Page 160, *supra*.

[9] Plooij, *De chronologie van het leven van Paulus*, p. 78, note 2: 'Octavia, the wife of Nero, who was repudiated for the sake of Poppaea, died on 9th June 62. Nero died *die quo quondam Octaviam interemerat* in the year 68 (Suetonius, *Nero*, c. 57). Nero in the first place divorced Octavia alleging that she was barren, and then he married Poppaea *duodecimo die post divortium Octaviae* (Suetonius, *Nero*, c. 35). Soon afterwards Octavia was banished to Campania and there put under military guard. Because of outspoken and incessant remonstrances among the people Nero was obliged to call her back (Tacitus, *Annales*, xiv.60 f). On a false charge that she had been guilty of adultery Nero condemned her to banishment in the island of Pandataria, where a few days later, on 9th June 62, she was put to death. All these happenings can hardly have taken place within less than a month. This enables us to calculate the date of Poppaea's marriage approximately, and obliges us to set the marriage in the beginning of May or perhaps somewhat earlier.'

Hasmonaean palace and the wall in the temple area were built in the interval between summer A D 61 and April A D 62, an interval that included the winter season. It is not possible to determine for what length of time bad weather may have held up building operations or how far Agrippa's addition to the palace had proceeded when the Jews set about counter measures. The added story may have been no more than a large summer-house or high tower, and need not have extended over the entire roof of the palace. On the other hand, while the wall erected by the Jews, if properly sited, need not have been very long, it must have been of considerable height to cut off Agrippa's view. The introductory words 'about the same time' have, however, a certain vagueness, and it may be that these buildings were begun when Felix was procurator, but were completed after Festus assumed office.[10] It is possible then that Festus was procurator only for one year, A D 61 (summer)–62,[11] and the following is ventured as a tentative calendar of events:

---

[10] Cf. Hoennicke, *Die Chronologie des Lebens des Apostels Paulus*, p. 8. The objection of Erbes, 'Die Todestage der Apostel Paulus und Petrus', *TU* n.f.IV.(1899), p. 20, that Josephus in his account of the procuratorship of Felix makes no reference to any disquiet occasioned by Agrippa's action, is not serious; but his suggestion that it may have been when Festus came with troops to Jerusalem for the Passover season that he conferred with Agrippa and ordered the Jews to pull the wall down, merits consideration.

[11] Cf. Hoennicke, ibid: 'And indeed the events mentioned in the *Antiquities*, xx,8.10–9.1 and the *Jewish War*, ii.24.1, can have followed one another within the space of a year.' H. von Soden, 'Chronology. B. New Testament', *Encyclopaedia Biblica* I.810: 'For the events related of Festus' term of office one year will suffice.'

The commencement of Festus's procuratorship is put in A D 61 by Cornely, *Introductio*, III.373; Clemen, *Paulus, sein Leben und Wirken*, I.410; E. Meyer, *Ursprung und Anfänge des Christentums*, III.54; Grieve in *Supplement to Peake's Commentary*, p. 19b. Wendt, *Die Apostelgeschichte* (5th edn. 1913), p. 64, gives summer A D 61 as its most likely date. Hoennicke op. cit. p. 25, puts it in A D 59, 60, or 61. Many, e.g. Ramsay, Goguel, Plooij assign it to A D 59, and perhaps even more, among them Anger, Wieseler, Lightfoot, Zahn, Brassac, to A D 60; see the comparative chronological tables in Hoennicke, pp. 69 ff and Plooij, facing p. 174.

A D		
61	Summer	Arrival of Festus as procurator. Rescript regarding citizen rights delivered in Caesarea.
62	April, 12th day	Passover. Deputation leaves for Rome immediately after Passover.
	May, early	Marriage of Nero and Poppaea.
	end	Deputation in Rome.
	June, 2nd day	Pentecost.
	end	Learning that Ismael the high priest is to remain in Rome, Agrippa appoints Joseph Kabi in his room.
	July, early	Death of Festus.
	middle	Ananus appointed high priest.
	August	Albinus nominated procurator.
	September, end	Deposition of Ananus. Arrival of Albinus in Judaea.
	October, 7th day	Tabernacles.

Two possible objections need, however, to be considered.

(*a*) If Ismael the high priest, who was a member of the deputation, left for Rome immediately after Passover,[12] then he was away from Jerusalem during Pentecost. The deputation,

---

[12] The assumption that the departure of the deputation was delayed until after Passover opens up the possibility that it may have sailed as far as Corinth on one of the pilgrim ships which quickly conveyed Jews of the Diaspora to and back from Palestine at this season. On these ships see Ramsay, ' Roads and Travel (in New Testament) ', *HDB*, extra vol., p. 399b.

it may be argued, is more likely to have gone to Rome in A D 61, probably between Pentecost and Tabernacles in which case the commencement of Festus's procuratorship would require to be carried back to the summer of A D 60.

But, in the first place, there must have been a standing arrangement for the overtaking of the duties of the high priest on occasions when he was unavoidably absent. In the second place, if the deputation went to Rome in A D 61, it was there several months before Poppaea became Nero's wife, and that obliges us to abandon the obvious meaning of the words in which Josephus describes her and to assume that he calls her Nero's wife euphemistically or proleptically.

(*b*) For some obscure reason Ismael the high priest was retained as a hostage in Rome. Josephus records that immediately on receiving this news Agrippa appointed Joseph Kabi, the son of Simon, in his room. He then proceeds. ' And now Caesar, upon hearing the death of Festus, sent Albinus into Judaea as procurator. But the king deprived Joseph of the high priesthood, and bestowed the succession to that dignity on the son of Ananus, who was also himself called Ananus' (*Ant.*, xx.196 f). That suggests that Joseph Kabi was high priest only for a short time; and indeed if the deputation went to Rome in April A D 62, he can have been high priest only for two or three weeks. But, it may be pointed out, when lower down Josephus records the deposition of Ananus, he notes that he had ruled but for three months; and if Joseph Kabi had held the office only for two or three weeks, that, it may be argued, would have been a more remarkable fact, and one that Josephus is hardly likely to have left unmentioned. Joseph Kabi, it may be concluded, must have been high priest for more than three months, and allowance can be made for that only by carrying back the commencement of Festus's procuratorship to summer A D 60.

But that is perhaps to build rather much on an omission. Josephus has not told us why the high priesthood was taken away from Joseph Kabi. It is conceivable that Agrippa had appointed him to the office somewhat unwillingly out of a desire to satisfy Festus, and that the death of Festus gave him an opportunity to replace him by a man of his own unfettered choice. Josephus may have thought it well to pass over this matter as far as possible in silence, and that may be why he has not called attention, as in normal circumstances he would have done, to the brevity of Joseph Kabi's tenure of the office.

It has been suggested that help towards answering the question, When did Festus succeed Felix as procurator of Judaea ? may perhaps be afforded by the coins of Palestine. In the *Palestine Exploration Fund Quarterly Statement* of 1914 [13] A. R. S. Kennedy points out that if it could be shown that there was an issue of coins of a new type when a procurator entered an office, then an issue made, after a considerable pause, in the fifth year of Nero may be taken as indicating that Festus became procurator in A D 59. There was in fact an issue of new coins about the time (*c*. A D 9) when Marcus Ambivius succeeded Coponius and another about the time (A D 15) when Valerius Gratus succeeded Annius Rufus. P. L. Hedley,[14] in an attempt to refute Eisler's contention that Pilate became procurator in A D 18, shows that coins of a new type which emerge first in A D 17/18 are still current in A D 24/25, and that there is no evidence of coins of a different type until A D 29/30. But since Pilate became procurator in A D 26,[15] this means that, so far as is known, there was no issue of new coins until he had been three years in office. It follows that the issue of the fifth year of Nero may not mark the commencement of the procuratorship of Festus, but may have been made in a year within the period of Felix's administration.

[13] Page 198, note 1.
[14] ' Pilate's Arrival in Palestine ', *JTS*, XXXV.(1934), pp. 56 f.
[15] See Schürer, *The Jewish People in the Time of Jesus Christ* I.ii.81 f, note 130.

CHAPTER TWENTY

To Rome

I—FROM CAESAREA TO FAIR HAVENS IN CRETE

THAT HE might appeal to Caesar, Paul was handed over to a Roman centurion, Julius, who was about to sail from Caesarea to Italy with a number of prisoners. All embarked on a ship of Adramyttium bound for ports in the province of Asia. The next day they touched at Sidon. Thence, because of a strong westerly wind, they sailed northwards under the lee of Cyprus and then, helped by land breezes and a westward current, hugged the southern coast of Asia Minor until they gained the port of Myra. There Julius transferred his convoy to an Alexandrian ship bound for Italy with a cargo of corn. The voyage from Myra was beset with difficulty from the outset. For many days they made little headway and were hard put to reach Cnidus. They were now exposed to the full force of the persisting west wind. Unable to make headway in the teeth of it, they set their course southwards and, rounding Salmone, the eastern promontory of Crete, struggled along the south coast of that island to the port of Fair Havens.

Since Paul was arrested in Jerusalem about the time of Pentecost and had been two years a prisoner in Caesarea when Felix was succeeded by Festus (Acts 24:27), it is to be concluded that Festus arrived in Palestine in summer, perhaps in late June or early July (A D 61).[1] Three days after taking up his appointment he went from Caesarea to Jerusalem, where he spent eight to ten days, and then returned to Caesarea. On the next day Paul was brought before him and appealed to Caesar (Acts 25:1, 6 ff). Four days being allowed for the journey up to and back from Jerusalem, this was the sixteenth or eighteenth day after

---

[1] Pentecost A D 59 was *c*. 5th June (Lewin, *Fasti Sacri*, p. 318).

Festus's arrival. An interval followed of some days (Acts 25:13 : ἡμερῶν δὲ διαγενομένων τινῶν) before Agrippa and Bernice arrived in Caesarea. They spent many days (Acts 25:14 : πλείους ἡμέρας) there, and on one of them they heard Paul speak for himself. Since some time needs doubtless to be added for final preparations for the voyage and for the arrival in the harbour at Caesarea of a suitable westward-bound ship, it seems unlikely that the departure can have taken place earlier than towards the end of August. According to the Western text of Acts 27:5 the voyage from Caesarea to Myra was one of fifteen days, which is regarded as a likely estimate. The slow progress from Myra as far as Cnidus may have consumed other fifteen days. If seven days are added for the continuation of the voyage thence to Fair Havens, the arrival in this port may be dated about the end of the first week in October.

2—FROM FAIR HAVENS IN CRETE TO MALTA

After recording the arrival at Fair Havens the writer of Acts proceeds: 'Now when much time was spent, and when sailing was now dangerous, because the fast was now already past (ἱκανοῦ δὲ χρόνου διαγενομένου καὶ ὄντος ἤδη ἐπισφαλοῦς τοῦ πλοὸς διὰ τὸ καὶ τὴν Νηστείαν ἤδη παρεληλυθέναι), Paul admonished them' (Acts 27:9 in the A V rendering). At a conference of the ship's officers Paul's counsel that they should stay where they were was not accepted. Instead it was decided that, as soon as weather permitted, they should sail to Phoenix, about forty miles to the west, where there was a more suitable harbour for wintering. Opportunity seemed to present itself when the weather cleared and a gentle south breeze began to blow. But when they were on the way to Phoenix, the weather changed again. A tempestuous gale, the North-easter, sprang up; and, unable to keep the ship's head to it, they let her drive before it and made for the shelter of Cauda (*Gozzo*). There no anchorage was possible, but in the lee of the island they were able to begin preparations to weather the storm. It continued with unabated fury for fourteen days, during which time they drifted no one knew whither, and then were shipwrecked on the coast of Malta.

In Acts 27:9 the reasons are given why there was a conference and, more particularly, why Paul's counsel was such as it was. Much time had been lost during the passage from Caesarea to Fair Havens. But the meaning of ἱκανοῦ δὲ χρόνου διαγενομένου seems to be that a considerable time had passed since the arrival at Fair Havens. There had been a waiting there day after day for many days in the hope that a change in the weather would permit a resumption of the voyage. But weather conditions were still unfavourable. Moreover, with every passing day a resumption of the voyage was becoming increasingly risky. The καί preceding τὴν Νηστείαν ἤδη παρεληλυθέναι apparently underlines the fact that the Fast (the Day of Atonement, 10 Tishri) had already gone by and so indicates that the season when navigation was recognized to be dangerous was already well advanced. There could be no question now of a resumption of the voyage. The only question now was where it would be best to winter. This conclusion that there was a stay at Fair Havens of some duration is perhaps confirmed by the mention of Lasea (Acts 27:8). It is referred to in a way which suggests that it was a place in which the crew and possibly also the prisoners and the soldiers who guarded them had spent leisure hours whilst awaiting in Fair Havens the coming of better weather.[2] If there was a stay there of about three weeks before the conference and another week passed before an attempt to reach Phoenix became possible, the shipwreck on Malta may have taken place in the end of November.

W. P. Workman[3] holds that the καί before τὴν Νηστείαν should be rendered 'as well as something else' or 'even': not only had the day generally recognized as marking the commencement of the season of hazardous navigation gone past,

---

[2] So Conybeare and Howson, *The Life and Epistles of St. Paul* (new edn., 1898), p. 640.
[3] 'A New Date-Indication in Acts', *Expository Times*, XI.(1899–1900). 316–19.

but even the Fast had already done so. It follows, so he maintains, that in this particular year the Fast must have been later than that day or at all events very late indeed. From two passages in Caesar [4] he infers that that day was the autumnal equinox, 24th (23rd) September. Now in the period A D 55–62 the Fast was later than the autumnal equinox only in A D 57, 59, and 62. Rejecting A D 57 and A D 62 on the ground that no one nowadays argues seriously for them, Workman concludes that Paul sailed from Caesarea for Rome in A D 59. But the autumnal equinox was not everywhere recognized as the first day of the season of hazardous navigation. According to Vegetius [5] that day was 14th September, and in the period just mentioned the Fast was later than 14th September in A D 55, 57, 58, 59, 60, and 62. This reasoning thus leads to no sure result.[6]

The writer of Acts apparently regarded the Fast as the first day of the season of hazardous navigation. That among the Jews of the first century of our era it was said proverbially that it was risky to go to sea after the Fast, is not unlikely. In later rabbinic literature the Feast of Tabernacles, which commenced five days after the Fast, is frequently regarded as the end of the period of safe navigation.[7] Recognizing that the conference at Fair Havens must have taken place at a time considerably later than the Fast, several older commentators either identified the $N\eta\sigma\tau\epsilon\iota\alpha$ with the $\Theta\epsilon\sigma\mu o\phi\acute{o}\rho\iota\alpha$, an ancient Athenian festival, or regarded the word as a nautical expression not found elsewhere but equivalent to *extremum autumni*.[8]

3—FROM MALTA TO ROME

All on board the vessel wrecked on Malta escaped safe to land.

---

[4] *Bell. Gall.*, iv.36 ; v.23.
[5] *De re militari*, iv.39.
[6] In A D 59 the Fast was late, about 5th October, but in A D 56, in which year there was possibly an intercalary month, it may have been still later, about 7th October.
[7] So Strack and Billerbeck, *Kommentar zum Neuen Testament aus Talmud und Midrasch*, II.771 ff.
[8] So Knowling in *The Expositor's Greek Testament*, II.520.

The people of the island showed them much kindness, and they remained there for three months. Thereafter (Acts 28:11) Julius with his prisoners embarked on the *Castor and Pollux*, a ship that had wintered in the island and was about to sail for Italy. If the shipwreck took place in the end of November, the departure from Malta must have taken place in March of the new year (A D 62), in all likelihood not earlier than the eleventh day of that month, the first day on which according to Vegetius the seas were again open to navigation. Those who date the shipwreck in the end of October or early in November and consequently hold that the *Castor and Pollux* sailed from Malta in February, quote in support of so early a putting to sea the words of Pliny (*H.N.* ii.47): ' Spring opens the seas to navigation. It commences when the west winds (*Favonii*) soften the wintry air ... on 8th February.' But the experience which Julius had had almost all the way from Caesarea, in particular in the attempt to reach Phoenix from Fair Havens, must have taught him caution. It may be assumed that, resolved to be safe rather than sorry, he did not sail until March.

From Malta they proceeded to Syracuse. The distance, about eighty miles, was covered apparently in one day. Probably because of an adverse wind they remained in Syracuse three days. Then, apparently in one day, they crossed to Rhegium. After they had been a day there, a south wind sprang up, and in two days, after an excellent run of 182 miles, they reached Puteoli (*Pozzuoli*), the port of Rome, in the Bay of Naples. According to Acts 28:14 there was a halt in this place of a week. Usually it is assumed that, immediately on disembarking, Julius forwarded to the officials in Rome intimation of his arrival and remained in Puteoli until he received from them instructions as to how he was to proceed. Loisy [9] objects that Julius had no need of instructions other than those he had received before setting sail from Caesarea and further that he was himself quite capable of organizing the journey from Puteoli to Rome; the statement

---

[9] *Les Actes des Apôtres*, p. 928.

that there was a week's stay in Puteoli thus lies under the suspicion of having been worked in to answer the question, How did the Christians of Rome get to know that Paul had arrived in Puteoli so as to be able to come out, some to Appii Forum and some to Tres Tabernae, to meet him ? But the statement can hardly be rejected simply because no entirely satisfactory reason for so long a halt is known to us. The march of 140 miles from Puteoli to Rome will have been completed in seven days. The journey from Malta to Rome thus occupied twenty-two days, and Paul's arrival in the capital may be dated early in April A D 62.

According to the best manuscripts the text of Acts 28:16 runs : Ὅτε δὲ εἰσήλθομεν εἰς Ῥώμην, ἐπετράπη τῷ Παύλῳ μένειν καθ' ἑαυτὸν σὺν τῷ φυλάσσοντι αὐτὸν στρατιώτῃ. No mention is made of the official or officials to whom Julius delivered Paul. The Western text fills in this lacuna. There, after Ῥώμην, the reading is ὁ ἑκατόνταρχος παρέδωκε τοὺς δεσμίους τῷ στρατοπεδάρχῳ, τῷ δὲ Παύλῳ ἐπετράπη κτλ. If by the stratopedarch is meant the prefect of the praetorian guard, the statement that Julius handed over his prisoners to him may be true. Certainly it consorts with what appears to have been the practice in the time of Pliny the Younger.[10] In a rescript the emperor Trajan instructed him to send a prisoner in chains to the prefects of the praetorian guard. From Tacitus (*Ann.*, xii.42 and xiv.51) it is known that ordinarily there were two prefects of the praetorian guard, but that from A D 51 to 62 there was only one such prefect, namely Afranius Burrus, who, according to a reckoning made by Wieseler,[11] died in January or February A D 62. To infer from the singular (τῷ στρατοπεδάρχῳ) in the Western text that Paul's arrival in Rome must be dated earlier than A D 62 is, however, extremely precarious. The reference in the Western text may be to the particular prefect to whom the prisoners were delivered or to that one of the two of them to whom the duty of receiving them was assigned.

[10] *Ep.*, x.57.
[11] *Chronologie des apostolischen Zeitalters*, pp. 83 ff, footnote.

In the Latin *Codex Gigas*, στρατοπέδαρχος in the Western text of Acts 28:16 is rendered *princeps peregrinorum*. According to Mommsen this was the commander of the Augustan or Imperial cohort (Acts 27:1), a body of officers, known as the *frumentarii* or *peregrini*, who superintended the corn supply and whose headquarters in Rome were on the Caelian Hill. An African inscription [12] discovered since Mommsen discussed this matter enables the existence of such a commander to be carried back from the third century to the days of Trajan and so lends support to his conjecture that there may have been such a commander at the time when Paul arrived in Rome. The *frumentarii* also discharged police and other functions. Actually, however, there is no evidence that these extra duties were assigned to them so early as the first century of our era. Moreover *princeps peregrinorum* is an interpretation rather than a translation of στρατοπέδαρχος; and, being a comparatively late interpretation, it may possess no historical value.[13]

Acts ends with a statement to the effect that Paul remained in Rome in easy imprisonment for two full years and with a brief account of how he spent that time. As recorded in this work, the apostle's history thus extends down to A D 64.

[12] See *Comptes rendus de l'Académie des Inscriptions et Belles-Lettres*, 1923, p. 197.
[13] On the subject of this paragraph see Mommsen and Harnack, ' Zu Apostelgeschichte 28,16 ', *Sitzungsberichte Berl. Akad.*, 1895, pp. 492 ff; Ramsay, *St. Paul the Traveller and the Roman Citizen*, pp. 347 ff; E. Meyer, *Ursprung und Anfänge des Christentums* iii, p. 480, note 2; T. R. S. Broughton in Jackson and Lake, *The Beginnings of Christianity* I.v, pp. 443 f; two articles in the *Journal of Roman Studies* xiii (1923), pp. 152–67 and pp. 168–87, the one, ' The Castra Peregrinorum ', compiled by P. K. Baillie Reynolds from notes made by T. Ashby, the other, ' The Troops Quartered in the Castra Peregrinorum ', written by P. K. Baillie Reynolds; A. N. Sherwin-White, *Roman Society and Roman Law in the New Testament* (1963), pp. 109 f.

CHAPTER TWENTY-ONE

The Sequel to Acts 28:30-1

IN ACTS the record of the missionary activity of Paul is carried forward to the end of his second year as a prisoner in Rome, at which time he was apparently still waiting the hearing of his appeal to Caesar. But although the record stops at that point, there are ways in which we may seek to ascertain what, had it been continued, the probable content of the continuation would have been. Three questions may be considered : (1) Are there in Acts any indications of what subsequently befell the apostle ? (2) Do the epistles attributed to him throw any light on his later history ? (3) What is the historical worth of early extra-canonical tradition on this matter ?

I

The last two verses of Acts fittingly conclude that work. There is in them a note of triumph. The writer has accomplished the task which he took in hand, namely, to give an account of the expansion of Christianity from Jerusalem to Rome. Having imprinted on the minds of his readers an unforgettable picture of Paul proclaiming the Gospel there, he lays down his pen. It is not surprising that commentators have incorporated in their expositions of these two verses the words of Bengel : '*Victoria Verbi Dei. Paulus Romae, apex evangelii*'.

It is true, nevertheless, that this conclusion of the book is abrupt, that it disappoints the reader's expectations and fails to satisfy his legitimate curiosity. The examinations of Paul that took place from the day of his arrest in Jerusalem to the time when he appealed to Caesar have all been recorded in some detail. He is now in Rome that his case may be finally settled. A trial is impending to which all the earlier ones are merely preliminary. But about the conduct and issue of this trial nothing is recorded.

Almost inevitably the reader feels that the writer has failed him in breaking off at a point so near the finale on towards which he has been leading him.

The last two verses being an appropriate conclusion, it is unlikely either that untoward circumstances obliged the writer to abandon his work or that he died before he had finished it.[1] It is conceivable that after Acts 28:29 he gave an account of Paul's trial, condemnation and martyrdom in Rome and that, to allow for further missionary journeys, this account was subsequently struck out and the present conclusion added by a later hand.[2] But the character of the present conclusion [3] and also the lack of any manuscript evidence of a longer text of Acts at this point, tell against that. Following Bengel, certain scholars [4] have suggested that the writer intended to add a third volume to his work *ad Theophilum* and in it to give an account of Paul's trial ending in his release and of subsequent missionary labours. It is, however, precarious to find evidence of such an intention in the word πρῶτον in Acts 1:1. According to Souter [5] πρῶτος is 'also used where there are two elements only, as πρότερος, the true comparative was dying out in New Testament times'. Moreover if the writer had projected a third volume, then, following the literary technique which he has adopted in the end of his Gospel and the beginning of Acts, he would have given a brief account of Paul's trial in the last chapter of Acts

---

[1] See on the other hand Hoennicke, *Die Apostelgeschichte*, p. 10; de Zwaan, 'Was the Book of Acts a Posthumous Edition?', *Harvard Theological Review*, XVII.(1924).95 ff; Lietzmann, *The Founding of the Church Universal*, p. 100.

[2] Cf. F. Pfister, 'Die zweimalige römische Gefangenschaft und die spanische Reise des Apostels Paulus und der Schluss der Apostelgeschichte', *ZNTW*, XIV.(1913).216–21.

[3] See Harnack, *Date of the Acts and the Synoptic Gospels* (E.T. of *Neue Untersuchungen zur Apostelgeschichte und zur Abfassungzeit der synoptischen Evangelien*), p. 94, note 1.

[4] Among them are Zahn, *Einleitung in das Neue Testament*, I.439, II.371, and Ramsay, *St. Paul the Traveller and the Roman Citizen*, p. 309.

[5] *A Pocket Lexicon to the Greek New Testament*, s.v.

to be followed by a fuller account of it in the opening chapter of the new volume.

The writer's statement, ' Paul dwelt two whole years in his own hired house ', undoubtedly suggests that Paul's circumstances changed at the end of that time, and further that the writer was aware of the nature of that change. He knew what happened to Paul at the close of his two-year imprisonment. But for some reason he has not recorded it. What can his reason have been ?

(1) He may have withheld what he knew because it was not the kind of information that he cared to communicate. Essentially this is the view of K. Lake. According to a theory which he published in 1909 and again in 1913,[6] it was the duty of the Jews to come from Palestine to Rome to state their case against Paul before the emperor. But they failed to come throughout a period of two years, and at the end of that time the case went by default. Paul was indeed set free, but this end of the trial was ' disappointing to Luke from the point of view of Christian Apologetic '. Accordingly, in the end of his book he has not mentioned the trial, but has given prominence instead to the freedom to preach the Gospel which, prisoner though he was, Paul enjoyed during the two years that preceded it.

It has, however, not been firmly established that two years was the statutory period within which accusers were required to state their case in Rome. Philo (*In Flaccum*, 128 f) refers to a man, Lampon by name, who was accused of impiety (ἀσεβεία) against Tiberius. Out of malevolence the prefect put off hearing his case and kept him a prisoner for two years (διετίαν), and this period is described as μήκιστον χρόνον. But this means not ' the longest time legally possible ', but simply ' a very long time '. Moreover Lampon's case is not parallel to that of Paul. He did not appeal to Caesar, and his trial was delayed not because his accusers failed to appear, but deliberately by the prefect.

---

[6] See Cadbury, ' Roman Law and the Trial of Paul ', in Jackson and Lake, *The Beginnings of Christianity*, I.v.326 ff, where Lake's words are quoted.

Pliny (*Ep.*, x.56 f) refers to a man who had been exiled for life by Bassus, the proconsul of Bithynia in A D 98. The judgements of Bassus were later rescinded, and all who considered that they had suffered unjustly from them were allowed a new trial provided they asked for that within two years. This man did not do so; and when Pliny inquired of Trajan what should be done in his case, the emperor replied that he had had two years given him in which to lodge an appeal if he felt aggrieved, and ordered him to be sent in chains to Rome. But here also there is no appeal to Caesar, and the period of two years mentioned here may have been decided upon by the Senate only for this particular situation. An edict (*BGU* ii 628, *recto*),[7] which deals with cases sent on appeal to the emperor, enacts for criminal cases coming from across the sea that if both the accused and the accusers fail to present themselves within one-and-a-half years, the appeal shall be dropped. But this is a shorter period of grace, and in the surviving text of the edict, which is badly mutilated, nothing is said as to what was to happen when only the accusers failed to appear. Moreover it is now recognized that this edict belongs not, as until recently some authorities thought, to the first but to the third century of our era. According to A. N. Sherwin-White, *Roman Society and Roman Law in the New Testament* (1963), p. 115, it deals with 'the late-empire system of *appellatio* after sentence and not with the early-empire system of *provocatio* before sentence'.

(2) Again the writer may have withheld what he knew because it would have been detrimental to his purpose.

In many places he has indicated that on the whole Roman officials did not hinder but rather facilitated Paul's missionary activities. According to some who maintain that he wrote in the early sixties when Paul's trial was pending, his aim in doing so was that his book might serve as an 'explanatory statement' for the information of readers somehow concerned for the

---

[7] The text as restored by Mitteis is given in Jackson and Lake, *The Beginnings of Christianity*, I.v.333 f.

decision of the case.⁸ But the composition of Acts can hardly be carried so far back.⁹

Others, who assign its composition to a later date, hold that in the passages just referred to the writer's aim was to mollify the attitude towards Christians of Roman officials in times of impending persecution.¹⁰ If now in the end of his book he had recorded a trial before the emperor at which Paul was found guilty and condemned to death, that would have hurt this aim most grievously, and he may well have held his peace because he recognized that. But had his purpose in underlining the favourable attitude of Roman officials been the one now before us, he is likely to have ended his narrative somewhat earlier, certainly before the disturbance in Jerusalem which, on Paul's last return there, led to his being taken into custody by the Romans.

It has been suggested¹¹ that the issue of Paul's appeal to Caesar may have been his banishment from Rome. In that case also the story of his trial would have hurt the apologetic aim which according to the theory now before us the writer of Acts had in view, and for that reason he may have refrained from telling it. But the evidence for banishment is meagre and doubtful. In Clement of Rome, *Corinthians* 5:6 φυγαδευθείς may refer merely to Paul's experience recorded in Acts 13:50; and while φυγαδευθείς is now the generally accepted reading, ῥαβδευθείς has also been conjectured (cf. 2 Cor. 11:25). According to Theodore of Mopsuestia¹² Paul was liberated by the judgement of Nero and ordered to depart in safety (*securus abire jussus est*). But it is not clear that the order given was to

---

[8] J. I. Still, *St. Paul on Trial*, pp. 35 f.
[9] See Moffatt, *Introduction to the Literature of the New Testament* (3rd edn., 1918), pp. 304 and 311–13.
[10] According to D. W. Riddle, 'The Occasion of Luke-Acts', *The Journal of Religion*, X.(1930).545–62 ' it was the foreboding of the Domitianic suppression which furnished the occasion of Luke-Acts '.
[11] E.g. by L. P. Pherigo, ' Paul's Life after the Close of Acts ', *JBL*, LXX.(1951).277–84.
[12] *Argum. in Eph.* 1.

depart from Rome. In the next sentence it is said that after stopping two years in the city, Paul departed from it. The statement of Pelagius [13] that on the first occasion Paul was sent away from the city (*quia prima vice sit ex urbe dimissus*), is merely an inference he makes from Paul's request to Philemon to prepare him a lodging. The hypothesis of Goguel [14] that Paul's trial ended in his condemnation to the mines appears to have commanded little attention.

(3) Yet again it is possible that the writer may have withheld what he knew simply because he was aware that it was already common knowledge.

Silence on this ground is particularly understandable if what was known was to the writer an occasion of sorrow. Acts is history and not biography. But Paul is the writer's hero throughout its second half, and he cannot have been unconcerned about the outcome of his trial. If he was released, his joy on that account would have constrained him to tell, if only in a sentence or two, the story of the trial, well-known as he knew that story to be. If on the other hand he was condemned, he may well have stopped short of an account of the trial and have turned elsewhere for a note of triumph on which to conclude his narrative.

While, however, the writer's feelings of regard for Paul may in part have moved him not to go beyond the end of the two-year Roman imprisonment, his principal reason for stopping there must undoubtedly be sought in the purpose that he had in view in writing the book, namely, to sketch the progress of Christianity from Jerusalem to Rome. That progress encountered obstacles; it was opposed by individuals and by multitudes; but it was according to the divine will and proved irresistible. The message of the Gospel was carried to Rome; the great missionary to the Gentiles himself reached Rome; and with a brief account of him proclaiming the kingdom of

---

[13] *Comm. in Philemon* v.22.
[14] *Introduction au Nouveau Testament*, IV.II.391.

God there the writer fittingly concludes his work. He has carried the story of the expansion of Christianity sufficiently far to let it be seen that the Church has no better *apologia* than its own history. A continuation of the narrative in which an account was given of Paul's trial and condemnation would have been an anticlimax, and would have been so even if an account had been added of his martyrdom and departure to the place of glory. On the other hand, a continuation in which it was recorded that the issue of his appeal to Caesar was his complete vindication would have been a peculiarly fitting coping-stone to the work, and only the fact that no such continuation was possible can adequately explain its omission.

It is conceivable that the knowledge that the writer of Acts had of what happened at the end of Paul's two-year imprisonment in Rome has coloured the account he gives of him in the years preceding his arrival there. Shadows of coming events have been discerned particularly in the story told in 20:4–21:15. It may be questioned, however, if these are sufficiently distinct to justify the giving of the title 'The Progress of a Martyr' to that passage.

But Paul's statement, as recorded, to the Ephesian elders, ' Behold, I know that ye all, among whom I have gone preaching the kingdom of God, shall see my face no more' (Acts 20:25) together with its moving effect upon them as recorded in Acts 20:36–8, occasions difficulty. The statement is remarkably positive. Paul does not say, 'I think it likely' or 'I am almost sure' but 'I know'; he does not say 'some of you' or 'most of you' but 'ye all among whom I have gone preaching the kingdom of God'; and he says οὐκέτι, by which he means 'no more' or 'never again'. This language, it may be urged, is but the expression of a strong personal conviction, and that conviction may have been falsified by subsequent events. But at this time Paul may not have had such a strong personal conviction. He was already minded to undertake missionary work in regions west of Rome. But there is no indication that he was resolved, once he reached these regions, to continue in them for the remainder of his years. On the contrary, because of his affection for his converts the likelihood is that he cherished the hope of being able one day to return and see them again. He was told that bonds and afflictions awaited him. But he need have had no absolute assurance that these would prevent him from ever visiting Ephesus again. He was prepared to die in the service of Christ (Acts 20:24), but that does not mean that he had abandoned the hope that he would live to continue in His service. In addressing the Ephesian elders he may perhaps have hinted that there was a possibility of his not seeing them again, and that may well have saddened them as they took leave of him. But the forthright terms in which according to Acts 20:25 he spoke to them and the moving story that follows of their sorrowful parting must be attributed to the writer, and he can have sharpened what Paul may have said to them and changed into the bitterness of tears the sadness which it may have occasioned them only because he knew that in fact Paul never did again visit Ephesus.

II

In epistles which, according to a view that is widely held, Paul wrote during his two-year imprisonment in Rome there are statements which indicate that he was then looking forward confidently to his release: I know that I shall abide and continue with you all for your furtherance and joy of faith (Phil. 1:25); I trust in the Lord that I also myself shall come shortly (Phil. 2:24); But withal prepare me also a lodging, for I trust that through your prayers I shall be given unto you (Philem, 22). For two reasons, however, no sure conclusion regarding the issue of Paul's trial can be built upon these statements: (1) they occur in epistles about the date and place of origin of which there is by no means a consensus of opinion, (2) there is no evidence that the confidence expressed in them was based on a knowledge that Paul had of steps then being taken in his favour by influential parties or in official circles. Thankful as he was for the opportunity to proclaim Christ which he had in his imprisonment (Phil. 1:12-13), he doubtless longed for the fuller opportunity which freedom would afford him. That longing may well have been the secret spring of his confidence, and in any consideration of the statements just quoted the extent to which wishful thinking may account for them cannot be overlooked.

It is, however, most of all in the Pastoral Epistles that evidence has been sought that Paul's two-year imprisonment in Rome ended in his release. In them reference is made to a series of events in his life for which a place cannot be found within the period of it recorded in Acts. Eusebius attempted a solution of this problem by maintaining that Paul was set free from his first Roman imprisonment, the one recorded in Acts 28:30-1, that he then engaged in a post-Acts ministry, and that finally he suffered martyrdom after a second Roman imprisonment. In his *Ecclesiastical History* II.xxii.2-3, he writes: ' But, as his [Felix's] successor, Nero sent Festus, in whose day Paul was brought in bonds to Rome, having first made his own defence. Aristarchus was with him, whom also somewhere in his epistles he suitably calls a fellow prisoner. And Luke, the same who delivered in writing the Acts of the Apostles, brought his history to a close at that point of time, after indicating that Paul spent two whole years at Rome without restraint, and preached the word of God, none forbidding him. Having, therefore, made his defence at that time, it is recorded that the apostle again journeyed on the ministry of preaching, and, having set foot for the second time in the same city, was perfected in his martyrdom. While still in bonds he composed his second epistle to Timothy, mentioning both his former defence and also his imminent perfecting.' [15]

[15] Trans. of H. J. Lawlor and J. E. L. Oulton, *Eusebius. The Ecclesiastical History and the Martyrs of Palestine* i (1927), p. 55. The words λόγος ἔχει, rendered by ' it is recorded ', do not signify that here Eusebius merely expresses his own opinion or again that here he refers to a tradition current in his own day. Rather, as Lawlor and Oulton, ibid., ii (1928) p. 73, note, ' the documents implied by this phrase are the Pastoral Epistles '.

Eusebius's argument is that the words 'first defence' in 2 Timothy 4:16 refer to Paul's trial at the end of his first Roman imprisonment and plainly indicate that, after a period of release, there was a second Roman imprisonment ending in a second trial. Paul wrote 2 Timothy during the second imprisonment. In it he recalls that at his first trial he was delivered out of the mouth of the lion (2 Tim. 4:17), but he has an inner awareness that the second trial which awaits him will end differently and writes: ' The Lord shall deliver me from every evil work, and will preserve me unto his heavenly kingdom.' (2 Tim. 4:18.)

This argument was accepted by Jerome,[16] Chrysostom [17] and several other early writers. Among those who have accepted it in modern times are Th. Zahn [18] and M. Meinertz.[19] But for the most part it is now rejected, the phrase ' first defence ' being understood in other ways. Some refer it to the *prima actio* or precognition, the first stage of Paul's trial at the end of his second Roman imprisonment, after which he was remanded in custody to wait for the second stage. According to others 2 Timothy 4:16–18 is part of an epistle which Paul wrote shortly after his arrival as a prisoner in Caesarea, and by his ' first defence ' he means the ἀπολογία recorded in Acts 22:1 ff, the second being the one recorded in Acts 23:1 ff. But besides this uncertainty as to the meaning of the phrase, there is the possibility that it does not come to us from Paul, but has been attributed to him and quite probably does not refer to any actual historical situation.

While some still attribute the Pastoral Epistles to Paul, the modern critical view, based on a thorough examination of their language and style, their doctrine, and the stage of church organization which they imply, is that while genuine Pauline

---

[16] *De vir. illust.*, 5 ; Migne, *PL.*, xxiii.617.
[17] *In 2 Tim. hom.*, 10 ; Migne, *PG*, lxii.657.
[18] *Einleitung* I.453.
[19] ' Worauf bezieht sich die πρώτη ἀπολογία ? ', *Biblica*, IV.(1923).390–4.

fragments may perhaps be incorporated in them,[20] they present a fictitious extension of the apostle's life made to serve religious ends and that for the history of Paul no more can be obtained from them than from the apocryphal Acts of Apostles.[21] It is by no means evident either that the author would not have ventured upon such an extension of Paul's life unless there had been a tradition that he engaged in a post-Acts ministry, or that by venturing upon it he testifies to the existence in his day of such a tradition.

III

Reference to an activity of Paul which may seem to belong to a time subsequent to the ' two whole years ' mentioned in Acts 28:30, is found in three early extra-canonical writings—Clement of Rome's *Epistle to the Corinthians* (*c.* A D 96), the *Actus Petri Vercellenses* (not later than A D 200), and the *Muratori Canon* (*c.* A D 200).

(i) Early in his *Epistle to the Corinthians* Clement writes, by way of admonition, about the evil that has been wrought by envy and jealousy. In Chapter 4 he takes examples from the Old Testament. Then in the two following chapters, which we quote in the translation of J. B. Lightfoot,[22] he gives examples from the immediate past.

5. But, to pass from the examples of ancient days, let us come to those champions who lived nearest to our time. Let us set before us the noble examples which belong to our generation. By reason of jealousy and envy the greatest and most righteous pillars of the Church were persecuted, and contended even unto death. Let us set before our eyes the good Apostles. There was

---

[20] See P. N. Harrison, *The Problem of the Pastoral Epistles*, pp. 113 ff; ' The Pastoral Epistles and Duncan's Ephesian Theory ', *NTS*, II.(1956).250 ff ; G. S. Duncan, *St. Paul's Ephesian Ministry*, pp. 184 ff. That there are in fact any such fragments may be questioned, see P. Wendland, *Die urchristlichen Literaturformen* (Handbuch zum NT, I.III.367) ; R. S. Easton, *The Pastoral Epistles*, pp. 76–8 and 106.
[21] Cf. E. Meyer, *Ursprung und Anfänge des Christentums* III.134.
[22] *The Apostolic Fathers* (edited and completed by J. R. Harmer), pp. 59 f.

Peter who by reason of unrighteous jealousy endured not one nor two but many labours, and thus having borne his testimony went to his appointed place of glory. By reason of jealousy and strife Paul by his example pointed out the prize of patient endurance. After that he had been seven times in bonds, had been driven into exile (φυγαδευθείς), had been stoned, had preached in the East and in the West, he won the noble renown which was the reward of his faith, having taught righteousness unto the whole world (δικαιοσύνην διδάξας ὅλον τὸν κόσμον) and having reached the farthest bounds of the West (ἐπὶ [23] τὸ τέρμα τῆς δύσεως ἐλθών); and when he had borne his testimony before the rulers (μαρτυρήσας ἐπὶ τῶν ἡγουμένων), so he departed from the world and went unto the holy place, having been found a notable pattern of patient endurance.

6. Unto these men of holy lives was gathered (συνηθροίσθη) a vast multitude of the elect, who through many indignities and tortures, being the victims of jealousy, set a brave example among ourselves. By reason of jealousy women being persecuted, after that they had suffered cruel and unholy insults as Danaids and Dircae, safely reached the goal in the race of faith, and received a noble reward, feeble though they were in body. Jealousy hath estranged wives from their husbands and changed the saying of our father Adam, *This now is bone of my bone and flesh of my flesh.* Jealousy and strife have overthrown great cities and uprooted great nations.

For the present our main concern is the meaning to be given to the expression τὸ τέρμα τῆς δύσεως in Chapter 5. Attempts have been made to show that it means Rome. It is pointed out that here Clement's language is exuberant: he piles up clauses in such a way as suggests that he is paying little attention to their sequence or association. It may be then, so it is maintained, that we ought to put a comma after ἐλθών and, regarding ἐπὶ τὸ τέρμα τῆς δύσεως ἐλθών as synchronous with μαρτυρήσας ἐπὶ τῶν ἡγουμένων, to interpret τὸ τέρμα τῆς δύσεως as the place

---

[23] The suggestion of Wieseler, *Chronologie des apostolischen Zeitalters*, p. 532 to read ὑπό instead of ἐπί before τὸ τέρμα τῆς δύσεως and to understand by this the highest authority in the West, i.e. Nero and his *consilium*, has seldom been adopted by later writers.

where Paul bore his testimony before the rulers, i.e. Rome. But it is equally possible that we ought to put a semicolon after ἐλθών, as Lightfoot does, and so to associate ἐλθών with the preceding διδάξας; Paul taught righteousness to the whole world and, in doing so, proceeded to the farthest bounds of the West. Others suggest that here Clement may be putting himself at the standpoint of Paul. Paul, who had been educated in Jerusalem, was already in land that was west for him when he crossed to Macedonia, and Rome may have seemed to him a distinctly western city, even τὸ τέρμα τῆς δύσεως. If, as his intimate acquaintance with the Old Testament Scriptures probably indicates, Clement was a Jew, that, it is maintained, would improve the possibility that he shared Paul's outlook in this matter. But even if he was a Hellenistic Jew—and the proof of that is not complete—he may, through his residence in Rome, have come to have such a sense of it as the centre of the Empire that by the time he wrote his *Epistle to the Corinthians* he would not naturally have referred to it as τὸ τέρμα τῆς δύσεως. Lightfoot adduces several passages from Strabo [24] in which expressions similar to τὸ τέρμα τῆς δύσεως undoubtedly indicate Spain or the western part of the inhabited earth. That admittedly does not necessarily determine the meaning of τὸ τέρμα τῆς δύσεως in Clement's epistle. Nevertheless it lends support to the view that by it he means not Rome but regions lying to the west of it.

The reference which he makes here to Paul is, however, rhetorical in character. Here he indulges in a panegyric on the apostle, and allowance needs to be made for exaggeration. Pfister [25] has shown that in later accounts of the achievements of outstanding conquerors, travellers and missionaries there is a marked tendency to break through the limit of historical fact and to represent their territorial extent as greater than it actually

---

[24] Strabo, ii.1; ii.4; iii.1; iii.5. Lightfoot, *Biblical Essays*, p. 423, note 2; *Apostolic Fathers* I.ii.30, also adduces Vellei. Pater. i.2: *in ultimo Hispaniae tractu [in] extremo nostri orbis*.

[25] Op. cit. (Note 2, *supra*), pp. 216 ff.

was. Thus it is said of Alexander the Great in 1 Maccabees 1:3 : 'And [he] went through to the ends of the earth' (καὶ διῆλθεν ἕως ἄκρων τῆς γῆς), and in the *Excerpta Latina Barbari*: 'He subjugated all races from the Caspian Gates, which are in the orient, to the outer bounds of Hercules, which are in the extreme western regions over against Cadiz.'[26] In the present passage the same tendency is seen in the statement that Paul taught righteousness unto *the whole world*, and quite possibly it is also to be seen in the following statement that he reached *the farthest bounds of the West*. It may be that, in eulogizing Paul's labours in the Gospel, Clement has overstepped the truth in the latter statement as he has undoubtedly done in the former. In consequence we cannot with any certainty infer from this passage that at the end of his two-year imprisonment in Rome Paul was released and then proceeded with his face toward the regions of the setting sun, carrying the Gospel into them.

It needs further to be noted that here Clement speaks in general terms : he says 'the farthest bounds of the West'; he does not say 'Spain'; and nothing suggests or indicates that he was speaking specifically of Spain. Here then there is no evidence, and there is none elsewhere, that the tradition of a journey of Paul to that land was current so early as the end of the first century.

(ii) By far the greater part of the *Actus Petri Vercellenses* is devoted to certain doings and experiences of Peter. But the first three chapters tell in some detail the story of the departure of Paul from Rome on a journey to Spain. Whether these chapters come to us from the pen of the author of these *Acts* or were taken over by him from the *Acts of Paul*, they point to the existence by the end of the second century of a tradition that Paul left Rome 'to become a physician in the body (i.e. by

---

[26] *Evsebi Chronicorum Libri Dvo*, ed. A. Schoene, I, appendix, p. 209 :
  et omnes gentes subjugavit a Caspiacas portas
  quae sunt in ortu solis usque in exteriores
  terminos Eraclii qui iacent in exteriores occi
  dentes partibus contra Garirum.

going in person) to them that were in Spain '. But this tradition need not have had, and in all probability did not have, any roots in history. It may have been, and in all probability was, a legend that arose and gained currency simply because it was wrongly assumed that Paul's purpose to visit Spain mentioned in Romans 15:24, 28 was in fact realized. Several other legends that can be accounted for in the same way are listed by Pfister. For instance, in the romance of Ps. Callisthenes a detailed description is given of a journey of Alexander the Great to Ethiopia, a journey which, according to certain authors,[27] the king at one time purposed, but which in fact he never undertook.

Pfister also adduces an illuminating statement from Jerome: '(Paul) who... was brought to Italy also and, as he himself writes, to Spain in foreign ships.'[28] Here Jerome has Romans 15:24 in mind, and here we find him doing precisely what was apparently done by those among whom, already before his time, the legend of a journey of Paul to Spain had originated. He assumes that Paul carried out his intention to go to Spain. He changes the fact, Paul wrote that he purposed a journey into Spain, into the legend, Paul went to Spain as he himself writes.

(iii) Reference to a journey made by Paul to Spain is found in the following passage (lines 34–9) of the *Muratori Canon*:

acta autē omniū apostolorum
sub uno libro scribta sunt lucas obtime theofi
le comprindit quia sub praesentia eius sincula
gerebantur sicuti et semote passion ēpetri
euidenter declarat sed et profectionē pauli ab ur
be ad spaniā proficiscentis.[29]

[27] Arrian, *The Anabasis of Alexander* vii.1: 'Some authors also have stated that he was meditating a voyage round the larger portion of Arabia, the country of the Ethiopians, etc.'

[28] *Com. in Jes.*, ii.10, Migne, *PL*, xxiv.151.

[29] 'The Acts, however, of all the Apostles are written in one book. Luke puts it shortly to the most excellent Theophilus, that the several things were done in his own presence, as he also plainly shows by leaving out the passion of Peter, and also the departure of Paul from town on his journey to Spain' (Trans. H. M. Gwatkin, *Selections from Early Christian Writers*, p. 85).

This canon was composed in Greek *c.* A D 200 and translated into somewhat barbarous Latin so that at a considerable number of points its interpretation is difficult. Although the word *semote* has occasioned much discussion, the meaning of the lines now before us is fairly clear. The writer states that in Acts Luke gives an account only of the events of which he had himself been an eye-witness and plainly shows this by leaving out the passion of Peter and the departure of Paul from the city on his journey to Spain. But Luke has undoubtedly recorded things that were not done in his own presence, and his reason for not recording the death of Peter or a journey made by Paul to Spain, if such a journey was actually made, may have been other than this writer suggests. It can, however, be urged that the present lines testify to the existence by the end of the second century of a tradition that Paul visited Spain. As we have seen, such a tradition is accepted and elaborated in the opening chapters of the *Actus Petri Vercellenses*, and according to M. R. James [30] ' whatever be the true meaning of the clause in the Muratorian Fragment which relates to Acts, it seems clear enough that the author knew of books in which the " passio Petri " and the " profectio Pauli ab urbe ad Spaniam proficiscentis " were set forth in detail ; and these books must surely have been Acts of Peter and Acts of Paul '.

In Spain itself no reliable traces of a missionary activity of Paul have been found.[31] Even the legends say nothing about this. The tradition that the Gospel was first preached in the country by James the son of Zebedee is late and untrustworthy. Indeed it cannot be proved that Christianity was brought there earlier than the end of the second century.

---

[30] In *Texts and Studies*, II.III.50.
[31] P. P. Gams, *Die Kirchengeschichte von Spanien* (1862 ; reprint, 1956), recognizes that ' nowhere in Spain does one come upon a trace of the preaching of Paul ' (p. 7), that ' nowhere in Spain is a firm tradition found regarding his stay there ' (p. 59), and that ' even the Mozarabic or early Spanish liturgy of the feast of Peter and Paul gives no account or indication of a journey of Paul to Spain ' (p. 59).

CHAPTER TWENTY-TWO

The Date of Paul's Martyrdom

OUR INQUIRIES in the three directions indicated in the opening paragraph of the foregoing chapter have led us to conclude that in all probability Paul suffered martyrdom at the close of his two-year imprisonment in Rome. The abrupt ending of Acts points to that conclusion, and neither the references made in the Pastoral Epistles to certain post-Acts activities of Paul on the Aegean seaboard nor the references to a journey he made to Spain found in certain early Christian writings stand in the way of it. Accordingly, having already concluded that Paul arrived in Rome in A D 62, we now assign his martyrdom there to A D 64.

We proceed (1) to note that this date of the martyrdom is perhaps confirmed by Clement of Rome, and (2) to consider a later date of it given by Eusebius.

I

The passage from Clement of Rome's *Epistle to the Corinthians* quoted on pp. 188 f above in the translation of J. B. Lightfoot contains the earliest reference to the apostle's martyrdom that has come down to us. In studying it two points need to be remembered—the one that here Clement does not attempt a history of the events to which he refers, but merely cites them in illustration of the hurt that is wrought by jealousy and envy, the other that these events were well known to his readers in Corinth. These facts explain why he does not say explicitly where these events took place or date them precisely.

There is practically no room for doubt that one of the events which Clement cites here is the Neronian persecution of A D 64. He states that a vast multitude of the elect suffered indignities and tortures ; and, so far as is known, there was no persecution of such a multitude of Christians prior to A D 96 except the Neronian. Tacitus in his account (*Ann.*, xv.44) of this persecution also speaks of a vast multitude (*multitudo ingens*), and what Clement writes about women being insulted as Danaids and Dircae answers to what Tacitus writes about Christians being put to death with insult, dressed up in the skins of beasts to perish by the worrying of dogs (*ut ferarum tergis contecti, laniatu canum interirent*). Since Clement wrote from Rome, we gather from his words, ' A vast multitude of the elect ... set a brave example *among ourselves* ', that the persecution to which he refers took place in that city.

The fact that the examples which Clement adduces in Chapter 4 from the Old Testament are given in chronological order may suggest that those which he adduces in Chapters 5 and 6 are also given in that order. But that does not necessarily follow, and whether it is strictly the case may be questioned. The last two of these examples, the estranged wives and the overthrown cities, seem to belong to all ages and not to be drawn merely from the immediate past. It is also possible that Clement has mentioned Peter before Paul simply because he was in the habit of naming them in that order, and that no inference ought to be made from this as to the order in time in which these two suffered martyrdom. But a close connection in time does seem to be suggested between the sufferings of these two and those of the many whom Clement mentions immediately after them. In this connection the words, ' Unto these men of holy lives was gathered (συνηθροίσθη) a vast multitude of the elect ', are of special importance. They ought not to be taken to mean, to the examples of these men there falls to be added that of a vast multitude of the elect. Nor do they refer simply to the gathering of these men and this multitude in the place of glory. ' They mean ', writes F. H. Chase,[1] ' " *to* these " rather than " *with* these " " there was gathered ", and thus seem to imply that the apostles were among those " who were seized first " (Tacitus

---

[1] ' Peter (Simon) ', *HDB*, III.769b.

Ann., xv.44), the first fruits of a too abundant harvest. Thus the obvious interpretation of Clement's words is that St. Peter and St. Paul were martyred in the Neronian persecution.' E. Meyer [2] maintains that when the Roman authorities decided in A D 64 to proceed against the Christians, they immediately dealt with Paul's case, passed judgement against him, and had him put to death, as a Roman citizen, with the sword. Further he maintains that Clement, in the passage where he writes that a vast multitude of the elect was gathered unto the holy men, Peter and Paul, declares as unambiguously as possible that these two suffered in Rome at the time of the Neronian persecution. Among others who have reached the same conclusion are Harnack,[3] Lietzmann [4] and O. Cullman,[5] who in his book on Peter investigates very fully the passage from Clement of Rome's *Epistle to the Corinthians* that has been before us.[6]

II

In the Armenian version of the *Chronicle* of Eusebius there stands over against the 13th year of Nero, i.e. A D 67, the note, ' On top of all his crimes Nero was the first to provoke persecutions of Christians ; under him the apostles Peter and Paul suffered martyrdom in Rome ',[7] and in Jerome's version over

---

[2] *Ursprung und Anfänge des Christentums* III.501 and 498.
[3] *Geschichte der altchristlichen Litteratur bis Eusebius*, II.1.242.
[4] ' Ein neuer Fund zur Chronologie des Paulus ', *Zeitschrift für wissenschaftliche Theologie* n.f.XVIII(1911).345–54 ; *Petrus und Paulus in Rom.* pp. 167 ff.
[5] *Peter : Disciple—Apostle—Martyr* (2nd edn., 1962), pp. 91–110.
[6] M. Smith, ' The Report about Peter in 1 Clement v.4 ', *New Testament Studies* VII.(1960).86–8, suggests that Clement has rounded off Acts 12:17, ἐπορεύθη εἰς ἕτερον τόπον, with the words, ἐπορεύθη εἰς τὸν ὀφειλόμενον τόπον τῆς δόξης, and so remodelled the story of Peter's release into a story of his martyrdom and ascension. But in this study Clement's words, ' Unto these men . . . was gathered a vast multitude of the elect ', have not been adequately discussed.
[7] Ed. Schoene, II.156 : *Nero super omnia delicta primus persecutiones in Christianos excitavit, sub quo Petrus et Paulus Apostoli Romae martyrium passi sunt.*

against the 14th year of Nero, i.e. A D 68, there is a note to the same effect, 'On top of all his evil doings Nero is the first to occasion a persecution of Christians, in which persecution Peter and Paul gloriously entered into rest in Rome.'[8] Here there is the same close association which we have observed in Clement of Peter and Paul with the others who suffered martyrdom in Rome in the Neronian persecution. The date which Eusebius gives here for that persecution is, however, not A D 64 (Tacitus *Ann.*, xv.33, 44), but either A D 67 or A D 68 and so a year very near to the close of Nero's life. This later date for the martyrdom of Paul, which is also found in Jerome, *De Viris Illustribus*, 5, has been accepted by many of the scholars who maintain that Paul fulfilled his intention to go to Spain and also revisited the East, as it seems to them, the Pastoral Epistles indicate.

Tacitus (*Ann.*, xv.44) sets the Neronian persecution in a causal connection with the burning of Rome. Eusebius, who made little, if any, use of the works of Latin authors, seems to have been unaware of this connection. In the Armenian version of his *Chronicle* the great fire in the city is spoken of vaguely as 'many conflagrations which occurred in Rome,[9] which are put in the 9th year of Nero; in Jerome's version it is said more explicitly, 'That he might contemplate a likeness of burning Troy, Nero set fire to a very large part of the city of Rome ',[10] and the date given is the 10th year of Nero. Eusebius thus put the burning of Rome in A D 63 or 64, but the Neronian persecution in A D 67 or 68.

Why did he date this persecution and with it the martyrdoms of Peter and Paul so near to the close of Nero's life? As has already been noted,[11] he is the first writer to state expressly that Paul was released at the end of his two-year imprisonment in

---

[8] Ibid. p. 157 : *Primus Nero super omnia scelera sua etiam persecutionem in Xpianos facit in qua Petrus et Paulus gloriose Romae obcubuerunt.*
[9] Ibid. p. 154.
[10] Ibid. p. 155.
[11] Page 186, *supra*.

Rome and did not suffer martyrdom until after a second imprisonment there. In *H.E.*, II.xxii, he says that during the interval between the two imprisonments Paul 'was sent again to the ministry of preaching', but he does not indicate where he preached or for how long and so in this place provides us with no answer to our question.

In Jerome's version of the *Chronicle* of Eusebius the commencement of the procuratorship of Festus is put in A D 56, and, as has been indicated,[12] this may be regarded as the date which Eusebius himself gave for it. It may then be assumed that he put Paul's arrival in Rome in A D 57 and the end of his first imprisonment there in A D 59. From then to the end of his second imprisonment is an interval of 8 or 9 (= 67 [68] − 59) years. Eusebius may have learned from some source or himself have estimated that it had been so long, and thus have arrived at A D 67 or 68 as the date of the apostle's martyrdom. But it is at least as likely that for some independent reason he was committed to this date for the martyrdom and consequently to an interval of this length.

In the Armenian version of the *Chronicle* the arrival of Peter in Rome is put in the third year of Caligula, i.e. A D 39, and in the same place it is noted that his episcopate there was one of twenty (*viginti*) years.[13] Neither of these particulars can come from Eusebius himself. In *H.E.*, II.xxiv he writes that the all-good and gracious Providence led Peter to Rome during the reign of Claudius, i.e. at some time between A D 41 and A D 54; and his date for the martyrdom of Peter is A D 67 or 68 and not A D 59 (= 39 + 20). According to Jerome's version Peter arrived in Rome in the second year of Claudius, i.e. A D 42, and the length of his episcopate there was twenty-five (xxv) years.[14] There is no good reason why these particulars should not be carried back to Eusebius himself. If he meant by Paul's departure for Rome his departure to another place mentioned in Acts

[12] Page 154, *supra*.
[13] Ed. Schoene II.150.
[14] Ibid. p. 153.

12:17, then he had to choose for it a year in the reign of Agrippa I, therefore in the interval A D 41–4, and he may well have decided upon A D 42;[15] and A D (42 + 25) = A D 67. This, however, does not answer our question, since the length (twenty-five years) given to Peter's episcopate remains unaccounted for.

Two possibilities here present themselves.

(1) In the apocryphal *Acta Petri et Pauli* [16] we read that at the time of Peter's death certain men addressed the people saying, 'Know ye that this Nero will be utterly destroyed not many days hence and his kingdom given to another', and then that thereafter the multitudes rose against him so that he fled to the wilderness, where he died of hunger and cold and his body was eaten by wild beasts. That is of course legend. But it is not difficult to discern what very possibly lies behind it, the thought, namely, that Nero, the instigator of a great crime against the people of God, cannot have lived on after its perpetration but must have been cut off almost immediately. As Chase indicates, this thought may have led to the carrying down of the persecution to A D 67 or 68, thus to the setting of it about a quarter of a century after A D 42 and so to the assigning to Peter of a Roman episcopate of that length of time.

(2) It has often been suggested that in this matter Eusebius was indebted to the work of an earlier writer. Working back from his own time and using the periods for which the earlier bishops of Rome were assumed to have held office, this writer concluded that Linus became bishop in A D 67/68. Eusebius, according to whom Linus obtained the episcopate after the martyrdom of Paul and Peter,[17] took this as the year of their martyrdom; and

---

[15] Eusebius was aware of the tradition (on which see v. Dobschütz in *TU*, XI.i.51 ff, and Harnack, op. cit. (note 3, *supra*), II.i.243 f) that the Lord had commanded His disciples not to depart from Jerusalem for twelve years (*H.E.*, V.xviii.13). But since he put the crucifixion in A D 33 (*Chronicle*, ed. Schoene, II.148), his choice of A D 42 for Peter's departure for Rome cannot be put down to the influence upon him of that tradition.

[16] *Acta Apostolorum Apocrypha*, ed. Tischendorf (1851), p. 38.

[17] *H.E.*, III.ii.

assuming that Peter came to Rome in A D 42, he concluded that he was bishop there for twenty-five years.

Carried away by his appreciation of Paul's missionary labours, Clement of Rome spoke in exaggerated terms of their territorial extent. But while he could be sure that those of his readers who noticed this would make due allowance for it, he is not likely to have ventured a date for the martyrdom of Peter and Paul which many who had been alive at the time of it could immediately call in question. In whatever way then Eusebius may have been led to assign the martyrdom to A D 67 or 68, there need be little doubt that the date which Clement indicates for it is to be preferred.

Chronological Outline

	A D		A D
Birth of Paul	between 5 and 14	Marullus, Procurator of Judaea	37–41
The Crucifixion	33	Claudius, Emperor	41–54
Paul's Conversion	35 (34)	Herod Agrippa I, King of Judaea	41–44
Paul's First Visit to Jerusalem after his Conversion	38(37)	Herod's Persecution of the Church	43
Paul in Syria and Cilicia	38(37)–45	Guspius Fadus, Procurator of Judaea	44–46
Paul's Ministry with Barnabas in Syrian Antioch	45	Tiberius Alexander, Procurator of Judaea	46–48
Famine Relief Visit to Jerusalem	Winter 45–46	Cumanus, Procurator of Judaea	48–52
First Missionary Journey	46–47	Claudius's Expulsion of the Jews from Rome	49(?)
The Jerusalem Conference	48	Agrippa II, King of Northern Territory	50–93 (100)
Second Missionary Journey	48–51	Gallio, Proconsul of Achaia	51 (May)–52
Paul in Syrian Antioch	51–53	Felix, Procurator of Judaea	52–61
Third Missionary Journey	53–59	Nero, Emperor	54–68
Paul arrested in Jerusalem	59	Festus, Procurator of Judaea	61–62
Paul a Prisoner in Caesarea	59–61	Albinus, Procurator of Judaea	62–64
Paul Sails for Rome	61	The Neronian Persecution	64
Paul arrives in Rome	62		
Paul a Prisoner in Rome	62–64		
Martyrdom of Paul	64		
Pontius Pilate, Procurator of Judaea	26–36		
Marullus, Procurator of Judaea	36–37		
Gaius (Caligula), Emperor	37–41		

Index of Authors

Aland, K., 80
Alford, H., 14, 45
Allo, E. B., 139
Anger, R., 114, 167
Aphrahat, 84
Arndt and Gingrich, 5
Arrian, 192
Ashby, T., 177
Augustine, 91
Aurelius Victor, 50

Bacon, B. W., 96, 97, 140, 145
Ballance, M., 70
Balsdon, J. P. V. D., 99
Baronius, C., 147, 148
Bartlet, J. V., 47
Baur, F. Ch., 32
Bell, H. I., 100
Bengel, J. A., 45, 178, 179
Benoit, P., 54, 78, 88
Bernard, J. H., 84, 85
Beare, F. W., 32, 82
Binnie, W., 15, 47, 92
Blass, Fr., 147, 154
Blinzler, J., 11
Boeckh, P. A., 137
Bonnard, P., 38, 94
Bormann, M., 149
Bourguet, E., 104, 105
Bousset, W., 94
Brassac, A., 105, 107, 167
Broughton, T. R. S., 177
Bruce, F. F., 4, 144
Buck, C. H., 90

Cadbury, H. J., 101, 114, 121, 128, 180
Caesar, 174
Cerfaux and Dupont, 122
Cesnola, L. P. Di, 62
Chandler, R., 137
Charles, R. H., 83
Chase, F. H., 81, 82, 195, 199
Chrysostom, 143, 187
Clavier, H., 10
Clemen, C., 47, 65, 167

Clement of Alexandria, 30, 91
Clement of Rome, 182, 188, 189, 190, 191, 194, 195, 196, 197, 200
Conybeare and Howson, 68, 131, 143, 173
Cornely, R., 167
Cullmann, O., 81, 95, 196

Deissmann, A., 103, 104, 105
Dibelius, M., 37, 47, 72, 95, 117
Dindorf, W., 99, 152
Dion Cassius, 17, 41, 50, 63, 99, 100, 101, 110, 111, 138
Dionysius Petavius, 147, 148
Dittenberger, W., 105, 107
Dobschütz, E. von, 28, 120, 199
Duncan, G. S., 13, 136, 188
Dupont, J., 26, 34, 38, 47, 54, 122

Easton, B. S., 188
Eaton, D., 130
Eckhel, 50
Eisler, R., 170
Emmet, C. W., 47, 56
Erbes, C., 153, 159, 167
Eusebius, 50, 51, 54, 80, 85, 91, 99, 151, 152, 153, 154, 186, 187, 196, 197, 198, 199, 200
Euting, 16

Fascher, E., 4
Féret, H.-M., 92
Field, F., 18
Findlay, G. G., 37, 87, 90, 118, 122
Foster, J., 60
Fotheringham, J. K., 143
Fries, S. A., 13
Frontinus, 109
Funk, R. W., 47, 48
Furneaux, H., 149

Gams, P. P., 193
Gapp, K. S., 52
Gatti, 61
Georgius Hamartolus, 85
Gerhardt, O., 140, 141, 143

201

INDEX OF AUTHORS

Geyser, A. S., 77
Ginzel, F. K., 136, 137, 141
Goguel, M., 10, 11, 12, 26, 47, 65, 86, 96, 97, 117, 126, 128, 131, 167, 183
Greeven, H., 37, 117
Gregory of Nazianzus, 84
Gregory of Nyssa, 84
Grieve, A. J., 47, 167
Grimal, P., 109
Grimm-Thayer, 5
Groag, E., 63, 110
Gutschmid, von, 16
Gwatkin, H. M., 192

Haenchen, E., 7, 8, 11, 17, 26, 41, 45, 47, 48, 49, 65, 68, 76, 116, 117, 121, 122, 128, 143, 148, 157
Harnack, A. von, 26, 28, 29, 30, 73, 78, 95, 102, 103, 147, 154, 157, 177, 179, 196, 199
Harmer, J. R., 188
Harrison, P. N., 188
Hedley, P. L., 170
Hegessipus, 85
Heussi, K., 80
Hicks, E. L., 18, 19
Higgins, A. J. B., 31
Hippocrates, 7, 132
Hoennicke, G., 40, 45, 50, 148, 155, 167, 179
Hogarth, D. G., 62, 63
Hogarth, W. D., 101
Holtzmann, O., 147
Holzmeister, U., 5, 42
Hopfl and Gut, 7, 47
Howard, W. F., 84

Ideler, L., 137
Irenaeus, 29, 85

Jackson and Lake, 42, 50, 81, 114, 116, 121, 128, 129, 140, 144, 147, 177, 180, 181
Jacquier, É., 65
James, M. R., 193
Jeremias, J., 2, 26, 54, 74, 78
Jerome, 2, 91, 102, 151, 154, 187, 192, 196, 197, 198
Jones, A. H. M., 22
Jones, W. H. C., 132
Josephus, 1, 4, 8, 12, 17, 18, 19, 22, 39, 40, 51, 52, 54, 55, 66, 67, 86, 99, 100, 102, 103, 115, 149, 152, 153, 154, 155, 158, 159, 160, 161, 162, 163, 164, 165, 169
Jowett, B., 96
Julius Africanus, 102, 103, 154, 155
Justin Martyr, 79, 80
Justus of Tiberias, 152, 153, 154

Katzenmeyer, H., 80
Kellner, H., 40, 147
Kennedy, A. R. S., 170
Kilpatrick, G. D., 31
Knopf, R., 7
Knowling, R. J., 14, 77, 174
Knox, J., 37, 38, 47, 90, 101, 131
Knox, W. L., 26
Kornemann, E., 61

Lagrange, M.-J., 14, 91
Lake, K., 17, 42, 47, 59, 64, 81, 82, 114, 116, 121, 128, 129, 140, 144
Lampe, G. W. H., 117, 144
Lawlor and Oulton, 186
Lersch, B. M., 137
Lewin, T., 7, 19, 22, 40, 41, 66, 101, 115, 137, 140, 150, 157, 171
Liebenam, W., 41, 52
Lietzmann, H., 56, 179, 196
Lightfoot, J. B., 5, 25, 54, 167, 188, 190, 194
Lipsius and Bonnet, 60
Lohmeyer, E., 25
Loisy, A., 17, 128, 147, 175
Lucian, 17
Lumby, J. R., 143

McGiffert, A. C., 73
Manson, T. M., 47
Marcus, R., 55
Margoliouth, D. S., 1
Marquardt, J., 18, 20, 149
Meinertz, M., 187
Menoud, P. H., 88
Merrill, E. T., 80
Metzger, H., 66, 135
Meyer, E., 19, 65, 73, 78, 139, 149, 167, 177, 188, 196
Migne, 1, 145, 187, 192
Minear, P. S., 90
Mitteis, 181
Moffatt, J., 17, 24, 182
Momigliano, A., 101

Mommsen, T., 20, 21, 111, 177
Morton, H. V., 66, 123
Moulton and Milligan, 66, 131

Naber, S. A., 51
Niese, B., 51
Nikitsky, A., 104
Nonne, 40

Oepke, A., 3, 7, 8
Ogg, G., 30, 37
Origen, 19, 91
Orosius, 50, 54, 102, 103

Paley, W., 15, 47, 91
Papias, 85
Parker and Dubberstein, 40
Pelagius, 183
Perowne, S., 22
Pfister, F., 179, 190, 192
Pherigo, L. P., 182
Philippus Sidetes, 85
Philo, 7, 41, 99, 154, 180
Pliny the Elder, 49, 60, 67, 110, 175
Pliny the Younger, 176, 181
Plooij, D., 17, 45, 54, 62, 64, 71, 105, 107, 140, 141, 148, 152, 153, 166, 167
Pomtow, H., 104
Prat, F., 105
Ps. Callisthenes, 192
Ps. Chrysostom, 1

Rackham, R. B., 71, 143
Ramsay, W. M., 44, 45, 46, 47, 50, 60, 65, 68, 69, 70, 103, 117, 121, 134, 140, 144, 167, 168, 177, 179
Reiche, B., 90
Reifenberg, 40
Reinach, A. J. de, 105
Renan, E., 7
Rendall, F., 97
Reynolds, P. K. B., 177
Riddle, D. W., 90, 91, 182
Rigaux, B., 7
Robertson, A., 143
Robinson, D. F., 32, 79
Robinson, J. A., 84

Sabatier, A., 90
Sanday and Headlam, 139
Sanders, J. N., 34, 82, 134

Schlatter, A., 2
Schlier, H., 43, 44, 45, 72, 76
Schoene, 30, 50, 80, 85, 99, 152, 196, 197, 198, 199
Schürer, E., 4, 20, 21, 22, 51, 102, 149, 154, 170
Schwartz, E., 19, 42, 58, 147, 150
Seneca, 110
Sevenster, J. N., 90
Sherwin-White, A. N., 177, 181
Smaltz, W. M., 74
Smith, D., 131
Smith, M., 196
Soden, H. von, 21, 147, 167
Souter, A., 179
Spitta, F., 11, 73
Still, J. I., 182
Strabo, 18, 67, 123, 190
Strack and Billerbeck, 2, 3, 174
Streeter, B. H., 80
Suetonius, 41, 49, 99, 100, 101, 103, 148, 155, 157, 158, 166
Süskind, 45
Syncellus, 99, 152

Tacitus, 50, 61, 99, 101, 110, 138, 148, 149, 155, 156, 157, 158, 159, 166, 176, 195, 197
Taylor, V., 84
Theiner, A., 147
Theodore of Mopsuestia, 182
Thouless, R. H., 8
Thucydides, 136
Tischendorf, C., 199
Torrey, C. C., 50
Trocmé, E., 95
Turner, C. H., 25, 71, 92, 93, 144, 154, 157

Unnik, W. C. van, 6, 36, 90

Vegetius, 125, 156, 174, 175
Vellei, Paterculus, 63, 190
Venables, E., 85
Vossius, G., 1

Weber, V., 47, 148
Weiss, J., 6, 32, 36, 94, 117, 151
Weizsächer, C. von, 35, 73, 78, 128, 129
Wendland, P., 188
Wendt, H., 167

Westberg, F., 12
Wetzer and Welte, 147
Whiston, W., 1
Wieseler, K., 25, 40, 54, 69, 89, 101, 102, 113, 114, 131, 135, 140, 148, 151, 161, 165, 176, 189

Workman, W. P., 173, 174

Zahn, T., 1, 18, 25, 45, 61, 167, 179
Zangemeister, C., 102
Zwaan, J. de, 50, 179

Index of New Testament Passages

Matthew
4:24 f	25
9:25	93
13:26	93
26:42	56

Mark
9:1	84
10:39	84, 85

Luke
3:1	116
24:50	124

John
4:54	56
18:31	3
21:16	56

Acts
1–8	24, 26
1:1	179
1:3	28
2:41	24
4:1–22	26
4:1	26
4:4	24
4:5 f	26, 27
4:18	27
5:17–42	26
5:17 f	26
5:21	26
5:33	27
5:34 ff	6
5:40a	27
5:40b	27
6:1–8:4	74
6:1	24, 74
6:5	24
6:8–8:3	11
6:9 ff	33
7:58	4, 6
8	80
8:1	24
8:5–40	74
8:12	93
8:18–24	60
8:20–24	80
9:1–30	74
9:1–2	2, 9
9:2	26
9:19a	14
9:19b–22	14
9:19b	14
9:20	14
9:21	14
9:22	14
9:23–25	16
9:23	14, 15, 34, 114
9:26–30	31, 32, 33, 35, 43
9:26	16
9:27	34
9:28	34
9:29	33
9:30	36
9:31–11:18	74
9:31	118
9:32–11:18	81, 82
9:43	114
10:1–11:18	95
10:1–23	94
10:15	56
10:24–48	94
11	56
11:1	95
11:19–30	74
11:19–28	54
11:19–26	81
11:20	34
11:22	34
11:25	33, 36
11:26	38, 78
11:27–30, 12:25	32, 33, 43, 49, 58, 74, 82, 92
11:27–30	39, 49, 78, 81
11:27	78
11:28	49, 54
11:28b	45
11:29	44, 48
11:30	43, 45, 53, 75
12	54
12:1–24	39, 42, 53, 54, 74, 81, 86
12:1–19	79
12:1	53
12:2	74, 85
12:3	42, 86
12:17	74, 79, 81, 82, 196, 199
12:19	42
12:23	42
12:24	73
12:25–14:28	74
12:25	39, 43, 44, 48, 53, 58, 75
13–14	44, 58, 65, 78, 87, 88
13:1–14:28	82
13:4–14:26	71
13:4–12	59
13:5	66
13:6–12	61, 62, 63, 64
13:6	66, 67
13:13–14:25	58, 59
13:13	67
13:14	68
13:15	3
13:44	68
13:45	68
13:49	68
13:50	182
14:4	79
14:6 f	70
14:14	79
14:19	70
14:21	70
14:25	71
14:28	72, 73, 74, 78
15	46, 47, 49, 53, 90, 91, 92
15:1–39	92
15:1–35	78
15:1–33	74, 78, 79
15:1–29	43, 46, 58, 72
15:1	78, 92
15:3–33	78
15:5	27
15:7 ff	74
15:7	82
15:9	91

Matthew

Reference	Page(s)
15:19	77
15:23–29	75
15:23	44, 73, 75, 76, 77, 79
15:24	92
15:33	79, 112
15:34	112
15:35 ff	74
15:35	72, 74, 78
15:36 ff	96
15:36	78, 87 112, 115
15:39	90
15:39b	59
15:40–16:4	58, 59
15:40	79, 112
15:41	36, 44, 77, 118
16:1–4	118
16:4	76, 77, 79
16:6–10	117
16:6	116, 118, 133
16:7	116
16:12–40	119
16:12	119
16:13	119
16:14	119
16:16	119
16:18	119
17:1–10	121
17:1	120
17:2	121, 122
17:14 f	125
17:14	120, 124
17:15	125
18:1–18	113, 126
18:1–17	104
18:1 f	99
18:2	102
18:5	126
18:11	114
18:12 ff	38
18:18–23	127–132
18:18–22	90
18:18	69, 114, 115, 129
18:19	128
18:19b–21a	127
18:21	129
18:22	128
18:23	116, 118, 132, 133, 134
18:24–28	54
18:26	127
19:1–41	135
19:1	134
19:8	135
19:10	135
19:21–22	135
19:21	135
19:22	135
19:23–41	135, 137
19:24	137
19:38	138
20:1–3	117
20:1	130
20:2	139
20:3–21:16	129
20:3	129, 139
20:4–21:15	184
20:5	140
20:6	139, 140, 143, 144
20:7	139, 140, 143
20:16	140, 144, 145
20:16b	129
20:24	185
20:25	184, 185
20:31	135, 159
20:36–38	184
21:4	144
21:5	124
21:10	144
21:14	129
21:17	156
21:25	76, 77, 78
21:27–22:29	146
21:38	164
22:1 f	187
22:3	1, 6
22:5	2
22:12	26
22:30–23:35	146
24	146
24:10–21	150
24:10	148, 150, 151, 162
24:17	139
24:22	151
24:23	151
24:25	151
24:27	147, 150, 151, 171
24:27a	159
25:1–27:2	146
25:1	171
25:6 ff	171
25:13	172
25:14	172
26:10	3
26:11	124
26:12	2
27:1	177
27:2	156
27:5	172
27:7	114
27:8	173
27:9	172, 173
28:11	175
28:14	175
28:16	176, 177
28:29	179
28:30–31	178, 186
28:30	147, 188

Romans

Reference	Page(s)
14	76, 77
15:19	139
15:24	192
15:28	192
16:7	28

1 Corinthians

Reference	Page(s)
2:3	131
5:9	135
6	76, 77
8	76, 77
9:5	79
9:6	90
10	76, 77
15:8	29
15:32	135
16:5–8	137
16:7	132
16:8	136
16:9	138

2 Corinthians

Reference	Page(s)
1:8	135
2:3	135
2:9	135
2:13	139
7:5–7	139
7:8	135
7:12	135
8:1	120
11:8 f	113
11:23 ff	10
11:25	182
11:32 f	16
11:32	18, 19, 22

INDEX OF NEW TESTAMENT PASSAGES

Galatians
1:11–2:10 ... 56
1:11–24 ... 57
1:15 ... 93
1:16 ff ... 13
1:16 ... 14
1:17 ... 44
1:18–24 ... 31, 32, 35, 43, 44
1:18 ... 14, 15, 43, 44, 56, 86, 93, 114
1:20 ... 35
1:21 ... 44, 73, 78, 93
1:22 ... 6, 34
1:23 ... 36
2:1–14 ... 92
2:1–10 ... 43, 45, 46, 47, 57, 72, 74, 76, 77, 87, 89, 92, 131
2:1–10a ... 47
2:1 ... 30, 56, 72, 86, 93, 131
2:6 ... 76
2:7 ... 93
2:9 ... 57, 74, 131
2:10 ... 47
2:10a ... 48
2:10b ... 47
2:11–14 ... 89, 92, 93, 94
2:11 ... 91, 93, 94
2:12 ... 92, 93
2:14 ... 97
3:23 ... 18
4:4 ... 93

Ephesians
6:20 ... 5

Philippians
1:12–23 ... 186
1:25 ... 185
2:24 ... 185
4:7 ... 18
4:16 ... 122

1 Thessalonians
1:9 ... 122
2:9 ... 122
2:17 f ... 123
2:18 ... 122
3:1 ... 125, 131
3:6 ff ... 113
4:10 ... 120

2 Timothy
4:16–18 ... 187
4:16 ... 187
4:17 ... 187
4:18 ... 187

Philemon
v. 9 ... 5
v. 22 ... 185

1 Peter
1:5 ... 18

www.ingramcontent.com/pod-product-compliance
Lightning Source LLC
Chambersburg PA
CBHW070322230426
43663CB00011B/2196